NORTH CAROLINA
STATE BOARD OF COMMUNITY COLLEGES
LIBRARIES
WAKE TECHNICAL COMMUNITY COLLEGE

 Y0-CUO-009

WAKE TECHNICAL COMMUNITY
COLLEGE LIBRARY
9101 FAYETTEVILLE ROAD
RALEIGH, NC 27603-5696

WITHDRAWN

BUCKNELL REVIEW

# Self, Sign, and Symbol

STATEMENT OF POLICY

BUCKNELL REVIEW is a scholarly interdisciplinary journal. Each issue is devoted to a major theme or movement in the humanities or sciences, or to two or three closely related topics. The editors invite heterodox, orthodox, and speculative ideas and welcome manuscripts from any enterprising scholar in the humanities and sciences.

This journal is a member of the Conference of Editors of Learned Journals

BUCKNELL REVIEW
*A Scholarly Journal of Letters, Arts, and Sciences*

*Co-Editors*
MARK NEUMAN
MICHAEL PAYNE

*Assistant Editor*
DOROTHY L. BAUMWOLL

*Editorial Board*
PATRICK BRADY
WILLIAM E. CAIN
JAMES M. HEATH
STEVEN MAILLOUX
JOHN WHEATCROFT

*Assistant to the Editors*
JANE S. LENTZ

Contributors should send manuscripts with a self-addressed stamped envelope to the Editors, Bucknell University, Lewisburg, Pennsylvania 17837.

BUCKNELL REVIEW

# Self, Sign, and Symbol

Edited by
MARK NEUMAN and MICHAEL PAYNE

LEWISBURG
BUCKNELL UNIVERSITY PRESS
LONDON AND TORONTO: ASSOCIATED UNIVERSITY PRESSES

© 1987 by Associated University Presses, Inc.

Associated University Presses
440 Forsgate Drive
Cranbury, NJ 08512

Associated University Presses
25 Sicilian Avenue
London WC1A 2QH, England

Associated University Presses
2133 Royal Windsor Drive
Unit 1
Mississauga, Ontario
Canada L5J 1K5

The paper used in this publication meets the
requirements of the American National Standard for
Permanence of Paper for Printed Library Materials Z39.48-1984.

**Library of Congress Cataloging-in-Publication Data**

Self, sign, and symbol.

  (Bucknell review; v. 30, no. 2)
  Includes bibliographies.
  1. American literature—History and criticism.
2. Symbolism in literature.  3. Self in literature.
4. Semiotics.  5. French literature—20th century—
History and criticism.  I. Neuman, Mark, 1935–
II. Payne, Michael.  III. Series.
AP2.B887 vol. 30, no. 2    051 s [810'.9]    86-47606
[PS169.S9]
ISBN 0-8387-5108-3 (alk. paper)

**(Volume XXX, Number 2)**

Printed in the United States of America

This issue of *Bucknell Review* is dedicated to Harry R. Garvin, who retired as editor in 1984. Under his direction the *Review* expanded to well over one hundred pages for each quarterly number and then in 1976 began to be issued in a hardback topical format twice each year. During the period of Professor Garvin's editorship, the *Bucknell Review* attained national stature as an interdisciplinary journal in the humanities. The essays in this issue are among the last manuscripts selected for publication during Professor Garvin's editorship.

# Contents

| | | |
|---|---|---|
| Notes on Contributors | | 11 |
| Introduction | MARK NEUMAN<br>MICHAEL PAYNE | 13 |
| Dream Symbolism and Literary Symbolism | DAVID J. GORDON | 19 |
| Opening the Closure, and Vice Versa | JOSEPH MARGOLIS | 34 |
| *The Rime of the Ancient Mariner:* Coleridge's Scientific and Philosophic Insights | L. M. GROW | 45 |
| Young Man Hawthorne: Scrutinizing the Discourse of History | JOHN FRANZOSA | 72 |
| James, Browning, and the Theatrical Self: *The Wings of the Dove* and *In a Balcony* | ROSS POSNOCK | 95 |
| Eliot, Burglary, and Musical Order | MICHAEL BEEHLER | 117 |
| The Dynamics of Vision in William Carlos Williams and Charles Sheeler | WILLIAM MARLING | 130 |
| The Joy of Textualizing Japan: A Metacommentary on Roland Barthes's *Empire of Signs* | HWA YOL JUNG | 144 |
| Ponge on Braque: The Visible Object | SERGE GAVRONSKY | 168 |

Recent Issues of BUCKNELL REVIEW

*Phenomenology, Structuralism, Semiology*
*Twentieth-Century Poetry, Fiction, Theory*
*Literature and History*
*New Dimensions in the Humanities and Social Sciences*
*Women, Literature, Criticism*
*The Arts and Their Interrelations*
*Shakespeare: Contemporary Approaches*
*Romanticism, Modernism, Postmodernism*
*Theories of Reading, Looking, and Listening*
*Literature, Arts, and Religion*
*Literature and Ideology*
*Science and Literature*
*The American Renaissance: New Dimensions*
*Rhetoric, Literature, and Interpretation*
*The Arts, Society, Literature*
*Text, Interpretation, Theory*
*Perspective: Art, Literature, Participation*

# Notes on Contributors

MICHAEL BEEHLER: Teaches at Montana State University. Main professional interests: contemporary Continental criticism, modern poetry and drama, and science fiction. Published articles on T. S. Eliot, Wallace Stevens, Joe Orton, and Stanislaw Lem in *Sub-stance, Boundary 2, Genre,* and *Criticism,* and on "Stevens' Boundaries" in *The Wallace Stevens Journal.* He has recently completed a book-length study of writing and representation in Eliot and Stevens.

JOHN FRANZOSA: Teaches at Wayne State University. He has published articles on Hawthorne and other figures of the American Renaissance in *American Imago, ESQ, Genre,* and *Texas Studies in Literature and Language.*

SERGE GAVRONSKY: Teaches at Barnard College. Publications include *Poems and Texts* (1969); *Lectures et comptes rendus, poèmes* (1973); *Francis Ponge and the Power of Language* (1979); and *Culture/Ecriture, essais critiques* (1983). Forthcoming: *The German Friend,* a novel, to be published by SUN, in New York and by Spirales Editions, in Milan. His chapter on "L'oeil du regard: Ponge et l'art" will appear in the volume on Francis Ponge published by L'Herne in Paris.

DAVID J. GORDON: Teaches at Hunter College and the CUNY Graduate School. He is the author of *Literary Art and the Unconscious* and a monograph on D. H. Lawrence. Currently he is preparing two books on Bernard Shaw and the comic sublime and a group of essays in literary psychoanalysis.

L. M. GROW: Teaches at Broward Community College, Fort Lauderdale, Florida. Published: *The Prose Style of Samuel Taylor Coleridge* and the articles "The Rime of the Ancient Mariner: Multiple Veils of Illusion," "Book Learning versus Personal Experience in *The Rime of the Ancient Mariner,*" and "The Consistency of the *Biographia Literaria.*"

HWA YOL JUNG: Teaches at Moravian College, Bethlehem, Pennsylvania. The present paper stems from his interest in comparative philosophy and the methodology of the comparative study of cultures, especially Western commentaries on Oriental (East Asian) culture. At present he is completing a book manuscript, *The Diatactics of Language: A Prolegomenon to Political Philosophy*, part of which involves an examination of post-structuralist and deconstructionist criticism toward the development of *politextuality*—the hybridization of the "political" and the "literary." His article "Misreading the Ideogram: From Fenollosa to McLuhan and Derrida" appears in *Paiduma*.

JOSEPH MARGOLIS: Teaches at Temple University. Author of *Philosophy Looks at the Arts, The Language of Art and Art Criticism, Negativities: The Limits of Life, Art and Philosophy*, and other books.

WILLIAM MARLING: Teaches at Case Western Reserve University. Author of *William Carlos Williams and the Painters, 1909–23* (1982) and *Dashiell Hammett* (1983) as well as numerous scholarly articles. Recently a Fulbright Lecturer at the Universidad de Deusto in Bilbao, Spain.

ROSS POSNOCK: Teaches at the College of William and Mary. He has recently completed a book on James's literary and psychological relation to Browning, and has published articles on both writers. His review essay on recent James criticism appeared in the annual *Review*, 1982. His current project concerns theatricality as a social, cultural, and literary theme in late nineteenth-century English and American literature.

# Introduction

IN the current complex state of literary theory it may be useful to recall that it was once possible to think of texts as virtually autonomous structures suspended between authors and readers. Although the author was thought to be more or less detached from the text, the authorial presence in a work could be explained as the author's fictional projection in the form of a speaker. The reader in turn was fictionally shaped, manipulated, or created as a presence in the text by the rhetorical powers of the author. Whatever communication there might be between author and reader took place in the rarified, pure atmosphere of a virtual world. The art of writing consisted of the ability to create such self-sustaining worlds that readers found it pleasurable or enlightening to enter.

This view of texts—a synthesis of Cleanth Brooks, Susanne Langer, Walker Gibson, Wayne Booth, and Walter Ong—has been confounded in a number of significant ways during the past twenty years. If the text is autonomous can it offer us knowledge? If texts are detached from biography and history then why is it possible to identify individual styles and to detect widespread interest in particular genres and other conventions that are more pronounced in one age than in another? Why is it that certain texts—indeed, some of the most profound ones—appear to turn in on themselves, as though in parody of their own self-sufficiency? *Self, Sign, and Symbol* wrestles with these postformalist questions from a variety of discrete but related points of view.

David Gordon takes up Freud's often neglected concern with philology and the capacity of language to retain traces of universal human history. Lacan, in contrast to Freud, holds that no stable meaning exists in either dreams or literary texts. Reaffirming Freud's position, Gordon finds in Freud a respect for analogical integrity of disciplines, whereas Lacan looks for the common denominator of all human sciences. Joseph Margolis also challenges the current state of literary theory (the "circus of literary theory," as he calls it) with a revisionist critique of semiotics and deconstruction.

Assiduously avoiding any reference to contemporary theoretical debate, L. M. Grow examines what Foucault might have called Coleridge's archaeology of the human sciences, his attempt to provide a philosophical basis for science. By concentrating on *The Rime of the Ancient Mariner,* Grow shows that for Coleridge form evolves organically from within by processes that are both material and mental. Coleridge might well agree with Foucault's assertion that discourse is an attempt to translate and overcome contradiction, which is "the very law of its existence."

John Franzosa applies the methodology of Erik Erikson's psychohistory to a rhetorical interpretation of Hawthorne's historical sketch "Endicott and the Red Cross" in order to show "how Hawthorne's writing attempts to occupy the space between arbitrary signs and luminous symbols." Despite Hawthorne's ironic employment of symbolic structure in his tale, his "organicism" is as strong as Coleridge's. In significant contrast to this point of view, Ross Posnock finds in Henry James's *The Wings of the Dove* a rewriting of Browning's *In a Balcony,* which reveals both writers' interest in theatricality. James's comments on the necessity of roles, manners, and conventions anticipates Lacan's conception of symbolic order, the substitution of an alien, impersonal social system that defers direct communication.

Just as Browning lies beneath the surface of James's novel, so Nietzsche is an informing presence in Eliot's *The Waste Land* and in much of his criticism, especially, Michael Beehler argues, the criticism that explores the place of meaning in poetry and music. William Carlos Williams, on the other hand, found in painting rather than in music his sense of the essence of creative process. William Marling shows that Williams's visual thinking was significantly influenced by his friendship with the painter Charles Sheeler and that their work and friendship mutually influenced each other. Williams finally distances himself from Sheeler, whose preoccupation with his own technique failed, in Williams's view, to come to terms with the rough intractable stuff of the American urban scene.

Hwa Yol Jung shows that for Roland Barthes the entire culture of Japan becomes an "empire of signs." Man, for Barthes, is a system of signs, and semiology becomes the means of knowing what can be known. A further step toward the objectification of the self by the world of signs (or the subjectification of the observable world by language) is taken in Serge Gavronsky's study of Francis Ponge's praise of Georges Braque's pictorial world.

The order of these essays would seem to constitute a new argument for the self-sufficiency of the text that may have been only faintly imagined by the American New Critics. In their recent view of textual theory in America, however, Robert Scholes and T. Todorov have warned that semiology and deconstruction may have at last revealed their antihumanism. The recovery of an interest in the meaning of texts and in the human exchange between writer and reader that texts make possible may become the next new criticism.

Mark Neuman<br>Michael Payne

BUCKNELL REVIEW

# Self, Sign, and Symbol

# Dream Symbolism and Literary Symbolism

## David J. Gordon
*Hunter College*

IN his *Introductory Lectures on Psychoanalysis* Freud wrote: "A constant relation . . . between a dream-element and its translation is described by us as a 'symbolic' one."[1] But he was always uneasy about "these portions of dream-interpretation . . . that . . . could really be understood without the dreamer's associations."[2] They dispensed with the subtle technique he had so carefully and brilliantly developed, and suited a popular handbook. Moreover, dream symbolism raised a difficult question about the origin of our knowledge. If different people from different societies unconsciously represented the body, parents, siblings, birth, life, and death by means of the same image,[3] then certain ideas, certain connections, apparently were inherited.

Although Freud resisted the Jungian inference of a Collective Unconscious, he never quite resolved the epistemological question. (He was still wrestling with it in *Moses and Monotheism*.) But, as John Forrester has shown in *Language and the Origins of Psychoanalysis*, he found in philology an attractive middle ground between individual and racial memory.[4] Primitive literary productions like folklore and fairy tales, not to mention jokes and common obscene humor, seemed to prove that the words of the languages we acquire retain traces of an archaic and psychologically universal history. In the years of his association with Jung, culminating in *Totem and Taboo* (1912) and in such papers as "Dreams in Folklore" (1911) and "The Occurrence in Dreams of Material from Fairy Tales" (1913), Freud was stimulated to go beyond what he had said in *The Interpretation* about "typical dreams" and explore what might be called the cultural aspects of dream symbolism.

The little folk and fairy tales cited in those articles do not quite resemble dreams in that they are, however crudely, dramatic and coherent rather than narratively disjointed and affectively distorted. The symbolic connections they imply (e.g., excrement as gold) are palpable enough to become the source of simple humor or simple parable, to be of literary use. Such tales may be placed just to one side of a borderline between literature and dream. Just to the other side we may place typical dreams and others whose symbolic meaning is so thinly disguised that it leaps to our waking mind. I once heard a college girl naively report a dream in which the automobile of an instructor she was known to like crashed into her garage. Those listening laughed at once, and the girl herself, after blushing, laughed too. Here was unconscious humor that was almost a form of joking, almost a social act.

Thin as the borderline is, however, it is seldom blurred altogether. "Kubla Khan" is often, and understandably, called a "dream poem," but it has too much rhetorical art to look like an actual dream,[5] and the numerous dreams reported by Freud and his followers contain, as a rule, too little rhetorical art to be considered even simple forms of literature. But there are suggestive analogies between dream symbolism and the major modes of literary symbolism: myth, allegory, and the surcharged images of realistic literature. I will comment on these analogies, and finally on some implications of the change initiated by Jacques Lacan in the very meaning of psychoanalytic symbolism. Roughly speaking, these modes correspond to Vico's three eras within an historical cycle: "the age of the gods," when there was little separation between subject and object and language was naturally metaphoric; "the age of the heroes," when subjective and objective were paralleled according to a transcendent scheme; and "the age of men," when, in deference to a primary external reality, the inner world is merely intimated or presented as fantasy.[6]

The analogy between dream symbolism and myth may be probed most effectively through the *Oedipus Rex,* so closely bound up with the history of psychoanalysis, though the Homeric texts illustrate more precisely what Vico meant by poetry in the age of the gods. Freud habitually treated the play as a disguised version of underlying dream thoughts. It dramatized reactive horror to the primordial wishes of parricide and incest, which was then rationalized "for theological purposes," constituting "a misconceived secondary revision" of the original material. He appreciated its marvelous articulation—the "ever-mounting excitement," "cunning delays" and "skillfully prolonged inquiry"—but the genetically oriented psychologist was trying to reconstruct an older form of the story whereas the literary critic can hardly wish to read the powerful end result of a creative process as "misconceived . . . revision."[7]

Freud was sure that the power of Sophocles' play came from the resonance of the original material unconsciously perceived by the spectator or reader. The trouble with this assumption is that there is nothing subtle about the motifs of parricide and incest in the play. The horror of their gradual discovery is dramatized, but they are presented as grave social taboos rather than hidden wishes. Oedipus' self-blinding cannot really be interpreted as a symbol of castration, though Freud does persuade us that blinding carries this symbolic suggestion in E. T. A. Hoffmann's "The Sandman"[8] and other later narratives as well as in dreams. Here, it is a fitting response, understood by the Chorus, to the completed knowledge of his acts.

Some critics, Freudian and otherwise, have not resisted the temptation to think of the characters of the play realistically.[9] There is, to be sure, the famous realistic touch when Jocasta distinguishes between dreaming of incest and actually committing it. But a general expectation of realistic cause-and-effect involves us in absurdities: why didn't Oedipus or Jocasta ever suspect the truth from the fact of his pierced ankles? why, if each was anxious to evade the oracular pronouncement, did he or she marry a spouse of questionable age? why did Oedipus never connect the oracle with the memory of having killed a man who might have been Laius? why does no one comment on the presumable physical resemblances? We understand, or should, that these questions are out of bounds. We cannot condescend to Oedipus as we do to a character in a realistic text who is presented to us as deficient in self-knowledge, like Henry James's Hyacinth Robinson or Saul Bellow's Tommy Wilhelm. The supposed conflict between his unconscious wish and an inhibition derived from his moral sense is really a conflict or gap in his world between the will of the gods and the will of man. As Meredith Skura finely puts it: "The horrible deeds are not Oedipus's fault, but rather a vast Freudian slip of the universe which exposes the unconscious truth, substituting father for stranger and mother for wife in a story where they do not belong. . . . Oedipus's world acts feelings out for him and makes it impossible to distinguish psychology from cosmology."[10]

This mythic story, then, is symbolic as a whole rather than in parts. Inner world and outer, wish and act, merge. But, unlike the dream, it is a product of a waking imagination, which takes as much pleasure in evoking the power of constraint as of instinct, and has no need of a disguising and distorting censor. Freud's prejudice against "theological purpose," which prompts his scornful sentence "The attempt to harmonize divine omnipotence with human responsibility must naturally fail in connection with this subject matter just as with any other," prevents him from seeing that the play, though it dramatizes the power of the gods, by no means shows man's humility before them. As Bernard Knox firmly objected, there is nothing humble about Oedipus, and it is his daring that wins our admiration and sympathy.[11] Ironically, when Freud forgets about the play as such and about his unsatisfactory theory of art based on the model of the daydream,[12] he himself not only identifies with the heroic Oedipus (solver of the riddle of the Sphinx) but also invokes with Miltonic majesty the power of stern Necessity. Indeed, in his enthusiastic study of Michelangelo's *Moses,* he celebrates the sculpture for depicting the noble renunciation of egotistic impulse.

If in the world of mythical narrative, inner and outer worlds are scarcely distinguishable, in the allegorical narratives that flourished during the Middle Ages and into the Renaissance, they are sharply separated yet constantly related to one another in explicit schemes of equivalence. From a modern point of view, myth and allegory make a contrast within a larger frame of similarity because both are products of a religious world view that joins human and divine. In the world of myth, the actions of men and of gods influence one another; they may be said, in pictorial terms, to occupy the same plane. In the layered world of allegory, as Northrop Frye following Vico pointed out, the system of equivalences is justified with reference to a transcendent reality that organizes them conceptually.[13] Image is linked to concept, and, as the image moves in a narrative, the concepts make up an explanation.

Consider the encounter in *The Faerie Queene* between the weakened Redcrosse Knight and the superficially daunting giant Orgoglio:

> But ere he could his armour on him dight,
> Or get his shield, his monstrous enimy
> With sturdie steps came stalking in his sight,
> An hideous Geant horrible and hye,
> That with his talnesse seemd to threat the skye,
> The ground eke groned vnder him for dreed;
> His liuing like saw neuer liuing eye,
> Ne durst behold: his stature did exceed
> The hight of three the tallest sonnes of mortall seed.
>
> The greatest Earth his vncouth mother was,
> And blustring *Aeolus* his boasted sire,
> Who with his breath, which through the world doth pas,
> Her hollow womb did secretly inspire,
> And fild her hidden caues with stormie yre,
> That she conceiu'd; and trebling the dew time,
> In which the wombes of women do expire,
> Brought forth this monstrous masse of earthly slime,
> Puft up with emptie wind, and fild with sinfull crime.
>
> So growen great through arrogant delight
> Of th'high descent, whereof he was yborne,
> And through presumption of his matchlesse might,
> All other powres and knighthood he did scorne.
> Such now he marcheth to this man forlorne,
> And left to losse: his talking steps are stayde
> Vpon a snaggy Oke, which he had torne
> Out of his mothers bowelles, and it made
> His mortall mace, wherewith his foemen he dismayde.
> [1.7.8–10]

The naive dramatic interest of these stanzas is apparent. On another level, they express a symbolic meaning that we understand according to the ready hints that Orgoglio represents at once the sin of pride and the Catholic Church, both "puft up with emptie wind."

There is a suggestive resemblance between the interacting levels of such literary allegory and the interacting texts of an interpreted dream, the manifest dream and the latent dream thoughts. In both instances, a latent text comes into being during the process of interpretation but is not simply to be substituted for the manifest one. A just interpretation focuses on the relation between the given and emergent texts.[14] Symbolism being in question, one could say of both dreams and allegories that there is a constant relation between certain elements of the given text and their translation in the emergent text. In each case, an alogical, nonmimetic narrative translates into, or means again as, a discursively articulated narrative, and in each case the symbolism is definite and determinate.

But the symbolism of allegory is what Freud, from his psychoarchaeological perspective, would call imposed from above. It is a connection between image and concept rather than between image and image. The knowledge required to understand allegorical symbolism is public, though not necessarily popular. (To understand Orgoglio, one must know a little about the Catholic Church in the sixteenth century and about the tradition of the deadly sins.) The knowledge required to understand dream symbolism, on the other hand, is usually private, as in one of my dreams the recessed figure of a Negro at a social gathering symbolized the weak tincture of dark paint I was mixing into some white paint during the day. And its importance must usually be teased out: in my dream what mattered most was that someone at that gathering had told me of a black colleague who died after complaining of symptoms similar to ones that were worrying me at the time.

Our analogy between dream and allegory may be clarified by a brief comparison of our responses to the different kinds of wit found in them and in a nonsymbolic context. Wit in a dream, as in the parapraxes, is involuntary and prompts an embarrassed laugh. Wit in allegory gives us delayed pleasure when we have put together incongruous perspectives, the dramatic and the conceptual. (Orgoglio is formidable on one level but of course collapses like a punctured bladder.) And in overt wit, we relish the return of a repressed thought connection for the very incongruity it cleverly exploits. In his famous conceit of the worms that try the too-long-preserved virginity of the coy mistress, Andrew Marvell makes his worms function *like* a penis, and sophisticatedly mocks the idea of *symbolic* equivalence. The similarity in physical action between the worm doing its wormy thing and the penis doing its thing highlights the screaming dissimilarity in value between grim repulsiveness and keen pleasure, barren death and buoyant life.

During the Middle Ages and Renaissance, the terms allegory and symbolism were virtually synonymous. But in the eighteenth century there developed a certain disdain for the explicitness of allegory, a preference for a more subtle symbolism. William Blake spoke emphatically for the new sensibility:

> Fable or Allegory are a totally distinct & inferior kind of Poetry. Vision or Imagination [we would say symbolism] is a Representation of what Eternally Exists, Really and Unchangeably. Fable or Allegory is Form'd by the daughters of Memory. Imagination is surrounded by the daughters of Inspiration, who in the aggregate are called Jerusalem.[15]

The vehemence of this pronouncement overrides Blake's acknowledgment a paragraph later that great allegories contain Vision, not to mention the fact that his own major poems must be described as allegorical. (Blake's practice of the subtler symbolism is probably best illustrated by the earlier lyrics, for example "The Sick Rose" where the word "crimson" suggests by receding degrees the rose's vivid beauty, the blush of its erotic joy, the hectic flush of disease, and the petalled reddishness of its sex destroyed by the secret storm-swoop of the phallic worm.) But an important shift in the conception and use of symbolism is nonetheless indicated. Blake repudiates allegory's practice of deriving symbolic truth from historical tradition, and, like Yeats, the French Symbolists and Jung after him, seeks a psychological—more exactly a psycho-metaphysical—basis for the world of permanent forms evoked by imagination. "Jerusalem," "The Great Memory" (or "Spiritus Mundi"), "the unity of poetic experience," and "The Collective Unconscious" all have a curious ontological status, inside and outside the mind at once, an ambiguity that in theory preserves for literature, as once for religion, the sense of mystery. These are among the more radical responses to the encroaching prestige of realism and positivist science, but it may be said that post-Englightenment symbolism generally, placed in the same situation, typically and characteristically worked by suggestion, implicitly admitting a primary truth status to the physical world perceived by our senses.

This is well illustrated by the following passage in Conrad's story "Heart of Darkness":

> Going up that river was like travelling back to the earliest beginnings of the world, when vegetation rioted on the earth and the big trees were kings. An empty stream, a great silence, an impenetrable forest. The air was warm, thick, heavy, sluggish. There was no joy in the brilliance of sunshine. The long stretches of the waterway ran on, deserted, into the gloom of overshadowed distances. On silvery sandbanks hippos and alligators sunned themselves side by side.

The broadening waters flowed through a web of wooded islands; you lost your way on that river as you would in a desert, and butted all day long against shoals, trying to find the channel, till you thought yourself bewitched and cut off forever from everything you had known once—somewhere—far away—in another existence perhaps.

We notice particularly, in the present context, the backgrounding function of Conrad's similes: "Going up that river was like travelling back . . ."; "you lost your way . . . as you would in a desert." Despite the sense of mystery established by the comparisons, there is no question that this is a "real" journey up a tropical river, that the weather report is "truthful," that there "are" hippos and alligators on the sandbanks. Yet the passage does richly accumulate symbolic resonance: through phrases that tend to dissolve present time and place ("earliest beginnings of the world," "another existence perhaps") enforced by the hypnotic rhythm of the sentences; through its association of human feeling with the nonhuman ("empty stream, great silence, impenetrable forest"); and through direct metaphor ("When vegetation rioted on the earth and the big trees were kings").

It is a critical commonplace to speak of Marlow's journey as symbolic. But it is not easy to say what the journey is symbolic *of.* The difficulty is not so much a matter of critical acumen as of critical tact. Any blunt equation is likely to make us wince or to prompt an eminently sensible commentator like Ian Watt to demur, "you either believe in night journeys and primal scenes or you don't."[16] Probably the best one can do, to compromise between an explanatory and a tactful impulse, is to peel off layers of suggestiveness by degrees, as with the "crimson" of "The Sick Rose." But I do not wish to imply that this is bound to lead us to a Jungian or Freudian core. We see what we are prepared to see, and if these frames of reference have no charm or cogency for us, we will not interpret literary texts accordingly. My point of concern is that the term *depth* as it might be used to refer to symbolic meaning in the surcharged images of modern realistic literature has a different sense from the use of the term in reference to dreams. The dream sense, like the sense of the term in Chomskyan linguistic theory, is analytic; it refers to the generative cause of a discernible effect, as the latent thought causes the manifest dream. The literary sense may be called phenomenological; it is a matter of respecting, for the sake of an accurate reconstruction of implied meaning, the veil or scrim between a foreground and a background, between what is plain and what is intimated, overt and covert.

Modern literary realism, in which psychic events, though they may be taken seriously, are not granted the same truth status as external ones, especially when they are expressed imagistically rather than analyzed in discourse (as in Freudian case history), is still a dominant convention of narrative fiction, though there is by now a good deal of literary symbolism that undermines it to one degree or another. In what is already a survey, I cannot begin to describe adequately newer developments, but we could hardly do so without tripping back over myth and allegory and attempting to make finer discriminations. I will briefly consider one such story, Kafka's "The Judgment," which may help us see how our already developed analogy between literature and dream is capable of extension and further refinement.

Georg Bendemann is planning to marry and is writing a supposed friend living an isolated life in Petersburg to invite him to the wedding, though he hardly expects the invitation to be accepted. Georg lives with his widowered father, who appears frail at first but seems to become angrier and stronger as he hears of his son's activity, and refers to the friend so ambiguously that we cannot be sure if he exists. It appears that the friend is an aspect of Georg in his relationship with his father, more specifically that he represents Georg's passive, nonmarrying, scarcely alive self who is, however, protected from the father's wrath whereas the decision to marry incurs it. The story has received so much sophisticated comment that I am diffident about using so slight and partial an interpretation as a basis for a wider point, but it does, I think, allow us to see that, despite the air of realism in the first two-thirds of the story, Kafka is somehow symbolic without attributing to his characters any suggestion of an inner life or of unconscious motives. The symbolism is more pervasive like myth and more schematic like allegory but too earthbound for the one and too elusive for the other.

Toward the end the story departs from the convention of realism more openly as the father declares: "An innocent child, yes, that you were, truly, but still more truly have been a devilish human being!—And therefore take note: I sentence you to death by drowning!" "Georg felt himself urged from the room," rushed past the astonished charwoman, "across the roadway, driven toward the water," and with a cry of love for his parents easily drowned out by traffic, "let himself drop." What strikes us chiefly about this denouement is the peculiar, unlifelike readiness with which Georg acts upon his father's outrageous statement. The father's disapproval of his son as a human being is suddenly expressed as a legal judgment, and the son takes the judgment literally and indeed compulsively, which would be incredible in real life. This is dream logic. The connections that would make for credibility ("Georg felt as if his father's disapproval were a sentence and as if he ought to obey him") are missing, and what we have is abrupt juxtaposition unconsciously signifying cause-and-effect relation itself, not any symbolic equation of image and image. (The pathetic touches of the astonished charwoman and especially the drowned outcry are like secondary revisions of primary process thinking.) Yet Kafka, if not Georg, knows clearly that the effect is absurd and even jokelike. One of the commonest techniques of joking is to take words overliterally, to shift expectation abruptly. Finally, then, Kafka's surrealism or expressionism or whatever label one wishes to use is unlike the impacted symbolic realism of a Conrad. Its symbolism, its rhetorical art generally, tends to be both excessively naive, like the dream, and self-mockingly sophisticated, like the joke.

I have been relating major instances of literary symbolism to the dream understood according to Freud's psychological model. But, as the Lacanians point out, the dream unlike the symptom is a verbal product, and may thus be discussed in the light of a linguistic model. For Lacan the unconscious is structured like a language, and the primary processes of condensation and displacement are homologous with metaphor and metonymy, though these seeming analogies become sanctions for placing the mind inside language rather than language inside the mind. The use of rhetorical terms may be misleading, for rhetoric is understood by the semiologist in Paul de Man's sense of "nonmimetic" rather than in the familiar sense of artful and cogent. The repressed is not what is unadmitted to consciousness, therefore, but what is unadmitted to discourse, which is above all the illusoriness of reference, for we lazily like to imagine language as a medium of exchange between the stable poles of self and other. Language is indelibly stamped by the period of early childhood when the idea of a self is forming, when the desire *for* the other is inextricably bound up with the desire *of* the other. It is this whole dialectical realm of language—or at any rate the more abstract form of it, *langue* rather than *parole*—that Lacan calls the symbolic.[17]

Like the arch-symbolist Mallarmé, Lacan would dissolve the universe into language, the world into the word. In Wordsworth's more Freudian poetics, "the mighty world of eye and ear," depending on the subsistent actuality of the physical world, would be called the Imaginary, derived from a preverbal experience of images. The true symbolic order is the ever-indeterminate relation of sign to image, signifier to signified. But unlike Mallarmé, who went from sign to image to the unity of poetic experience, Lacan does not seek an impossible ultimate unity. To be born into the symbolic order of language is to be born without the means of achieving unity and selfhood, for the unconscious is the discourse of the other. As Melanie Klein, from whom Lacan partly and self-avowedly derives, would have said, symbolizing requires learning how to tolerate the loss of an object rather than—as in earliest infancy, in psychosis and in dreams—hallucinating it. This link to Klein is worth pursuing briefly, as it helps to clarify, for an Anglo-American audience sketchily familiar with the Hegel to Heidegger tradition, the difference between Lacan and Freud.

In 1916, Ernest Jones tried to close out Jung's debate with Freud concerning the roles of biology and culture in symbol formation by asserting dogmatically that "only what is repressed is symbolized and only what is repressed needs to be symbolized." He wanted to restrict the psychoanalytic or "true" meaning of symbolization to a regressive as well as unconscious process. "All symbolism betokens a relative incapacity for either apprehension or presentation, primarily the former."[18] This position draws the line between dream and literary symbolism very sharply, ignoring the more or less transitional material that Freud found in typical dreams, folklore, and fairy tales. It was therefore bound to be modified even by psychoanalysts. But the Kleinians and, after them, Lacan, put forth an altered view that goes to the other extreme, and in theory draws hardly any line between dream and poem.

Thus Hanna Siegel, in her authoritative "Notes on Symbol Formation," distinguishes between what she calls Jones's "symbolic equation" and "the symbol proper":

In the symbolic equation, the symbol-substitute is felt to *be* the original object. The substitute's own properties are not recognized or admitted. The symbolic equation is used to deny the absence of the ideal object, or to control a persecuting one. It belongs to the earliest stages of development. The symbol proper, on the other hand, available for sublimation and furthering the development of the ego, is felt to *represent* the object; its own characteristics are recognized, respected and used. It arises when depressive feelings predominate over the paranoid-schizoid ones, when separation from the object, ambivalence, guilt, and loss can be experienced and tolerated. The symbol is not used to deny but to overcome loss.[19]

What Siegel's view shares with Lacan's, for all their differences, is the assumption that the infant experiences an irremediable loss or deprivation and that the best he or she can do is learn to tolerate it through symbol formation rather than, like a psychotic, to deny it. This view, playing down the later Oedipus complex and making the first eighteen months of life so determinative, relegates to abnormality the hallucinatory identification of wish and fact that Freud found in the dreams of normal people. The way is then open for a revisionary poetics that merges the dream into the literary text.

Geoffrey Hartman, for example, has argued that dreaming is as much a communication as a concealment; that it is concerned not only with considerations of *re*presentability, as Freud said, but also with considerations of *pre*sentability; that, in short, communication is a primary, instinctual need.[20] Bert States has suggested, in an essay called "The Art of Dreaming," that the dreamer's motive and the artist's are similar, though the dreamer's art may be crude. He cites the case of a man who dreamed he could not turn on his faucet, called a plumber who happened to be a woman and who turned on his faucet without difficulty, at which point he woke up with an emission. States infers that the dream solved what is essentially a narrative problem: how to bring a woman into proximity with a sexually aroused protagonist.[21]

Freud never denied that problem solving could take place in dreams, that dreams in fact could contain what he called secondary process thinking, indistinguishable from wakeful thought. But he did assert that the essential characteristic of dreaming was the dream work that disguised intelligibility sufficiently so that the alarm system of preconscious awareness would not be aroused and sleep could continue. Of course there is nothing to prevent a waker from touching up his recollection of a dream, from undoing condensation and displacement sufficiently so as to render it intelligible and even rhetorically adequate enough to be called literary. This possibility would only confirm for me what Hazard Adams has recently and eloquently argued against the deconstructionists, that language is inside man as well as man inside language, and can be used creatively.[22]

By expanding the meaning of symbolic as he does, Lacan effectually nullifies the distinction I would restore between dream and art as more or less unconscious, and therefore less or more intelligible uses of words. Despite his "return to Freud" slogan, he should, I think, be placed in a line of Freudian revisionists, going back to Jung, for whom primary and secondary process thinking were indistinguishable. But unlike Jung, and unlike Geoffrey Hartman and Bert States, he does not make a case for the communicative and creative functions of dreaming. He would show, rather, that no stable meaning can be established either in dreams or in literary texts. Weaving together a theory of pre-oedipal object relations with the sophistications of Hegelian dialectic and Saussurean linguistics, Lacanians seek to show that notions such as art and artist fall away with certain insecure psychological assumptions.

The difference between Freud and Lacan comes down to the question of whether or not to accept a provisional frame of reference. Freud would do so, for the sake of positive knowledge. Lacan would not, for the sake of the eternal play of the signifier, perhaps the equivalent in a skeptical age of Mallarmé's "unity of poetic experience." Though averse to philosophy, Freud understood that positive knowledge was dependent upon assumptions and therefore, from a more abstract point of view, could be called illusory. If told that his was only one theory of dreams—this is a counterstatement I have heard several times from philosophers—he would probably have shrugged and asked for another theory equally cogent. But Lacan's ideas are more congruent than Freud's with literary *theory*, where the concept of provisionality is important, and they have undeniably inspired much criticism of a remarkable generalizing power.

Two senses of the term *interdisciplinary* are at issue here. Lacan as a structuralist and semiologist is looking for the common denominator in all language-using fields, all human sciences, and finds it in the instability of any given frame of reference. Since this view is comprehensive, I doubt that it can be made compatible with the idea of literary criticism as a distinct discipline. Freud as the deviser of a particular discipline respects the integrity of every other. From a Freudian perspective, an interdisciplinary study would be essentially analogical, exploring likenesses while respecting differences. It does not have to be timid, however, and it is likely to be concrete.

## Notes

1. Sigmund Freud, *The Standard Edition of the Complete Psychological Works*, 24 vols. (London: Hogarth Press, 1953–74), 15:150. Hereafter *SE*.

2. Freud, *SE*, 15:150.

3. "The range of things which are given symbolic expression is not wide: the human body as a whole, parents, children, brothers and sisters, birth, death, nakedness" (*SE*, 15:153).

4. John Forrester, *Language and the Origins of Psychoanalysis* (New York: Columbia University Press, 1980). See particularly "Philology," pp. 166–210.

5. Elisabeth Schneider in *Coleridge, Opium, and Kubla Khan* (New York: Octagon, 1966) has argued convincingly that this poem was not composed in a state of sleep, drugged or otherwise, but "as other poems are" (p. 18).

6. *The New Science of Giambattista Vico*, trans. Thomas Goddard Bergin and Max Harold Fisch, 3d ed. (Ithaca, N.Y.: Cornell University Press, 1948), p. 18.

7. Freud, *SE*, 4:260–66, 17:230–31.

8. *SE*, 17:230–31.

9. The "some" is in fact so large a number that specific citation would be unfair, but we may mention as typical of such a view the idea that Oedipus moves from denying the harsh truth about himself to confrontation and self-acceptance; that he grows out of infantile megalomania into mature humility; that he betrays the insecurity of the self-made man and gets into trouble accordingly.

10. Meredith Anne Skura, *The Literary Use of the Psychoanalytic Process* (New Haven, Conn.: Yale University Press, 1981), pp. 51, 53.

11. Bernard Knox, "The Freedom of Oedipus," *The New Republic*, 30 August 1982, pp. 28–34.

12. The daydream model is particularly evident in "Creative Writers and Day-dreaming" (*SE*, vol. 9). It is sometimes said that Freud significantly altered his view of art thereafter, but it does not seem so to me. In "Formulations Regarding the Two Principles in Mental Functioning" of 1911 (*SE*, 12:224), he presents the artist as "a man who turns from reality" but "with his special gifts . . . molds his fantasies into a new kind of reality." As late as 1933 in the *New Introductory Lectures* (*SE*, 22:160), he refers to art as an "illusion" that "makes no attempt at invading the realm of reality" except in the hands of "a few people who are spoken of as 'possessed by art.'" This is to leave us without any middle ground between the escapist multitudes and the crazed few. The larger point here is that Freud's immense contribution to our intellectual life is as a psychologist, not as a literary critic or aesthetician.

13. Northrop Frye, *The Great Code: The Bible and Literature* (New York: Harcourt Brace Jovanovich, 1982), p. 5.

14. I am indebted in these few sentences to Meredith Skura's fine, extended discussion of dream and allegory in *Literary Use,* pp. 151–65.

15. *Blake: Complete Writings with Variant Readings,* ed. Geoffrey Keynes (London: Oxford University Press, 1966), p. 604.

16. Ian Watt, *Conrad in the Nineteenth Century* (Berkeley, Calif.: University of California Press, 1979), p. 239.

17. Jacques Lacan, *Écrits: A Selection,* trans. Alan Sheridan (New York: W. W. Norton, 1977). See particularly the essays called "The function and field of speech and language in psychoanalysis" and "The agency of the letter in the unconscious or reason since Freud." See also Paul de Man, *Allegories of Reading: Figural Language in Rousseau, Nietzsche, Rilke, and Proust* (New Haven, Conn.: Yale University Press, 1979), pp. 3–19.

18. Ernest Jones, "The Theory of Symbolism," *Papers on Psychoanalysis* (Boston: Beacon Press, 1961), pp. 116, 137.

19. Hanna Siegel, "Notes on Symbol Formation," *International Journal of Psychoanalysis* 38 (1957): 395.

20. Geoffrey Hartman, "The Dream of Communication," in *I. A. Richards: Essays in His Honor,* ed. Reuben Brower, Helen Vendler, and John Hollander (New York: Oxford University Press, 1973), pp. 157–77.

21. Bert O. States, "The Art of Dreaming," *Hudson Review* 31, no. 4 (Winter 1978–79): 571–86.

22. Hazard Adams, *Philosophy of the Literary Symbolic* (Tallahassee, Fla.: University Presses of Florida, 1983), p. 363.

# Opening the Closure and Vice Versa

## Joseph Margolis
*Temple University*

AT the moment, in the circus of literary theory, it is the moderate who is the gymnast of the center ring. One hardly blinks at the contortions of the severe structuralist or the even more severe deconstructionist—moralizers who move among us with their comfortable doomsday injunctions.

One warns us against the pretense of the aleatory, the tolerance of the contingently persuasive, the delusion of readers who deny their appropriately "docile" role by insisting on the seemingly independent structures of the objective texts they read or who exercise a penchant for the active and arbitrary and idiosyncratic response they believe can never be gainsaid. The proper reading of a text, we are advised, is controlled, regulated, imposed, ineluctably disclosed by our surrendering sensitively to the very structuring power of reading—"a text and its intertext being but variations of the same structure."[1] Reading a text "consists in pursuing such reference [of text to preexistent texts], in a recollective dialectic moving between the text one decodes and those other texts that one recalls."[2] Of course, there are many competing strategies recommended for such an edifying redemption; but that's not the point. The point is that the closure of a literary text, the very prospect of fixing its textuality, depends on its belonging to a "semiotic system," entering which we ourselves (shall we say?) are permitted to perceive its "unique significatory unity."[3] The initiation favors the filiating organization of human—semiotizing—subjects: not atomic external objects encountered somewhere, not solipsistic intelligences muttering to themselves, but the relational, totalized intertextual society of signs in which we live and have our being and which, thus encountered, forms the "necessary and sufficient" foundation, the "invariant" structure, that all our contingent, stylistically and generically variable texts instantiate (in being accessible as literary texts at all).[4]

The other redeemers, the deconstructionists, seduce us into a liberating "bliss" that strangely "discomforts," or invite us to practice a severe and exhilarating science "that runs the risk of never being established."[5] We are to forego the *"comfortable practice of reading"* (which, it needs to be said, remains forever available), because, thus positioned, "The text is never a 'dialogue' . . . there is not, behind the text, someone active (the writer) and out front someone passive (the reader); there is not a subject and an object. The text supersedes grammatical attitudes." We are offered "the untenable text, the impossible text," the text inaccessible to an orderly or progressive "cultural" criticism, the heady text that can only be entered "hysterically," confronting the "void," the text that permits only a "desperate plagiarism."[6] Put perhaps more safely but still opposed to the false safety of the structuralist, "the inter-text is: the impossibility of living outside the infinite text," meaning is not only "precarious" it is "revocable, reversible," and "discourse [ineluctably] incomplete," "the text undoes nomination" of every sort.[7] Closure is therefore impossible. One can almost formulate these happy tidings scholastically: "The hinge [*brisure*] marks the impossibility that a sign, the unity of a signifer and a signified, be produced within the plenitude of a present and an absolute presence."[8]

One would like to believe that these are the sounds of the war of the titans, but the truth is that the skirmishing is nearly inadvertent, backed into by shy creatures that would rather munch in their own territory. How is that, you'll ask? Well, there's the price of rhetoric, the demand of the pop world of academia, the charm of the memorable driving the sensible out of circulation, the sham contest of sham extremes enacted by lovely voices that either do or should know better. No doubt there *are* mistakes to be corrected. But nowadays, the corrections are no corrections: they are fandangos of some kind that circle around the obvious range of genuinely debatable issues that we (and they) never lose sight of, all the while we applaud these quite impossible masquerades. Could anyone literally believe these extraordinary pronouncements? I honestly doubt it.

This, then, is the confrontational obligation of the warrior moderate. He says—in his own voice: "There's closure and there's closure"; *"clôture and ouverture are one and the same";* "the reading of texts obtains, their defense obtains, all that comes to an end as all things must but the closure of a reading invites a new opening and every opening looks to its end." Now, is that a better thing to say?

The structuralist and the deconstructionist *say* impossible things. They pretend to be talking about the closure of reading particular texts. But the clever structuralist—certainly Lévi-Strauss through his excessive totalizing, even Althusser with his most improbable armature, also Riffaterre by way of his solo hermeneutic structuralism restructuring the Barthesian deconstruction of oldtime structuralism—*shows* the futility of closure in the very sense of closure he claims to favor. And the equally clever deconstructionist—certainly the Barthes of *S/Z*, equally certainly Derrida, the implacable critic of Husserl, Saussure, Lacan, the indefatigable reader of the *Phaedrus* and Mallarmé's *Mimique*—*shows* by the seriousness of his hyperbolic play that there is a measure of validity after all in the mock closure he imposes. The theory of closure shows only the infinite openness of texts; and the anti-theory theory of openness hardly disturbs the persuasive asymptotic drift of reading toward closure, coopting all resistance. One suspects, therefore, that these two could not possibly be merely pitted against one another: there must be a saner, more subterranean, agreement between them that deserves to be acknowledged (however discreetly, so as not to disturb the theater), which joins their struggle in the heroically ordinary.

The trouble is: the relatively unassailable doctrines in question are quite unfashionable, difficult even to be heard—unless they are at once attacked or supported from the vantage of either extreme. Still, they *are* secretly acknowledged by both sides, in a sense not really congruent with the public pose of either, though they are required by the viability of their quarrel. *And,* these propositions are just the ones to help us recover the sense in which the theory of reading cannot fail to be committed at once to both *clôture* and *ouverture*. The simple truth is that those notions simply are not incompatibles, certainly are not contradictories. Well, here are two salient such theses:

1. There is no discourse without reference.
2. There is no semiotic system.

The first insures some form of closure; the second, some form of openness. The first disables deconstruction; the second disables structuralism. The first entails the provision of structures; the second, the appeal to foundations. The first restructures deconstruction; the second deconstructs structuralism.

They are homely doctrines. One should not insist on too elaborate a reading. The first simply says that discourse must be about something to be discourse at all—that the apt speakers of a language must share the ability to agree about what they are talking about and whatever being able to do that entails. All the quarrels about truth and reality and method and knowledge and meaning presuppose that much at least—even the dispute between the structuralist and the deconstructionist. When Barthes, for instance, in his deliberately provocative way, usurping the structuralist's idiom in order to subvert it, says "the Text . . . practices the infinite deferral of the signified . . . its field is that of the signifier,"[9] we must not permit ourselves to forget that he himself begins this memorable essay: "Over the past several years, a change has been taking place in our ideas about language and, as a consequence, about the (literary) work, which owes at least its phenomenal existence to language."[10] The point is not to ask, Where is the infinite deferral there? but to realize that the thesis of the infinite deferral of reference is doubly controlled by the referential functioning of the "work" (in Barthes's vocabulary) and by the referential intent of his own essay offered to assist a certain habituated reader to get his new bearings within a certain changing literature. The "infinite deferral of the signified" is an artifact of some sort *of* ordinary referential skills. There is no other way. The pretense of the completely aleatoric is simply that.

On the other hand, the second proposition simply says that no mere human has ever been able to formulate an unchanging, comprehensive, single network of interconnected semiotic items of any sort that could provide a fixed internal place for every possible datum of human semiotic interest in any given domain of inquiry, or that any serious investigator has even actually used such a system or could plausibly claim to be doing so. All the quarrels about structures, relationships, categories, formative and transformative processes, kernels, cores, substrata, latencies, matrices, presuppose that much at least—including the dispute between the structuralist and the historicist.[11] When, therefore, Michael Riffaterre affirms, in an idiom that nearly combines the Russian Formalist and the French structuralist themes, that "the literariness of a work is inseparable from its textuality . . . hence at the semiotic level, words or texts have other texts as their referents,"[12] we must remember that the Formalists meant by their pronouncement precisely *not* to isolate what they (never quite successfully) took to be the distinctive functioning of literary texts, *not* to isolate the functioning of literary texts from that ulterior *reference* to the living history of a people in virtue of which alone the text affords its characteristic illumination; *and* we must remember that Riffaterre himself acknowledges, within the very remark already cited, that "at the representational level at which the reader grasps words discursively, words do seem to have as referents things or nonverbal conceptions of things."[13] The point is not to ask for the precise "pineal" connection between literary and nonliterary uses of language but to realize that the pursuit of semiotic referents from text to intertext—pursuing, say, "the expansion of a single matricing phrase" through "the entire text," even if it is reasonably successful or even if it is only one promising strategy among many (without privilege)—implicitly concedes that "closure" and "canonical forms" and "exclusive signifying unity" and "semiotic system" are exaggerated idealizations within the very flux of effective natural language.[14] The apparent containment of the semiotics of literary texts within the total semiotics of literary intertexts is nothing but an expression of the interpreter's exhuberance or caution, certainly not a judgment of the actual disconnection between language and the world. There is no other way.

The falsely Nietzschean pronouncement, ironically attractive to the deconstructionist, that reference is a lie or a fiction or a delusion, is either incoherent and self-defeating or just a preposterous or heroic pose to insure a proper respect for the literary text itself *and* for the deconstructionist's own pronouncement. Only equivocation could save those well-known dicta of Paul de Man that appear to have us inhabit forever the fictional world of literature, within which we are drawn to deny that fictionality itself.[15] Similarly, once structuralism is responsibly linked to the systematic review of literary history so that genres are relatively fixed *for* a period of literary evolution and so that the historical development of forms is rendered intelligible relative *to* literary structures assumed to be in place—once, as Todorov says, "the factitious opposition between 'structure' and 'history' vanishes"[16]—the study of structures can no longer be construed in the manner of structuralist closure (*pace* Todorov). The deconstructionist (de Man) is tempted by "the possibility of referential meaning as the *telos* of all language."[17] He must resist if he is not to concede too much to the structuralist. And the structuralist, for his part (Todorov), must remember to search for "the *laws* of variability, which concern the transition of one literary 'epoch' to another,"[18] if he is not to make an historicized shambles of his own essential conviction. Both structuralism and deconstruction are, for utterly different reasons, tempted by the isolation and sufficiency of a purely textual world. And both see the need to resist that temptation.

This is the sense in which an honest deconstructionism concedes the necessity of closure—however much it resists. This is the sense in which an honest structuralism concedes the unlimited openness of whatever provisional closure it proposes. Hence, this is the sense in which structuralism and deconstruction are hardly opposed to one another. Closure *is* openness tested for plausibility, and openness *is* closure with a tolerance for what is yet to come. The history of the standard contests of literary theory is utterly misleading, skewed for purposes of recruiting adherents to much glossier global doctrines, prepared to tolerate (for advertising purposes) a verbally crippling picture of the viability of reading and critical practice—from which, after all, it safely draws its own life. Ironically, this is the kindest account of all, for, literally construed, both deconstruction and structuralism are incoherent for humans. Structuralists pretend that the closure of texts is a function of a totalized and single system of relata, any change in which constitutes a change of system; but they cannot specify any such system and, therefore, on their calculation, their own would-be approximations are utterly meaningless. And deconstructionists, defending the infinite openness of texts, abjure every use of logocentric reference and metaphysically compromising predicates and, therefore, speaking (as they must, to make their point), they violate their own constraint.

What, then, is meant by closure and its denial? There are a great many answers, and it is important to realize that no single line of reflection, however important, can satisfy us. Terry Eagleton, for instance, notes "the *contradictory* nature of [Lukác's] *oeuvre,* whose neo-Hegelian categories [he says] now challenge, now ratify the Stalinist closure."[19] He means, obviously, by "closure" the suppression of honest differences within an official line (of any sort) that pretends to a privileged authority. Well, no one seems to be in favor of that nowadays. On the other hand, at the very beginning of *Grammatology*—speaking of that pretended science ("the science of writing," in the profoundly profound sense we have all learned to love), Derrida observes that every attempt to grasp the "unity of its project or its object . . . is, in principle, more or less covertly yet always, determined by an historico-metaphysical epoch of which we merely glimpse the *closure*. I do not say the *end*."[20] Here, of course, he is simply (that is, not so simply) warning us to be on guard against the temptation to take any posited structures (our own, one dares imagine) to be timelessly anchored in a cognitively transparent world—for there is no such world. Well, no one seems to deny that that warning is well taken.

There are many ways of summarizing the message. Try three. First of all, discourse requires structures, but not structuralism; foundations, but not foundationalism; essences, but not essentialism; universals, but not universalism; cognition, but not cognitivism; and so on.[21] Deconstruction rightly opposes closure of the second sort of each pair, but cannot do without closure of the first sort even in rendering its own bill of particulars; and closure of that sort is hardly opposed to openness—it positively dotes on it. Secondly, the *clôture/ouverture* idiom is equivocally, or multivocally, designed to test allegiances on such issues as these: Is there a fixed and reliable demarcation between what is "inside" and what is "outside" a particular text? Is there some certain or privileged or primary cognitive stance with respect to which the semiotic function of particular texts can be specified? Is there an exhaustive system of structural relations with respect to which all efforts to understand parts of the literary tradition can be understood in spite of the contingent histories of particular texts and of particular readers? Can we separate once and for all the properties of the real world and the conceptually organizing function of the human mind? Is there an ideally convergent reading of any particular text that all responsible interpretations approximate? A negative answer on all those questions—*and* an affirmative answer on cognate questions consistent with that—is quite capable of reconciling closure and openness, which, after all, is really all that is needed. Thirdly and perhaps most obviously, the two propositions offered earlier are inextricably connected, for there can be no reference unless there are structures to hold reference in place, and there can be no structures that disallow reference. Reference and structure are hardly more than a slightly displaced admission of the predicative nature of natural discourse used by gifted animals who manage to survive—in part by its successful functioning. Closure, so seen, is nothing more than the abstracted acknowledgment of that continuous deed, and openness, the speculation of how little that entails. Moderation, therefore, is hardly a literary theory, but it is the sine qua non of any that would be viable.

The curious thing is that intertextuality is the common property of the extreme structuralist and the extreme deconstructionist: one has only to compare Barthes and Riffaterre. In Barthes's hands, reference to the intertextual signifies "the infinite deferral of the signified," the hopelessness of any uniquely correct, ideally convergent, finitely completable reading of a text; in Riffaterre's, reference to the intertextual signifies the disciplined, ulterior, and ultimate "passivity" of readers arranging their critical training for the reception of larger, systematic structures subtly fastened by an historically enriching semiosis to the local contingencies of a particular text. The first yields *une jouissance* in the live impossibility of closure; the second, an apotheosis in the re-cognition of the great system perceptible even now in the seemingly unstructured vagaries of any idiom. In the one, we are led to doubt the fixed identity of authors, readers, texts, intertexts, signifiers, and signifieds; in the other, granting the theoretical limitation of reference to authors and texts, and granting the contingency of readers' bias, of authors' intention, of communities' history, we find our safe haven finally in the "only one universal of literariness . . . textuality . . . the complex of formal and semantic factors that characterize a self-sufficient, coherent, unified text and legitimize its forms, however aberrant they may be, by removing any hint of the gratuitous."[22]

The trouble here is double trouble. We cannot really do without texts or authors or readers or intentions or signs or languages or histories. When, for instance, Foucault worries the question of the historical recency of the idea of an individualized author, not nearly as much is threatened in the practice of criticism as one may suppose. It hardly matters whether

Foucault's grasp of the history of that development is accurate or not, for the conceptual apparatus required to make the point already entails the referential reliability (not the timeless fixity) of the production and identification of texts. Although he concedes in a telltale moment that "The word 'work' and the unity that it designates [the focus of Barthes's deconstructive theme] are probably as problematic as the status of the author's individuality," Foucault presses the point that the literary work "is an interplay of signs arranged less according to its signified content than according to the very nature of the signifier"—that is, arranged less according to an individualized author's expression or intention than to the "rules" and dialectical "transgression" of the rules of the apparently operative system of writing that is in place.[23] In this sense, Foucault is a poststructuralist but not a deconstructionist. In the same sense, Stanley Fish's candid confession of early error regarding Text, Reader, Author and his present search for the Reading Community (predictably doomed for the same reasons he himself details for the already discarded "universals"—to press into service Riffaterre's term) are too sanguine (both in the old rejection and the new adoption) for what is needed.[24] On the other hand, Riffaterre rejects the totalizing sufficiency of the same triad of concepts as does Fish, but *he* does so not merely for the sake of objectivity but also (and more decisively) for the sake of a structured system that alone makes objectivity possible. He is, therefore, not alarmed by the openended contingencies—and the threatening relativism—of history: he coopts *ouverture* as a form of necessary and provisional sensitivity to the idiosyncratic properties of local texts in order to reimpose the ulterior intertextual closure that we *know* in advance awaits us. This is the sense in which Riffaterre offers an emboldened version of the fusion of Russian Formalist and Czech Structuralist practices—in reaction to the excesses of French deconstruction.

But Foucault would be wrong if he supposed that confirming the historical novelty of individualized authorship calls into radical question all versions of the "authoring" principle (in effect, the deconstructive move); and what he offers (assuming he is correct) is conceptually too slight to help provide even a reasonable account, *here and now,* of how to construe the responsible reading of texts. And Riffaterre is surely wrong in supposing that intertextuality is not open to precisely the same conceptual worries that afflict the notions of text and reader and author and the rest (that's just the structuralist disorder all over again). In this sense, Riffaterre is a regressive structuralist in contrast, say, to Jakobson's being a progressive structuralist. Similarly, Barthes is a progressive deconstructionist in contrast, say, to J. Hillis Miller's being a regressive deconstructionist (that is, as in worrying the Foucault-like but not Foucauldian question, "Who, however, is 'Shelley'?"—in trying to present deconstruction as itself a kind of supple critical discipline, the effective use of the system of rhetoric but without the false conviction of metaphysics).[25]

Well then, here's the coda without musical closure:

1. There is no discourse without reference.
2. There is no semiotic system.
3. Text and intertext are methodologically identical and only relationally distinct.
4. Text and intertext cannot escape reference to the world, which is never more than partly and variably captured textually.

To suppose otherwise is theologically curious but critically uninteresting.

## Notes

1. Michael Riffaterre, "Sémiotique intertextuelle; l'interprétant," *Révue d' Esthétique*, Nos. 1–2 (1979), p. 132. English translations here are my own.
2. Ibid., p. 128.
3. Ibid. See also, Michael Riffaterre, *Semiotics of Poetry* (Bloomington, Ind.: Indiana University Press, 1978); and "The Self-Sufficient Text," *Diacritics* 3 (1973).
4. "Sémiotique intertextuelle," p. 132.
5. Roland Barthes, *The Pleasure of the Text*, trans. Richard Miller (New York: Hill and Wang, 1975), p. 14; Jacques Derrida, *Of Grammatology*, trans. Gayatri Chakravorty Spivak (Baltimore, Md.: Johns Hopkins University Press, 1976), p. 4.
6. Barthes, pp. 16, 22.
7. Ibid., pp. 4, 36, 45.
8. Derrida, p. 69.
9. Roland Barthes, "From Work to Text," in Josué V. Harari, ed., *Textual Strategies* (Ithaca, N.Y.: Cornell University Press, 1979), p. 76.
10. Ibid., p. 73.
11. See for instance Claude Lévi-Strauss, *The Savage Mind*, trans. (Chicago: University of Chicago press, 1966), chap. 9; and Jean-Paul Sartre, *Critique of Dialectical Reason*, ed. Jonathan Rée, trans. Alan Sheridan-Smith (London: NLB, 1976), bk. 2, chap. 3, p. 3.

12. Riffaterre, p. 128.
13. Ibid.
14. Ibid.
15. Paul de Man, *Blindness and Insight*, 2d ed., rev. (Minneapolis: University of Minnesota Press, 1983), p. 18; *Allegories of Reading* (New Haven, Conn.: Yale University Press, 1979), p. 201.
16. Tzvetan Todorov, *Introduction to Poetics*, trans. Richard Howard (Minneapolis: University of Minnesota Press, 1981), pp. 59–63; see also, Gérard Genette, *Narrative Discourse*, trans. Jane E. Lewin (Ithaca, N.Y.: Cornell University Press, 1980).
17. de Man, *Allegories of Reading*, p. 201.
18. Todorov, p. 63.
19. Terry Eagleton, "Towards a Revolutionary Criticism," *Walter Benjamin or Towards a Revolutionary Criticism* (London: NLB, 1981), p. 89.
20. Derrida, p. 4.
21. I have tried to develop these themes systematically in a number of places: most recently, in "Pragmatism without Foundations," *American Philosophical Quarterly*, forthcoming; "Relativism, History, and Objectivity in the Human Studies," *Journal of the Theory of Social Behavior*, forthcoming; "Historicism, Universalism, and the Threat of Relativism," *The Monist*, forthcoming.
22. The statement is from Michael Riffaterre, "For an Intertextual Definition of Textuality," presented at the 1983 MLA convention in New York. I've taken the liberty of making use of it here for the sake of roundness and accuracy. My own paper, presented at the same symposium, "Text Closure: A Reassessment," was prepared without foreknowledge of Riffaterre's remarks.
23. Michel Foucault, "What Is an Author?", trans. Josué V. Harari, in Josué V. Harari, ed., *Textual Strategies*, pp. 144, 142.
24. See Stanley Fish, *Is There a Text in This Class?* (Cambridge, Mass.: Harvard University Press, 1980).
25. J. Hillis Miller, "The Critic as Host," in *Deconstruction and Criticism* (New York: Seabury Press, 1979), p. 243 (read in the context of the entire essay).

# *The Rime of the Ancient Mariner:* Coleridge's Scientific and Philosophic Insights

## L. M. Grow

### *Broward Community College*

I

IF a book entitled *Coleridge the Scientist* appears in the near future, the reason will not only be that many other categories of the thinking of a man who literally "took all knowledge for his province" (Read, p. 96) have proved worthy of full-length studies.[1] The reason will also be that relatively recent scholarship has returned with increasing interest to his scientific or quasi-scientific pronouncements[2] in a surprisingly comprehensive range of disciplines (see Barfield, p. 37; Ball, p. 20; and Read, p. 97). Coleridge often devoted extensive labor to intellectual problems with bases in the natural sciences. Among the most prominent products of Coleridge's labors are, of course, his aesthetic dicta stemming from the biological concept of organic form, such as the "coadunating" power of the imagination" (Watters, p. 93). But he also did work in physics (Abrams, 1972), meteorology (Mann), astronomy (Lowes), chemistry (Coburn), and medicine (Harris). This does not mean that Coleridge's efforts lacked direction or coherence. His scientific work is one aspect of his philosophical thinking. He intended his philosophy to be comprehensive and so he did not partition scientific insights and philosophic insights into sepa-

---

I am grateful to Dr. Alan Friedman, Director of the New York Hall of Science, for reviewing the scientific content of this article and for many helpful suggestions about the presentation of the scientific material.

rate categories. Rather, he attempted "to give a philosophical basis to science" (Miller, p. 86).

Part of what has delayed a full-length study of Coleridge's science, I suspect, is a prevalent opinion that "To most modern readers, Coleridge's writings on science appear as incomprehensible nonsense, pure gibberish" (Miller, p. 77). Even "against the knowledge of his age" Coleridge is not always given high marks. Boulger, for instance, thinks that Coleridge's "approach to science . . . often approaches the ludicrous . . . [his approach] appears trivial or irresponsible in [its] desire to move from primitive knowledge to grand ontological view" (p. 312). But this assessment is certainly not unanimous. Critics of the stature of Abrams, Ball, and Barfield consider Coleridge's scientific jottings anything but "nonsense":

> Once we recognize the elements of scientific curiosity in so many of the descriptive entries in the Notebooks, we begin to modify the idea that Coleridge might be just an accurate observer of the world, one brilliantly capturing the miscellany as it comes. . . . he would be unfaithful to his philosophic self were it otherwise, and false too to his concept of what constitutes a genuine scientific interest in phenomena. . . . Hence it is not surprising to find a strong current of intellectual speculation coursing through the Notebooks, giving many entries the status of experiments, not merely descriptions. [Ball, p. 28]

In fact, it is quite possible to see Coleridge's scientific assumptions in a favorable light, especially if we do not unfairly pit him against the standards and discoveries of science in our own time. As Snyder (1924) suggests, Coleridge's cosmogony is, in historical context, forward-looking. Potter is even more enthusiastic, crediting Coleridge with sensing "the significant currents of thought in the civilized world," even though Coleridge's perceptions were sometimes more instinctive than conscious (p. 379). My own sympathies lie with Potter. I can find nothing in Coleridge, aside from portions of the letters and occasional notebook jottings (none pertaining to science) to justify such strong epithets as "ludicrous" and "trivial." Certainly nothing in the works consciously intended for publication merits such a valuation.

## II

Another of the traditional reasons for looking askance at Coleridge's scientific writings has been an unresolved dispute about whether he plagiarized at least some of them. By far the preponderance of opinion on the part of those who have made in-depth studies of Coleridge's interactions with other thinkers is that he did not appropriate materials unchanged. When he translated or adapted passages, he often embellished or extended the ideas and even disagreed with the conclusions reached by the person whose material he was utilizing.[3]

But what of Coleridge's scientific thought, in particular? Beach's challenges to Coleridge's originality may disincline us to accept, on behalf of Coleridge's scientific writings, at least, the traditional defenses for his compositional procedure. Here, however, it seems to me that Snyder's judgment has not been superseded:

> The annotations as a whole evince a critical attitude toward the material presented, an attitude not compatible with any merely fanciful playing with cosmic theories or cosmic images. Even those that are somewhat facetious in tone show Coleridge's philosophic imagination hard at work, ever challenging and then accepting or rejecting as the case may be. [1924, p. 621]

Sankey (p. 67) favorably compares Coleridge to Darwin in this regard:

> Both Coleridge and Darwin devoted themselves to the interpretation of nature. Neither man had the habit of simply responding to the scenery, taking pleasure in the emotions aroused by natural surroundings; they were too busy attempting to understand what they saw. It might even be argued that Darwin's scientific work was a successful application of Coleridge's methodological program: the illuminating insight, applied to a variety of formerly unrelated fields, and supported by a careful review of all relevant experience.

Whatever picture might exist of Coleridge as a copyist who had not the training or the talent even to assimilate, much less originate, scientific hypotheses simply must be repainted. Beach's apparently devastating proof of the pilfering of the *Theory of Life* from Schelling and Steffans does not shake this judgment. Even McFarland (no fan of Coleridge's science) finds, if Abrams's discoveries about the dominance of Coleridge's "metaphysical consciousness" are taken into account, "this strange and borrowed work curiously Coleridgean" (p. 325). Overall, the most sensible judgment about the charge of "literary buccaneering," a judgment which Hume (p. 489) and McFarland accept, is that the "source of Coleridge's mature thought is his own earlier ideas. As Potter says (p. 395), "It is not as an originator but as a reflector—a many-faceted reflector—that Coleridge is important." Coleridge is dramatically original in perceiving a mediating function for the powers of the mind; his empirically-based, philosophic analysis of consciousness, for instance, is a significant contribution to the "dialect of the imagination" (Freedman, p. 217; Metzger, p. 783).

## III

Although the preponderance of Coleridge's scientific musings are found in his prose,[4] reflections of science are also evident in his poetry. Coleridge, ". . . more than any other creative writer of his time sought some reconciliation between science and literature" (Evans, p. 44), and Coleridge felt that the poet and the scientist worked in similar ways.[5] Coleridge saw the poet's need for symbiosis of idea and instance, a reciprocity of concreteness and transcendence, as virtually identical with the scientists', the only difference being the order (of chronology, not priority) in which the two elements are used: ". . . where Coleridge calls the process of the scientists 'meditative oberservation,' he calls the creative power of the poet 'observant meditation'" (di Pasquale, p. 495). As Miller remarks, ". . . in nearly all his works Coleridge utilizes for illustrative purposes concepts and imagery drawn from the sciences. He applies the concept of cyclical imagery to an atom, a magnet, a poem, a state, and the Trinity, maintaining a remarkable consistency of imagery throughout" (p. 78). In his literary criticism, Coleridge adopts the conceptual framework and the terminology of natural science:

> Hence the strong hold which in all ages chemistry has had on the imagination. If in SHAKESPEARE we find nature idealized into poetry, through the creative power of a profound yet observant meditation, so through the meditative observation of a DAVY, a WOOLLASTON, or a HATCHETT . . . we find poetry, as it were, substantiated and realized in nature. [*The Friend*, 1:471][6]

Convergence of scientific and literary principle in Coleridge occurs most prominently in the concept of organic unity,[7] a concept which has important implications for *The Rime of the Ancient Mariner*. It is crucial to keep in mind that, although in our own time "organic unity" has been applied to justify the connection in one work of any elements otherwise inexplicable, for Coleridge the term had a precise and useful meaning. It was a recognition that (1) the components of an integer are both parts and whole, totally interpenetrated in each other yet remaining discrete; (2) the form originates internally, rather than being dictated by prefabricated rules; and (3) each work develops in its own way and must be approached by the reader in that way, not with the model of some other work in mind. Now this allows for unlimited flexibility and expansibility, since each newly-created entity can develop its own individual structure, but it must at the same time maintain precise, definable, and defensible internal patterns as well as relationships to all other entities.

Both the strictness of Coleridge's formulation of his theory of organic unity and its applicability to a literary work emerge quite clearly if we turn our attention to his Shakespearean criticism, long recognized as the meeting ground of philosophical principles and literary constructs for Coleridge:

> Shakespeare shaped his characters out of the nature within; but we cannot so safely say, out of *his own* nature, as an *individual person.* No! This latter is itself but a *natura naturata,* an effect, a product, not a *power.* It was Shakespeare's prerogative to have the *universal* which is potentially in each *particular,* opened out to him in the *homo generalis,* not as an abstraction of observation from a variety of men, but as the substance capable of endless modifications, of which his own personal existence was but one, and to use *this one* as the eye that beheld the other, and as the tongue that could convey the discovery. [*Miscellaneous Criticism,* pp. 43–44]

Here the notion of the one-in-many and the many-in-one is a criterion for literary excellence, not only because there is a "happy balance of the generic with the individual" (*Biographia Literaria,* 2:187), but also because more profoundly, ". . . here is an example of the reconciliation of opposites which the imagination embodies. The character is neither an individual nor a class alone, but, as it were, 'a class individualized'" (Badawi, p. 104). As Coleridge's remarks about character motivation, imagery, and the need for good actors in all roles, not just the major ones, make clear (Badawi, pp. 92, 114, 162, 163), he is espousing the symbiosis of individual and class, one and many, not merely bringing them together as contraries offsetting each other, or existing in a relationship of immovable object and irresistible force.

## IV

That Coleridge was able to apply scientific hypotheses to literary criticism is a circumstance that might lead us to wonder whether he ever extended the applications of the science with which he was acquainted, and used these hypotheses in the *writing* of literary works, such as *The Rime of the Ancient Mariner.* Although I think that such may have been the case, the possibility that he did so is only a possibility. My present contention is that scientific thought enables us to understand the structural (and perhaps thematic as well) workings of at least one Coleridge poem, *The Rime of the Ancient Mariner,* more clearly. I do not ascribe to Coleridge any conscious intent to apply scientific method, though what may have, as Lowes would have it, bubbled up from the well of the unconscious, is a metaphoric forerunner of modern quantum and field theory,[8] based on Coleridge's own convictions about organic unity operative both ontologically and epistemologically.

This scientific outlook especially yields dividends in explaining one of the most puzzling features of *The Rime of the Ancient Mariner*—the prose gloss. Until very recently, this prose gloss was explained in terms of Coleridge's tendency to append marginalia, notes, and prefaces to his poems (Martin, p. 71). At times Coleridge could become almost humorously frenetic where such addenda were concerned: "'The Motto—! —Where is the Motto—? I would not have lost the motto for a kingdom twas the best part of the Ode'" (Stephens, p. 402). Although it is frequently justifiable to regard this apparatus as trivial, pedantic, or purely exculpatory (Schulz, 1961, pp. 53–54), we must not be misled into the error of thinking, as many of Coleridge's contemporaries did, that this is true of *The Rime of the Ancient Mariner* (Stevenson, p. 31). As recently as 1969, Dunn assumed that "It was precisely to compensate for the lack of 'artful transitions' and 'full and extended connection of parts' that the gloss was added in 1815–1816." The temptation not to distinguish the "editorial" paraphernalia of *The Rime of the Ancient Mariner* from similar productions elsewhere in his works is made greater by the temporal coincidence of Coleridge's addiction to penning marginalia and his revisions of *The Rime of the Ancient Mariner.*[9]

Dyck's view of the gloss as narrative device by which two versions of the same story (the mariner's and the glosser's) may be compared is a major step in what I consider the right direction, though I think in one important respect she too misses the mark.[10] Comparing the narrative stance of the poem to Browning's *The Ring and the Book,* she views the tale as having a telling and a retelling. This is not true, precisely, for *The Rime of the Ancient Mariner*, since the glosser's tale is simultaneous with, not sequent to, the mariner's version. It is this major difference that I think works against not only this comparison but also others which on the surface might be similarly attractive. One thinks immediately of *The Moonstone*, in which each of the narrators supplies a portion of the story, no one by himself being in possession of all the facts; or of *The Grapes of Wrath*, its dichotomous structure of narrative and intercalary chapters seeming to parallel the ballad and the gloss, respectively, of *The Rime of the Ancient Mariner*.[11]

In applying the findings of quantum theoreticians to *The Rime of the Ancient Mariner*, even as loosely as an illustrative purpose permits, we are conscious of utilizing discoveries from the microworld of subatomic physics in the larger world of the mariner. This, of course, represents no handicap for modern theoreticians, since it is assumed that the laws of nature are constant; it is only because particles in the macroworld are so massive compared to atoms that the classical (i.e., Newtonian) physics can account adequately for observed behavior (Schlegel, pp. 222–23; Baker, pp. 190–91). Though Coleridge, naturally, had no way of foreseeing the revolutionary developments of subatomic physics, it is interesting that he did recognize a difference in manifestation of macro- and microreality:

> Thus the finite and infinite are the two necessary forms of Being, Manifested—which can never be divided—the instances in which either is assumed singly, will be found mere abstractions; or else those forms of subjective imagination, such as an atom, or Infinite Space. And what is Space? a something with the attributes of Nothing! but in real Science we must say
>
> 1. Being
>    or identity of Finite and Infinite
> 2. The Finite in the Infinite   —   [12]
>
> This is the proper answer to the argument in these pages. Finite & infinite are not contrary things but opposite correlative forms [Terms?] of the same Reality—just as Attraction and Repulsion are the antagonist *forces* of one & the same *Power*. [Kurtz, p. 211]

That the poet's coalescent vision could (in fact must) employ the observations of one realm to probe the other imaginatively—in a recognition that the laws of aesthetics, like those of other aspects of nature, are also constants with differing manifestations—is deducible from Coleridge's poetic statement as early as 1800. Whether Coleridge had all this so systematically asserted when he actually composed *The Rime of the Ancient Mariner* and when he made the major revisions we know from two letters written less than a month before he started composition of the 1798 version of the poem:

> —I can *at times* feel strongly the beauties, you describe, in themselves, & for themselves—but more frequently *all things* appear little—all the knowledge, that can be acquired, child's play—the universe itself—what but an immense heap of *little* things? I can contemplate nothing but parts, & parts are all *little*—!—My mind feels as if it ached to behold & know something *great*—something *one & indivisible*—and it is only in the faith of this that rocks or waterfalls, mountains or caverns give me the sense of sublimity or majesty!—But in this faith *all things* counterfeit infinity!— [*Collected Letters*, 1:349]

> For from my early reading of Faery Tales, & Genii &c &c—my mind has been habituated *to the Vast*—& I never regarded *my senses* in any way as the criteria of my belief. I regulated all my creeds by my conceptions not by my *sight*—even at that age. Should children be permitted to read Romances, & Relations of Giants & Magicians & Genii?—I know all that has been said against it; but I have formed my faith in the affirmative.—I know no other way of giving the mind a love of 'the Great', & 'the Whole'.—Those who have been led to the same truths step by step thro' the constant testimony of their senses, seem to me to want a sense which I possess—They contemplate nothing but *parts*—and all *parts* are necessarily little—and the Universe to them is but a mass of *little things*. [*Collected Letters*, 1:354]

This latter excerpt, juxtaposing as it does comments about works of the literary imagination with the questions of the relations of parts to whole and small to large, shows Coleridge considering the same issues that, if my reading of *The Rime of the Ancient Mariner* is correct, are given play there. The cosmological problem of size was very much in his mind, then, and we can be sure, on the basis of internal evidence alone, that other scientific data in the poem were carefully grounded in comprehensive reading and thoughtful infusion of fact in creative process (see Lowes, passim, and Jeffrey, p. 3).

Coleridge also believed that an objective, physical cosmos could not exist as a dead mechanism of matter, independent of the observing mind. That the act of measurement or observation could influence the entity observed Coleridge remarked in his notes on John Smith:

> Thus Cudworth, Dr. Jackson ... Henry More, this John Smith, and some others.... What they all wanted was a pre-inquisition into the mind, as part organ, part constituent, of all knowledge, an examination of the scales, weights, and measures themselves abstracted from the objects to be weighed or measured by them.... [Shedd, 5:266–67]

This belief coincides with one of the implications of quantum theory: "a genuine ontological dependence which does indeed force the scientist-observer in some measure to be responsible for the particular micro-events which he describes" (Schlegel, p. 218). If quantum theory is correct, "The spectator of an objective, unchanging natural world would have become an impossible myth, replaced by the participant scientist whose measurement procedures and state of motion contribute to the intrinsic properties of what he observes" (Schlegel, p. 226). Coleridge realized that many different states of matter exist simultaneously. Which state strikes the observer as "reality" at any given moment depends upon the mind set of the observer:

> How opposite to nature & fact to talk of the one *moment* of Hume; of our whole being an aggregate of successive single sensations. Who ever *felt* a *single* sensation? Is not every one at the same moment conscious that there co-exist a thousand others in a darker shade, or less light; even as when I fix my attention on a white House on a grey bare Hill or rather long ridge that runs out of sight each way.... [*Notebooks*, 2:2370]

Analogously, in quantum theory, "... the micro-particle generally is in a superposition of different states before observation brings it into some one velocity state.... And, it is in the possibility of physical systems existing in a superposition of different states, for a given observer and at one and the same time, that quantum theory breaks irrevocably with classical physics" (Schlegel, pp. 220–21). Coleridge's rebellion against seeing fixed and rigid particles of matter as reality permitted him to move in the direction of a physics of energy states:[13]

> ... in radical opposition to the picture of a world composed of particles of matter in motion, to whose impact an alien mind is passively receptive, Coleridge sets up what, following Schelling, he calls a 'vital,' or 'dynamic,' or 'constructive' philosophy. The elements of this philosophy are not moving material particles but inherent energies, or 'powers,' that polarize into positive and negative 'forces' (often called 'thesis and antithesis') which operate according to 'the universal law of Polarity or essential Dualism.'[14]

Coleridge's energy state physics is the key to the "quantum principle of superimposition" (Spisani, p. 9):

> ... the *superimposing* of one or more states, leading to different results observable at different times (but not to a predeterminable, sole, objective result); hence one must no longer expect any *model* to exist, in the usual sense of the word.
>
> If one or more 'states' are placed one over the other, till they form a new one, the *result* which may now be hypothesized will not be different from the result of one of the original 'states.' Yet it is not possible to know, determinately, which one it corresponds to, at an exact instant *(n)* of the *observer's time (t)*, since the *result* will be identical to one of the results of the 'states' superimposed, even supposing for the moment that it may appear at the same time, as *a* and non-*a*, that is as *identical* and as *different*, in the same instant $(t_n)$ of *different observes* [sic]. [Spisani, pp. 9, 11]

As a result, "One concludes that when, in the case of $p$ and $q$ (the one relating to *time*, the other to *space*), the more the value of one of them is defined, the less can the value of the other be determined" (p. 21).[15]

*The Rime of the Ancient Mariner,* like other voyage poems, involves the reader's sensations of motion: "With the reservation that one finds a whole variety of 'coalescent' experience in *The Ancient Mariner,* one is tempted to say that it is as much *about* motion as, say, Turner's *The Shipwreck* (1804) or his *Calais Pier* (1803); the immediate, all-pervasive 'texture' through which the inner meaning shines forth is primarily expressed in the sense of movement" (Cornwell, p. 227). The quantum-theory comparison which I am proposing may be applied to the poem to explain the elements of velocity and position in it. The reader of the poem is the observer and the mariner's tale and the gloss, respectively, are the different states of velocity and position simultaneously present.[16] The "particle" may be any segment of text taken as a unit by the eyes of the reader; the parameters of "particle" will vary from reader to reader, though most readers will probably perceive the individual groupings of gloss, and text glossed, respectively, as the basic units of measure. The velocity is the speed at which the reader perceives the tale to progress, and the position is narrative distance, varying from the total emotional involvement of the mariner to the at times almost indifferent state of the glosser.

The reader electing to scan the Mariner's tale first, without reference to the gloss, will have an entirely different sensation of velocity from that experienced by the reader choosing the opposite approach. The reader of the mariner's story by itself will be for the most part carried along by the breathlessly, perhaps even thumpingly, rhythmic ballad. A sluggish narrative conveys the same basic story to the reader of the gloss only. If due allowance is made for the diction, the glosser's version sounds something like a high-school student's book report. Here, for example, in prose form, is the gloss to Part 1 of the seven parts of the poem:

> An ancient Mariner meeteth three Gallants bidden to a wedding feast, and detaineth one. The Wedding-Guest is spellbound by the eye of the old seafaring man, and constrained to hear his tale. The Mariner tells how the ship sailed southward with a good wind and fair weather, till it reached the Line. The Wedding-Guest heareth the bridal music; but the Mariner continueth his tale. The ship driven by a storm toward the south pole. The land of ice, and of fearful sounds where no living thing was yet to be seen. Till a great sea-bird, called the Albatross, came through the snow fog and floating ice. The ancient Mariner inhospitably killeth the pious bird of good omen. [*Poetical Works,* pp. 187–89]

In only two spots thereafter is the somnolent drone of subject-verb-object interrupted, first for the breathtaking "No twilight within the courts of the Sun" (*Poetical Works,* p. 195) and then for the lovely

> In his loneliness and fixedness he yearneth towards the journeying Moon, and the stars that still sojourn, yet still move onward; and every where the blue sky belongs to them, and is their appointed rest, and their native country and their own natural homes, which they enter unannounced, as lords that are certainly expected and yet there is a silent joy at their arrival. [*Poetical Works,* p. 197]

My explanation for the abrupt departure from the agonizing tedium otherwise exhibited in the gloss is twofold: (1) the two departures serve as a "control group," tipping the reader that the turgidity of the rest is an intentional effect rather than inept composition, something that a writer with Coleridge's reputation for obscure prose might well wish to provide; (2) they underscore the microcosm-macrocosm differential. Both of the passages personify the elements, and the resulting celestial giantism further dwarfs the mariners. This consistent miniaturizing of the human figures ("as idle as a painted ship / Upon a painted ocean," lines 117–18, p. 191, *Poetical Works*), while inflating the personifications of nature ("At one stride comes the dark," line 200, p. 195, *Poetical Works*), is carried on within the mariner's tale as well as the gloss.

The reader who goes back and forth from gloss to ballad will encounter the start-and-stop situation so familiar to city commuters in heavy traffic. Whether the experience of the gloss or the experience of the mariner's tale actually materializes for a given reader will of course depend upon choice of reading order, just as in physics the state of a particle is only established in the act of observation or measurement of it.[17] Furthermore, the alert reader will discover as he reads the gloss that he is much better informed of the position of the ship and mariner on the voyage than is one starting with the text. In the mariner's tale, the six positional signals[18] are of limited information value, are less specific than those of the gloss, or merely repeat information obtainable earlier from the gloss.[19] Conversely, however, the reader of the mariner's tale is given a time indication at thirteen points in the text,[20] as compared to only two such indicators, neither adding to the data of the tale, for the gloss.[21] In short, just as in quantum measure the more determinable is the position of a particle the less determinable is its time of occurrence, and vice versa, so in *The Rime of the Ancient Mariner* the more determinate is the ship's position, via the gloss, the less determinate is the time of incidence in that position, knowable via the mariner's tale.[22]

This phenomenon manifests itself in the way the reader perceives the genre of the poem, and in the way he sees the symbolism. Fogle (1957) has identified *The Rime of the Ancient Mariner* as ". . . in kind a romantic poem, in the special sense in which Coleridge calls *The Tempest* a romantic poem—a drama of purest imagination, as free as the imagination can make it from the trammels of time and space" (p. 111). Freedom from time and space, I submit, is only an illusion arising from the fact that our ordinary perceptual processes may not immediately pick out the trammels of indeterminacy. The symbolism of the poem seems to be worked out in a similar way. The values of the sun and the moon, for instance, Delson shows to have ". . . alternatingly benevolent and malevolent associations, sometimes in the same scene. . . . If construed, as representing nature, their chief cumulative attribute as they affect the Mariner and his crewmates is of an instability so repetitive as to assume treacherous proportions" (p. 719).

Obviously the comparison which I have been drawing deliberately ignores what would be an essential distinction, were the purpose of the comparison not simply illustrative: in *The Rime of the Ancient Mariner* gloss and tale, position and time, are available to the reader-as-observer simultaneously, whereas in quantum determinations precise measurement of both factors at the same time is impossible, not merely a process which involves two separate measurements fused artificially into one. If we consider, however, the locus of the mariner-as-observer and the glosser-as-observer, the comparison sharpens considerably. Assuming the generally agreed upon identification of the mariner as a figure from the Age of Discovery and the glosser as a seventeenth-century character, and also adopting the admittedly far from tenuous assumption that these two figures are representatives of their times, it is easily enough concluded that neither historical era permits a vantage point perceptually sufficient to establish both space and time positions at once.[23] In addition to his constant desire to fuse the many discrete moments into the oneness of eternity, consistent with his belief in "a possible experience of time itself as organic and not merely linear . . ." (Barfield, p. 255 n.46), Coleridge was able, here, to show them as non-overlapping integers.

It is certain that Coleridge perceived the movements of entities (particles) comprising natural phenomena: "What a sight it is to look down on such a Cataract!—the wheels, that circuminvolve it—the leaping up & plunging forward of the infinity of Pearls & Glass Bulbs—the continual *change* of the *Matter,* the perpetual *Sameness* of the Form—. . ." (*Collected Letters,* 3:853). It is equally certain that Coleridge applied to literary works his observations about natural phenomena, as Brooke's analysis of Coleridge's *Biographia Literaria* comments about *Venus and Adonis* makes clear:

> . . . with more than the power of the painter, the poet gives us the liveliest image of succession with the feeling of simultaneousness. . . . the effect of the shooting star . . . is there and not there, and yet the sudden vivid movement in the vast unmoving sky leaves an impression of stillness; and in the *difference* between that and Adonis running apace one grasps the dramatic effect of the lines, the effect of his departure in Venus' mind. Not that Adonis really does move like a shooting star, but that to Venus his movement, under shock, has that effect; he is there, he is not there; and in between her whole sense of life collapses—but there is no 'in

between', the shock gives the feeling of simultaneousness. . . . [Pp. 65–66]

Brooke's description shows Coleridge's literary criticism fitting modern particle theory and observer entry into the situation under observation.

Coleridge's insistence that a literary work's structure ". . . must have the rhythm of a snake or the oscillation of sound waves, and its final effect is to be spiraling rather than merely encircling . . ." (Gilpin, p. 640) is again suggestive. Wave motion (essential to quantum conceptualization) is readily observable in bodies of water and, in this form, often exhibits a rhythm which finds a traditional parallel in musical compositions and in poems which, like *The Rime of the Ancient Mariner,* have regular metric character.[24]

V

Taken only this far, Coleridge's observation is patently simple; it took no Sage of Highgate to trace such a pattern. And yet within it are contained all the modern scientific implications which I have tried to argue provide a profitable vantage point for seeing *The Rime of the Ancient Mariner.*[25] In our own time, a theoretical superstructure and a critical terminology have been developed, by which we can systematically deal with space, time, and narrative stance, as these are autoreflected in a work of art. Not everyone will accept Lang's account, of course, but he does explain, in a systematic and comprehensible way, the works of art constructed in what he terms the "Performative mode":

In the Performative mode, the interior space and time of the work are not laid out *for* the activity which takes place; they may only be laid out by it. This contingency which turns on the unit of force, the sense of intimacy established between the latter and the structure which finally emerges, involves the viewer as well. The contingency of interior space and time is shared. Those features and the structure which depends on them emerge only in the act of constitution. There are alternate procedures which that act may follow; it is as if the resulting structure has *chosen* its form, conveying the sense of individuality which such choice ever marks out. Such apparent inconcisiveness does not deny the activity of the unit of force—that unit now represents a process which creates the conditions of its own coming to be, a network of space and time the sanction for which is finally a sanction for the structure itself. [P. 276]

If we see, as Ehrenpreis (pp. 10–11) does, *The Rime of the Ancient Mariner* as the "*chef d'oeuvre* of the whole genre," we expect tight structuring. What we find, paradoxically, is that "The Ballad's narration has been aptly compared to the film technique of montage; the story is advanced by a series of quick flashes, one distinct scene following another. There is no connecting tissue between the scenes, no explanation of events leading up to the crucial situation or following it."

Yet this is only the surface appearance of a set of relationships, disciplined in accordance with Lang's criteria for the Performative mode of discourse. The specific consequences, structurally speaking, of Lang's theory are that:

> a . . . purely analytical style, the objective of 'modern' philosophy, would be for Coleridge unthinkable. Further, the relative importance of philosophical certainty, of 'results' in an absolute sense is diminished, while what we might call the 'dramatic' element in philosophy, the process of search and its written enactment, assumes a larger significance. Much of Coleridge's best writing can be read as a dramatic monologue in prose, a mimetic representation, like Wordsworth's philosophical poetry, of the mind in the act of thinking something through: an attempt at truth, with the speaker uncertain what the exact destination of his argument will be. . . . it should not be thought surprising if his language can only point toward that object, imperfectly and by a series of approximations. . . . Even when Coleridge is at his most abstract, as in the essays 'On the Principles of Genial Criticism' or 'On poesy or Art' or, better still, in the *Treatise on Method*, he writes, I believe, with an acute aesthetic consciousness of what he is doing. . . . [Hunt, p. 834]

Hunt goes on to show the "poetic" rather than strictly logical structure of the *Biographia Literaria, The Friend,* and the *Aids to Reflection* (and, by implication, Coleridge's other prose works as well). He points out the endings of *Biographia Literaria* chapters (and some essays) in foreign languages and in scriptural quotations, as well as the resemblance between the eclectic condition of the *Biographia Literaria* and the similar way in which ancient biographies of the philosophers were written, and the resemblance between Coleridge's marginalia and the scholia tradition, "as if to suggest the moment when philosophy, having reached the limits of logical expression, must give way to a sacred language of some kind" (p. 835). Again, the way in which Coleridge handles symbol is that he, "like Keats of the great Odes," "turns it over in his own mind as he writes, as it were interrogating it until its symbolic implications are exhausted, without reaching a rational solution" (p. 837). Applying the most suggestive term "paralogical" to this approach, Hunt properly emphasizes that "Coleridge's very philosophical terms imply the process, the aspiration to vision, not the attainment. *Ese*mplastic power, co*ad*unating power, even etymologically, are terms of volition and transition, not of finality" (p. 836).

This "paralogical" structuring seems to me a perfectly natural outgrowth of Coleridge's scientific orientation and, in many respects, parallel (even analogous) to it. Coleridge's biological speculations manifest a similar belief in what we might term "logical discontinuity," although Coleridge believes that "all things strive to ascend, and ascend in their striving" (*Aids to Reflection*, p. 181). He also is convinced that there is a "wide chasm between man and the noblest animals of the brute creation, which no perceivable or conceivable difference or organization is sufficient to overbridge . . ." (*Theory of Life* [Shedd, 1:381–82]). Miller explains Coleridge's reconciliation of these two concepts in the belief that nature does not display "continuous progression," but "spurts" or "mutations" (p. 85).

This "paralogical" (or nonsequential) mode of progression is also extended by Coleridge to relationships governed by principles of physics: "The connection between the symbols of time, space and motion and the symbols of length, breadth and depth is not a logical one. Rather it must be seen, as he tells Tulk, as multiplications of the power, such as the square or cube" (Miller, p. 88). In more concrete terms, we can say that "Despite his errors, his struggles to give a philosophical basis to science are not without merit. Like the modern scientist, he feels the need to see matter as energy in a dynamic flux, operating within fixed laws and creating its own predicable patterns of relationships" (Miller, p. 86).

For Coleridge, then, the substance of reality is bound up with mind to such a degree that *natura* is not fully established until perceived. It is also not lifeless matter, the constitution of which has been imposed from outside by mechanical laws of cause and effect.[26] Rather it is, to apply quantum terminology, autoreflected. Form is organically evolved from within, by material and mental processes working in monadic concert. Applied to literary criticism and borne in mind, perhaps, during the composition of the gloss to a great poem, these principles yielded results of the utmost importance. Schlegel has traced

> ... the ultimate origin of the new physical philosophy in the *Critique of Pure Reason* published in 1787 by Immanuel Kant. For it was Kant [whose work Coleridge of course knew well] who first effectively argued that in knowing nature man significantly contributes to its properties. ... It is a nice thought, that what the sage of Konigsberg began, came to firm physical fruition some 148 years later, a few hundred kilometers across the Baltic Sea in Copenhagen. [Schlegel, p. 220]

Perhaps intermediated by the Sage of Highgate.

## Notes

1. The impressive range of books with interdisciplinary scope can be seen from the titles listed in References, following these Notes. See, e.g., Colmer, Barth, Sanders, Muirhead, Appleyard, William Kennedy, and Badawi. Authors and/or works cited in parentheses, in both text and Notes, receive full citations in References.

2. As in Abrams (1972), Ball, and Barfield. Although the scientific content of Coleridge's prose works has not gone unnoticed, only a few studies in past years have been more than peripherally concerned with it. Besides Sanders, one might single out Snyder (1924 and 1932), Evans, and Miller as representative in, respectively, the decades 1920–1970.

3. So Wells (p. 314) concludes about Coleridge's dealing with Herder and so Sankey (p. 63) concludes about Coleridge and Kant (cf., Chinol, Orsini, and Park). McFarland exonerates Coleridge from accusations of stealing from Schelling, often pointing out that Schelling himself refused to acknowledge the justice of charges that Coleridge had pillaged his works: "It seems to me, indeed, that Coleridge's total intellectual position is remarkably dissimilar to that of Schelling—that their thought is not only not identical, but also not even parallel" (p. xxxvi). On the same basis McFarland claims Coleridge's independence of Jacobi, Steffans, Friedrich von Schlegel, Herder, and Kant. Just three pages earlier, he disposes of the notion that Coleridge might be merely an offshoot of the Cambridge Platonist tradition (p. 24 n.1). Nor were Coleridge's links to English philosophy in general ironclad, as Wilma Kennedy (p. xvii) concedes.

Another contention that has been realized to its full potential for explaining the purpose of Coleridge's borrowings and mitigating their adverse consequences is that his borrowings are a technique of style. McFarland proceeds *in extenso* to explain that, vis-a-vis his *magnum opus*, Coleridge's borrowings constitute a "mosaic" organizational pattern (p. 27), the mere quarrying of stone to inlay the design of his philosophy (p. 195). That the *magnum opus* was never finished does not alter this argument. Hunt (p. 837) offers a reasonable explanation for the apparent facts that ". . . his theories are fragmentary and his borrowings seem ill-malgamated" (p. 485): when philosophical prose approaches the transcendental as subject matter, the prose inevitably starts to "function paralogically." Fruman's case against Coleridge does not seem to me to alter these conclusions.

4. The references are concentrated in the prose works, not only because prose is normally the appropriate medium for transmission of scientific data, but also because as Schulz (1963) observes, ". . . he drifted steadily between 1800 and 1810 from poetry to prose as his principal medium of expression . . ." (p. 141). A convenient compendium of selections from Coleridge's scientific writings in prose is to be found in chapter 7 (pp. 223–60) of *Inquiring Spirit*.

5. To a certain degree, Coleridge may be engaged in nothing more than typically estecean posturing, as he certainly is in his remark to Cottle in April 1797: "I should not think of devoting less than 20 years to an Epic Poem. Ten to collect materials and warm my mind with universal science. . . . So I would spend ten years—the next five to the composition of the poem—and the five last to the correction of it" (*Collected Letters*, I: 320–21). But he was totally in earnest in many other places, as when he solemnized: "I therefore go, and join head, heart, and hand, / Active and firm, to fight the bloodless fight / Of Science, Freedom, and the Truth in Christ" (Lines 60–62 of "Reflections on Having Left a Place of Retirement," p. 108 in the *Poetical Works*. Cf., *Collected Letters*, 2:864 and Zall, p. 67). Even though Coleridge is justly notorious for proposing vast writing projects which he never started, much less completed, and for projecting an inflated image of his own erudition, he *was* impressively erudite (Whalley, 1969, p. 251; Bush, p. 51), he *did* accomplish a great deal, and he *did* practice as well as espouse the idea that the scientist and the creative writer should proceed in similar ways about their common business: to expand the stock of human knowledge about the universe.

In the case of *The Rime of the Ancient Mariner*, the cautionary note sounded by Magnuson that "almost twenty years separate the publication of the poetry and the later prose that is often used to explicate the poetry" and that "the poetry was not written to exemplify the later program" may safely be muted, as Magnuson himself concedes: "he revised the poetry for *Sibylline Leaves* (1817) so that it would more nearly approximate his later theories: the gloss was added to 'The Ancient Mariner' . . ." (p. xiii).

6. This does not represent a critical bolt out of the blue, of course. Hazlitt (in 1818) has much the same conviction: "In Shakespeare there is a continual composition and decomposition of elements, a fermentation of every particle in the whole mass, by its alternate affinity or antipathy to other principles which are brought into contact with it. Till the experiment is tried we do not know the result, the turn which the character will take in new circumstances" (p. 51). Hazlitt's stress on the need for "experiment" enhances the modern sound of this passage.

7. The very term *organic* presupposes a connection to the world of nature, if not precisely to science. McKenzie's explanation of this concept remains one of the best.

8. Here and elsewhere in this essay I am employing the dominant "Copenhagen interpretation" of quantum theory which, however, continues to meet respectable dissent. A précis of the debate over the validity of this view is accessible in two nonmathematical treatments of the subject: Baker and March.

9. ". . . fluent annotation begins in 1801, and the most copious notes were written from 1808 onwards with rather heavy emphasis on the years from 1816 . . ." (Whalley, 1968, p. 430). Magnuson dates *The Rime of the Ancient Mariner* revisions from "late fall 1806 or early 1807. Thus at least by this time he was working on revisions that did not appear until 1817 . . ." (p. 53). It might be added that tinkering with *The Rime of the Ancient Mariner* continued well into the period when Coleridge was evolving his serious scientific notions. The beautiful "No twilight within the courts of the Sun" (gloss to lines 199–200; *Poetical Works*, p. 195), for instance, was composed as "an afterthought to the 1817 gloss to 'The Ancient Mariner' which was not printed with the gloss until 1828) . . ." (Johnson, p. 452).

Even the tone of the marginal notes of this period coincides with the feeling we get from the gloss to *The Rime of the Ancient Mariner*: "The habit of extensive annotation as a mode of self-communing, of breaking solitude by direct communication with the author of a book, begins in the Malta period 1804–06 . . ." (Whalley, 1961, p. 289).

10. It is only fair to add, however, that I did too. In an article (1977) accepted before Dyck's article appeared, I too was more inclined to see the narration of the poem in

terms of perspective (stance) than structural function. In another article (1973, p. 27), I likened the narrative to those in, respectively, *The Sound and the Fury* and *Pale Fire*. I now think that my comparisons have the same limitations that Dyck's comparison does.

11. In some ways, this comparison is closer than either of the other two. The specific tale of the Joads versus the generalized commentary of the interchapters has its counterpart in the bizarre tale of the mariner as opposed to the perfectly standard, even pedantically traditional, scholarly rendition of the glosser; the swift pace of the Joads' story in contrast with the more controlled tempo of the intercalary chapters fits a similar disjunction between the speed of the narrator's story and the torpor of the glosser's version; and the intercalary chapters' coverage of the same ground as the experiences of the Joads corresponds to the mariner-glosser situation in *The Rime of the Ancient Mariner*. Neither *The Moonstone* nor *The Ring and the Book* (or, for that matter, *The Sound and the Fury* or *Pale Fire*) has these features in common with *The Rime of the Ancient Mariner*.

12. Kurtz interprets this sign to mean "opposite" or "antithesis."

13. It may seem less startling to credit Coleridge with such a modern insight if we recall that comparisons between Coleridge's views and more recent science are a familiar part of Coleridge criticism; e.g., "If everything is the 'copula' of 'opposite energies,' then energy must be the sole basis of all existence and reality. For us, the concept of the atom may best illustrate what Coleridge means. Although entirely energy ($e = mc^2$), the atom presumably exists only when the free electron energy balances the 'passive' proton energy. . . . the prothesis of the atom—Coleridge would say today—is not the atom itself, but the force which gave birth to the two energies, negative and positive" (Miller, p. 81).

14. Abrams, pp. 27–49, based on utterances such as the following (from Egerton MS 2801 f. 151, quoted by Barfield, p. 204 n.28):

> It follows, therefore, that Body cannot be essentially *material*—but that Depth—e.g., a Power, manifesting itself in space, and contemplated in its *phenomena*, Length and Breadth, is what we mean by Body. The term, matter, therefore, taken separately, should be confined to the Phaenomena—i.e. to Length and Breadth without Depth—now as in bodies the only universal Evidence of Depth is Weight, therefore matter but not body should be attributed to imponderable Phaenomena—Light, Heat, Magnetism, Electricity are material but not corporeal.

15. A conclusion, however, which does not banish determinacy altogether:

> Yet when the classical representations are transformed by the postulates of quantum mechanics to obtain the probability amplitude, a means is provided for predicting the *probability* that a particular picture will be revealed, as the result of an observation. . . . Thus the quantum mechanical world provides an *exact* prediction of the *probability* of future events, despite the uncertainty of the events themselves. [Baker, pp. 222, 225]

16. To be perfectly precise, it would also be necessary to factor the contributions of the ballad narrator, the Wedding Guest, the First and Second Voices, the Hermit, the Pilot, and the Pilot's Boy, all of whose voices are heard at one time or another in the poem. Doing so, however, does not alter any of my conclusions; so, in the interest of clarity, I have omitted this interpretational refinement.

17. The givens of time and space in the poem are, of course, susceptible of other explanations; e.g., the influence of laudanum consumption on the poet (Abrams, 1934, pp. 27–29; Lefebvre, p. 441; Marks, passim). Fortunately, we are not enjoined to accept only one of the theories about the handling of time and space in *The Rime of the Ancient*

*Mariner*. After pointing out that in science two (incongruent) propositions cannot be retained to explain the same set of facts, Miner notes that "The opposite is true of literature. No pastoral elegy among those on the death of Sir Philip Sidney falsifies any of the others, no Impressionist still life an earlier one, no Viennese Waltz another Waltz" (p. 493). While it is obvious that an assertion about a work (especially about the causes of its unique structure) is not the same kind of "proposition" as that embodying the work itself, Miner goes on to add a condition equally valid for both sets of statements: "Aesthetic knowledge is virtually, not predictively, true. It therefore endures as not being falsifiable." Miner builds upon Meyer's distinction between "presentational" and "propositional" knowledge, illustrated in this way: "Thus, although only one true hypothesis accounts for the way that the refraction of light on water droplets produces the colors of a sunset, there are innumerable specific sunsets, each of which can be enjoyed for its own special effect" (p. 170). Meyer goes on to suggest the kind of "originality" offered by the "presentational manner": "The artist . . . is concerned not with the discovery of general principles but with their use. He employs the rules and regularities of a prevalent paradigm—the grammar, syntax, and formal procedures of an existing style—in order to create an original pattern of particulars: a work of art" (p. 173).

18. These are lines 22–24, p. 187 ("Merrily did we drop / Below the kirk, below the hill, / Below the lighthouse top"); lines 25–28, p. 197 ("The Sun came up upon the left, / Out of the sea came he! / And he shone bright, and on the right, / Went down into the sea:"); line 50, p. 188 ("And southward aye we led"); lines 83–86, p. 189 ("The Sun now rose upon the right: / Out of the sea came he, / Still hid in mist, and on the left / Went down into the sea"); lines 404–7, p. 204 ("Oh! dream of joy! is this indeed / The lighthouse top I see? / Is this the hill? Is this the kirk? / Is this mine own countree?"); and lines 570–71, p. 207 ("And now, all in my own countree, / I stood on the firm land!").

19. Schulz (1963, p. 70) mentions several unquestionably important pieces of information conveyed by the gloss: "We first learn from the gloss that the seamen 'make themselves accomplices in the crime' of the mariner when they justify his murder of the albatross, and that 'Death and Life-in-Death have diced for the ship's crew and she (the latter) winneth the ancient mariner." I cannot agree with him, however, that "Many such ambiguous parts of the narrative were eventually clarified by the gloss." My reaction to the information value of the gloss coincides with that of Watson (pp. 92–93) that the gloss is more confusing than helpful and adds very little data not ascertainable elsewhere by the reader.

The gloss has "The Mariner tells how the ship sailed southward with a good wind and fair weather, till it reached the line" (p. 187); "The ship driven by a storm toward the south pole" (p. 188); ". . . the ship . . . returned northward through fog and floating ice" (p. 189); ". . . the ship enters the Pacific Ocean, and sails northward, even till it reaches the Line" (p. 190); "The lonesome Spirit from the southpole carries on the ship as far as the Line . . ." (p. 201); ". . . the angelic power causeth the vessel to drive northward . . ." (p. 203); "And the ancient Mariner beholdeth his native Country" (p. 204).

20. Excluding such indefinite notations as "Day after day" or "all the night," we find: "'Higher and higher every day, / Till over the mast at noon—'" (lines 29–30, p. 188); "The glorious Sun uprist" (line 98, p. 190); "The bloody Sun, at noon, / Right above the mast did stand" (lines 112–13, p. 190); "The death-fires danced at night" (line 128, p. 191—because of the next reference, "There passed a weary time," line 143, p. 192, I take "at night" to mean "during one night," rather than the generic "at nighttime"—and "weary time" perhaps is also a questionable inclusion, since it is hardly more specific

than "Day after day"); "The western wave was all a-flame, / The day was well nigh done! / Almost upon the western wave / Rested the broad bright Sun" (lines 171–74, p. 193); "The Sun's rim dips; the stars rush out; / At one stride comes the dark" (lines 199–200, p. 195); "Seven days, seven nights, I saw that curse" (line 261, p. 197); "The moving Moon went up the sky, / And no where did abide; / Softly she was going up. / And a star or two beside—" (lines 263–66, p. 197); "For when it dawned—they dropped their arms" (line 350, p. 200); "Till noon we quietly sailed on" (line 373, p. 201; and "The Sun, right above the mast, / Had fixed her to the ocean" (lines 383–84, p. 201).

21. "At the rising of the Moon" (p. 195) and "By the light of the Moon he beholdeth God's creatures of the great calm" (p. 198). Read consecutively in this note and the one preceding, the time references are even more obviously vague and/or ritualistic than is apparent when they are encountered in their normal sequence in the poem. Whether they can with assurance be called time markers, as opposed to pattern points, may itself be disputable. This, however, enhances rather than distracts from the effectiveness of these signals according to the theory which I am advancing, since another of the offshoots of the quantum measures is "to make one foresee an 'area' in mathematical space in which objective time $(T_n)$ does not play an operative role" (Spisani, p. 111). The way in which the time references work is generally recognized in a novella recent enough to have been influenced by the milieu of quantum measurement, and a work otherwise very similar to *The Rime of the Ancient Mariner*, Ernest Hemingway's *The Old Man and the Sea:* "The some two hundred references to Santiago as 'the old man' have the cumulative effect of suggesting that he is preternaturally old. . . . His scars are 'as old as erosions in a fishless desert' (p. 10). Just how old are such erosions. . . . The fish also appears suspended in time and space. . . . In this manner, by various direct statements and by 'poetic' similes and images, Hemingway has made the visible a little hard to see" (Baskett, pp. 273–74). Cf., Montgomery, for a thesis about the impact of Werner Heisenberg's Principle of Uncertainty on Eliot.

22. A condition visible in different terms if one focuses on the diagrams sometimes drawn up to chart the Mariner's voyage geographically. Spisani's remarks (pp. 143–51) about endomorphic self-reflection versus exomorphic diagrammatic representation can be applied to the way in which, as reader-observers, we should view such schematic abstractions.

23. Though this remains the problem of the observer and in no way argues against the belief in their ultimate oneness. Quite the contrary: "For a Thing at the moment is but a Thing of the moment / it must be taken up into the mind, diffuse itself thro' the whole multitude of Shapes & Thoughts, not one of which it leaves untinged—" (*Notebooks*, p. 1597).

24. Coleridge consciously incorporated metrical duration into structural patterns in verse:

> The notebooks provide evidence from the voyage to Malta that Coleridge himself had an accurate sense of metrical duration that corresponds to the tonal discrimination that musicians call perfect pitch—a sense of the absolute duration of a given metrical unit (a line, say, of a certain pattern) providing a temporal matrix within which the words, finding their own unique rhetorical and dramatic values, declare in the fullest sense their meaning. [Whalley, 1969, pp. 271–72]

25. Obviously, it is also necessary to keep constantly in mind the limitations, as well as what I trust are the advantages, of the model, lest we inadvertently convert Coleridge into a nineteenth-century Bohr. For, at several specific points Coleridge rejects precisely the arguments needed to sustain a consistent field or quantum viewpoint; e.g.,

> Opposites ... are of two kinds, either logical, that is, such as are absolutely incompatible; or real, without being contradictory. A body in motion is something—Aliquid cogitabile; but a body, at one and the same time in motion, is nothing, or at most, air articulated into nonsense. [*Biographia Literaria*, 1:197]

> ... it is impossible that 'a succession of different states should be the effect of the same agents in the same proportions of agency.' [Unclassified MS at Victoria College, Toronto; quoted by Barfield, p. 205 n.2]

Earlier, Barfield points to another major departure of modern science from the inclination of Coleridge:

> To investigate scientifically the nature of Nature is to investigate the nature of phenomena as such. It is to ask the question: What is a phenomenon: True, 'Everything comes from other things and gives rise to other things.' Of any particular phenomenon we can say, tracing the chain of cause and effect: 'this comes from such and such another phenomenon or group of phenomena.' But if it is really the origin of phenomena *as such* that we are seeking to investigate, this answer will no longer serve: 'the solution of phenomena can never be derived from phenomena.' [P. 23; Coleridge citations are from *The Friend*, 1:500]

But we should not allow Coleridge's missteps to diminish the impressiveness of what he did foresee. Proper perspective emerges from some contemporary instances which indicate the difficulty of accurate scientific foresight. In a synopsis of the predictive value of science fiction from antiquity to the present, Asimov singles out two Heinlein stories for their remarkable anticipation of subsequent occurrences. The first, "Solution Unsatisfactory," appeared in the May 1941 issue of *Astounding Science Fiction*. Of it Asimov says:

> The story was written before Pearl Harbor, but Heinlein did not predict the American involvement in World War II. He *did* predict, however, the establishment of the Manhattan Project, and the development of a nuclear weapon. He was wrong in his details, but right in essence. Even more amazing, he went on to predict the nuclear stalemate that would exist after World War II, and got that quite correct. [Pp. 290–91]

Asimov lauds "Blowups Happen," from the September 1940 number of *Astounding Science Fiction*, for the same reason: This story contains an "astonishingly vivid description of a nuclear power plant and harrowing efforts to prevent it from destroying the environment. If these extrapolations are, respectively, "amazing" and "astonishingly vivid," coming as they do only a few months or a very few years in advance of the technology which realized them, and, nonetheless, are "wrong in details, but right in essence," how much greater does that make Coleridge's vision?

26. A. point put clearly in the *Theory of Life:*

> ... the bareness of the mechanic system ... which ... demanding for every mode and act of existence real or possible visibility, it knows only of distance and nearness, composition (or rather compaction) and decomposition, in short, the relations of unproductive particles to each other; so that in every instance the result is the exact sum of the component qualities, as in arithmetical addition. This is the philosophy of Death....

# References

Abrams, Meyer H. "Coleridge's 'A Light in Sound': Science, Metascience, and Poetic Imagination." *Proceedings of the American Philosophical Society* 116, no. 6 (21 December 1972): 458–76.

———. *The Milk of Paradise*, pp. 27–49. 1934. Reprint. New York: Harper and Row, 1970.

Appleyard, J. A. *Coleridge's Philosophy of Literature: The Development of a Concept of Poetry, 1791–1819*. Cambridge, Mass.: Harvard University Press, 1965.

Asimov, Isaac. "Prediction as a Side Effect," pp. 287–95. *Today and Tomorrow And*... Garden City, N.Y.: Doubleday, 1973. Orig. pub. in *Boston Review of the Arts* (July 1972).

Badawi, Muhammed Mustafá. *Coleridge: Critic of Shakespeare*. New York and London: Cambridge University Press, 1973.

Baker, Adolph. *Modern Physics and Antiphysics*. Reading, Mass.: Addison-Wesley, 1970.

Ball, Patricia M. *The Science of Aspects: The Changing Role of Fact in the Work of Coleridge, Ruskin and Hopkins*. University of London: Athlone Press, 1971.

Barfield, Owen. *What Coleridge Thought*. Middletown, Conn.: Wesleyan University Press, 1971.

Barth, J. Robert, S.J. *Coleridge and Christian Doctrine*. Cambridge, Mass.: Harvard University Press, 1969.

Baskett, Sam S. "Toward a 'Fifth Dimension' in *The Old Man and the Sea*." *The Centennial Review* 19, no. 4 (Fall 1975): 269–86.

Beach, Joseph Warren. "Coleridge's Borrowings from the German." *Journal of English Literary History* 9, no. 1 (March 1942): 36–58.

Boulger, James D. "Coleridge: The Marginalia, Mythmaking, and the Later Poetry." *Studies in Romanticism* 11, no. 4 (Fall 1972): 304–19.

Brooke, Nicholas. "Coleridge's 'True and Original Realism.'" *Durham University Journal* 22, no. 2 (March 1961): 58–69.

Bush, Douglas. *Mythology and the Romantic Tradition in English Poetry*. 1937. Reprint. New York: Norton, 1965.

Chinol, Elio. "Coleridge on Reason and Understanding." In *Friendship's Garland: Essays Presented to Mario Praz on His Seventieth Birthday*, 2:51–65. Rome: Edizione di Storia e Letteratura, 1966.

Coburn, Kathleen. "The Interpenetration of Man and Nature," pp. 95–113. *Proceedings of the British Academy* (1963; pub. 1964).

Coleridge, Samuel Taylor. *Aids to Reflection*. Edited by H. N. Coleridge. London: Moxon, 1836.

———. *Biographia Literaria*. Edited by John Shawcross. 2 vols. Oxford: Clarendon Press, 1907.

———. *Collected Letters*. Edited by Earl Leslie Griggs. 2 vols. Oxford: Clarendon Press, 1956.

———. *Complete Works*. Edited by W. G. T. Shedd. New York: Harper & Brothers, 1854 ff. *Theory of Life* included in vol. 1 (1854).

———. *The Friend*. Edited by Barbara E. Rooke. 2 vols. London: Routledge & Kegan Paul; Princeton, N.J.: Princeton University Press, 1969.

———. *Inquiring Spirit*. Edited by Kathleen Coburn. London: Routledge & Kegan Paul, 1951.

———. *Miscellaneous Criticism.* Edited by Thomas Middleton Raysor. Cambridge, Mass.: Harvard University Press, 1936.

———. *Notebooks.* Edited by Kathleen Coburn. Vol. 1. New York: Pantheon Books, 1957.

———. *Poetical Works.* Edited by E. H. Coleridge. London: Oxford University Press, 1912.

Colmer, John. *Coleridge: Critic of Society.* Oxford: Clarendon Press, 1959.

Cornwell, John. *Coleridge: Poet and Revolutionary 1772–1804: A Critical Biography.* London: Allen Lane, 1973.

Delson, Abe. "The Symbolism of the Sun and Moon in *The Rime of the Ancient Mariner.*" *Texas Studies in Language and Literature* 15, no. 4 (Winter 1974): 707–20.

di Pasquale, Pasquale, Jr. "Coleridge's Framework of Objectivity and Eliot's Objective Correlative." *Journal of Aesthetics and Art Criticism* 26, no. 4 (Summer 1968): 489–500.

Dunn, John J. "Coleridge's Debt to McPherson's Ossian." *Studies in Scottish Literature* 7, nos. 1–2 (July–October 1969): 76–89.

Dyck, Sarah. "Perspective in *The Rime of the Ancient Mariner.*" *Studies in English Literature 1500–1900* 13, no. 4 (Autumn 1973): 591–604.

Ehrenpreis, Anne Henry. *The Literary Ballad,* pp. 9–19. Columbia: University of South Carolina Press, 1970.

Evans, B. Ifor. *Literature and Science,* pp. 7–9, 58–65. London: George Allen & Unwin, 1954.

Fogle, Richard Harter. "The Genre of 'The Ancient Mariner.'" *Tulane Studies in English* 7 (1957): 111–24.

Freedman, Jack. "Eyesight and Vision: Forms of the Imagination in Coleridge and Novalis." In *The Rarer Action: Essays in Honor of Francis Fergusson,* edited by Alan Cheuse and Richard Koffler, pp. 202–17. New Brunswick, N.J.: Rutgers University Press, 1970.

Fruman, Norman. *Coleridge: The Damaged Archangel.* New York: Braziller, 1971.

Gilpin, George. "Coleridge and the Spiral of Poetic Thought." *Studies in English Literature, 1500–1900* 12, no. 4 (Autumn 1972): 639–52.

Grow, L. M. "*The Rime of the Ancient Mariner:* Multiple Veils of Illusion." *Notre Dame English Journal* 9, no. 1 (Fall 1973): 23–30.

———. "The Search for Truth: Book Learning versus Personal Experience in *The Rime of the Ancient Mariner.*" *Coranto* 10, no. 2 (1977): 3–12.

Harris, John. "Coleridge's Reading in Medicine." *Wordsworth Circle* 3, no. 2 (Spring 1972): 85–95.

Hazlitt, William. *The Complete Works.* Edited by P. P. Howe. Vol. 5. 1930. Reprint. New York: AMS Press, 1967.

Hume, Robert D. "Kant and Coleridge on Imagination." *Journal of Aesthetics and Art Criticism* 28, no. 4 (Summer 1970): 485–96.

Hunt, Bishop C. "Coleridge and the Endeavor of Philosophy." *PMLA* 91, no. 5 (October 1976): 829–39.

Jeffrey, Lloyd N. "'Human Interest and a Semblance of Truth' in the Slaying of Coleridge's Albatross." *CEA Critic* 30, no. 5 (February 1968): 3–5.

Johnson, Mary Lynn. "How Rare Is a 'Unique Annotated Copy' of Coleridge's *Sibylline Leaves*?: A Partial Answer, with a Variant of 'Lines on Donne.'" *Bulletin of the New York Public Library* 78, no. 4 (Summer 1975): 451–81.

Kennedy, William F. *The Economic Thought of Samuel Taylor Coleridge.* University of California Publications in English, vol. 17. Berkeley: University of California Press, 1958.

Kennedy, Wilma L. *The English Heritage of Coleridge of Bristol, 1798. The Basis in 18th Century English Thought for His Distinction between Imagination and Fancy.* Hampden, Connecticut: Archon Books, 1969. Orig. pub. New Haven, Conn.: Yale University Press, 1947 as *Yale Studies in English,* vol. 104.

Kurtz, Benjamin P. "Coleridge on Swedenborg with Unpublished Marginalia on the Prometheus." *University of California Publications in English* 14 (1943): 199–214.

Lang, Berel. "Space, Time, and Philosophical Style." *Critical Inquiry* 2, no. 2 (Winter 1975): 263–80.

Lefebvre, Molly. *Samuel Taylor Coleridge: A Bondage of Opium.* New York: Stein and Day, 1974.

Lowes, John Livingston. *The Road to Xanadu: A Study in the Ways of the Imagination.* 1927. Reprint. Boston: Houghton Mifflin, n.d.

McFarland, Thomas. *Coleridge and the Pantheist Tradition.* Oxford: Clarendon Press, 1969.

McKenzie, Gordon. "Organic Unity in Coleridge." *University of California Publications in English* 5, no. 1 (1939): 1–107.

Magnuson, Paul. *Coleridge's Nightmare Poetry.* Charlottesville: University Press of Virginia, 1974.

Mann, Peter. "Annotations of Coleridge in a Copy of *The Friend* (1818)." *Studies in Bibliography: Papers of the Bibliographical Society of Virginia* 26 (1973): 243–54.

March, Robert H. *Physics for Poets.* New York: McGraw-Hill, 1970.

Marks, Jeanette Augustus. *Genius and Disaster: Studies in Genius and Drugs.* 1926. Reprint. Port Washington, N.Y.: Kennikat, 1968.

Martin, Richard T. "Coleridge's Use of 'sermoni propriora.'" *Wordsworth Circle* 3, no. 2 (Spring 1972): 71–75.

Metzger, Lore. "Imitation and Illusion in Coleridge's Criticism." In *Proceedings of the IVth Congress of the International Comparative Literature Association,* 2:781–88. The Hague and Paris: Mouton, 1966.

Meyer, Leonard B. "Concerning the Sciences, the Arts—AND the Humanities." *Critical Inquiry* 1, no. 1 (Autumn 1974): 163–217.

Miller, Craig William. "Coleridge's Concept of Nature." *Journal of the History of Ideas* 25, no. 4 (October–December 1964): 77–96.

Miner, Earl. "That Literature Is a Kind of Knowledge." *Critical Inquiry* 2, no. 3 (Spring 1976): 487–518.

Montgomery, Marion. "Eliot and the Particle Physicist: The Merging of Two Cultures." *The Southern Review* 10, no. 3 (July 1974): 583–89.

Muirhead, John. *Coleridge as Philosopher*. London: George Allen & Unwin, 1930.

Orsini, G. N. G. "Coleridge, Fichte, and Original Apperception." In *Friendship's Garland: Essays Presented to Mario Praz on His Seventieth Birthday*, 2:67–74. Rome: Edizione di Storia e Letteratura, 1966.

Park, Roy. "Coleridge and Kant: Poetic Imagination and Practical Reason." *British Journal of Aesthetics* 8, no. 4 (October 1968): 335–46.

Potter, George R. "Coleridge and the Idea of Evolution." *PMLA* 40, no. 2 (June 1925): 379–97.

Read, Herbert. "Coleridge as Critic." In *Coleridge: A Collection of Critical Essays*, edited by Kathleen Coburn. Englewood Cliffs, N.J.: Prentice-Hall, 1967. Orig. pub. in fuller form in *Sewanee Review* 61, no. 4 (Autumn 1948): 597–624.

Sanders, C. R. *Coleridge and the Broad Church Movement: Studies in S. T. Coleridge, J. C. Hare, Thomas Carlyle, and F. D. Maurice*. Durham, N.C.: Duke University Press, 1942.

Sankey, Benjamin. "Coleridge and the Visible World." *Texas Studies in Language and Literature* 6, no. 1 (Spring 1964): 59–67.

Schlegel, Richard. "The Impossible Spectator in Physics." *The Centennial Review* 19, no. 4 (Fall 1975): 217–31.

Schulz, Max F. "Coleridge's 'Apologetic' Prefaces." *Tulane Studies in English* 11 (1961): 53–64.

———. *The Poetic Voices of Coleridge*. Detroit: Wayne State University Press, 1963.

Snyder, Alice D. "Coleridge's Cosmogony: A Note on the Poetic World-View." *Studies in Philology* 21, no. 4 (October 1924): 616–25.

———. "Coleridge's 'Theory of Life.'" *Modern Language Notes* 47, no. 5 (May 1932): 299–301.

Spisani, Franco. *Significato e struttura del tiempo; the Meaning and Structure of Time*. Azzoguidi-Bologna: Centro Superiore di Logica e Scienza Comparate, 1972.

Stephens, Fran Carlock. "Cottle, Wise, and Ms. Ashley 408." *The Papers of the Bibliographical Society of Virginia* 68 (Fourth Quarter 1974): 391–406.

Stevenson, Lionel. "The Mystique of Romantic Narrative Poetry." In *Romantic and Victorian: Studies in Memory of William H. Marshall*, edited by W. Paul Elledge and Richard L. Hoffman, pp. 26–42. Rutherford, N.J.: Fairleigh Dickinson University Press, 1971.

Watson, George. *Coleridge the Poet*. New York: Barnes and Noble, 1966.

Watters, Reginald. *Coleridge*. London: Evans, 1971.

Wells, G. A. "Man and Nature: An Elucidation of Coleridge's Rejection of

Herder's Thought." *Journal of English and Germanic Philology* 51 (1952): 314–25.

Whalley, George. "Coleridge's Marginalia Lost." *Book Collector* 17 (1968): 428–42.

———. "Harvest on the Ground: Coleridge's Marginalia." *University of Toronto Quarterly* 38, no. 3 (April 1969): 248–76.

———. "Portrait of a Bibliophile VII: Samuel Taylor Coleridge 1772–1834." *Book Collector* 10 (Autumn 1961): 275–90.

Zall, Paul M. "The Cool World of Samuel Taylor Coleridge: Dr. Beddoes the Bristol Brunonian." *Wordsworth Circle* 2 (1971): 67–73.

# Young Man Hawthorne:
# Scrutinizing the Discourse of History

## John Franzosa
### *Wayne State University*

> Words, or their inscriptions, unlike points, miles, classes, and the rest, are tangible objects of the size so popular in the marketplace, where men of unlike conceptual schemes communicate at their best.
> —William v. O. Quine, *Word and Object*

> Any character is better than none.
> —Nathaniel Hawthorne, *American Magazine of Useful and Entertaining Knowledge*

AS might be inferred from its title, this paper considers an important episode in Nathaniel Hawthorne's career, and more generally, a method for defining the contours of that episode as an object of study and a procedure for analyzing that object. That method is, of course, psychohistory, most specifically articulated by Erik Erikson in *Young Man Luther* (1958) and subsequent works as an attempt to comprehend the convergence of personality and history by grounding individual case study in an understanding of historical process. While a few literary critics—Richard Lebeaux, for example, in *Young Man Thoreau* (1977)—have specifically adopted Erikson's model, the method itself or in more general forms is not uncommon in literary or American studies investigations: an acknowledged masterwork is broken up through some interpretative scheme and its themes as identified and transcoded into personal and social terms; its form is then comprehended as a sign of the integration of the self of the author, which is also a symbolic resolution or articulation of social conflict. (Conversely, a formal "failure" is a sign of the failure to achieve this normative integration in the individual, the society, or between them.) The explanatory power of this model depends on its ability to frame the text, the psyche, and the society as homologies for one another so that "autonomy" and "independence," for example, may be examined in their literary, psychological, or social resonances without contradicting the significance of the terms of unsettling their values. But here is where the method runs into difficulties.

While the introduction of the historical and social determinants of individual behavior has had a salutary effect on psychoanalytic and literary studies, there are a number of difficulties—beside the obvious and largely misguided charges of "reductionism"—this model presents, particularly to the student of the American Renaissance. The first is this slipping from text to personality to society and back again that hinges on organic metaphors which prescribe such values as "growth," "development," "maturity," "integrity," and "functioning." The models of text and "personality" and "history" in psychohistory are easily traced to the early nineteenth century, when terms like "psychology," "society," "nationality" and "history" took on their modern significance. The writers who have been defined after the fact as the giants of the American Renaissance were not merely worried about issues that we now best understand in psychological and social terms; they defined those issues as particularly "psychological" and "social." Thus, a psychohistorical reading will not so much uncover a latent meaning as replicate the language of the American Renaissance, and reproduce a reading of literary works as examples of the growth of a national character expressing itself through individual authors whose biographies reveal them to be representative Americans.[1]

This organic yoking of personality and history would not be a problem—would not even be possible—if it were not for another problem, the older habit of figuring the individual as a representative of his culture. This again was a common feature of mid-nineteenth-century writing and would be trotted out whenever "character" was discussed, as in Emerson's *Representative Men* (1850) or E. P. Whipple's *Character and Characteristic Men* (1866). Sacvan Bercovitch, for one, has explored the importance of this relation by tracing its American origin to Cotton Mather's use of John Winthrop as exemplum, and implying that its Protestant roots may extend at least to Luther.[2] Although the roots clearly go much deeper, Bercovitch's observation effectively closes the circle: ironically, it may be said that

Luther is as much a founding practitioner as the first object of psychohistorical method and that the method from the first was tended to fold back in on itself by rediscovering its own assumptions about the relations of texts, individuals, and societies. Bercovitch and others interested in typology have offered a way out of this circularity, however, by opening a space in American Studies for a view of language as a sign system as well as symbolic communication. It is now possible—indeed, for pre-Romantic writing in America necessary—to detach the organic roots that the nineteenth century affixed to words and which have grounded the individual in his ontology, the nation in its phylogeny, and history in its teleology.

As part of the generation that was in the process of establishing such a ground, Hawthorne was ideally situated to scrutinize the rhetoric of such a project. Through a rhetorical reading of one of his historical sketches, "Endicott and the Red Cross," I would like to show how Hawthorne's writing attempts to occupy that space between arbitrary signs and luminous symbols even though, in the end, not even his ironic undermining of the symbolic structure of his tale could secure it from the organicism of his age or ours. My aim in this paper is not to provide a superior interpretation of Hawthorne's sketch, nor to stretch a psychohistorical narrative to cover Hawthorne as man and writer. Rather, I hope to retell a story of Hawthorne's tussle with a rhetoric of subjectivity embedded in the discourse of history and to praise the Pyrrhic achievements that are his ironic histories—not his ability to "communicate," as Quine would have it, in the cultural marketplace, but his attempts to resist such communication, or at least to name his own price.

Hawthorne scholars often think of 1837, the year of the great economic "Panic," as a critical year in Hawthorne's life as well as in American history.[3] *Twice-told Tales* was published in March and placed Hawthorne's name on his own work for the first time after nearly a decade of anonymity. He was able to break with his editor, Samuel Griswold Goodrich, and was about to plunge into the stream of contemporary politics. His days as a recluse and a bachelor were numbered, for by November, at the latest, he would be drawn into the sphere of the Peabody family and from there would be swept toward what he would call the "main current of life." The year 1837 often appears as a decisive break between the so-called "solitary years" when he lived and worked in the "chamber under the eaves" in his mother's house, and the more socially active period when he would obtain his first government position, challenge John O'Sullivan to a duel over a woman's reputation, court Sophia Peabody, and join a commune before settling down to married life in the Old Manse. A psychohistorical reading of such an episode might seize on such contrasts and through an interpretation of a representative text of the period, tease out the personal and social conflicts that text (as a symbol of the author's self) is presumed to represent and integrate. Hawthorne seems to have anticipated such a reading, however, which is why I think he was careful to destroy most documentary evidence of this period and why he helped fabricate the tradition of the solitary years in his melodramatic letters to Horatio Bridge, Henry Wadsworth Longfellow, and others.

In one surviving notebook passage he was fairly explicit about the nature of his personal and social conflicts: "in this dismal and squalid chamber FAME was won."[4] It might be interesting to intepret this famous passage and to speculate about issues of filth, secrecy, shame, enclosure, exhibitionism, appropriation, possession, transformation (perhaps a Freudian "anal birth fantasy" or a Lacanian wresting of the "name of the father" from the maternal womb). But I think we would do well to take Hawthorne's statement at face value and to assume that, like so many of his contemporaries reared on heroic tales of the revolutionary fathers, he wanted "fame."[5] Interestingly, such a perspective turns psychohistorical method and the rhetoric of subjectivity inside out, for if fame was to be won in the 1830s, the author's self could not be hidden or the determining conflicts repressed behind the text to await the analyst's superior scrutiny; rather, they had to be displayed through the text. Or, to put it another way, if fame was to be won through writing, the text had to be constructed so that any contemporary reader would be enticed to seek out a congenial authorial presence in order to confer on it the social and historical significance which is fame.

The text, for Hawthorne's contemporaries, was the site of an exchange where, by way of the authorial presence figured in it, the self of the author is produced as a subject of critical scrutiny and converted into the famous author as social object. The author's self is then a commodity—not much of a problem if the "author" is "the author of 'The Gray Champion'" or "The Author of 'The Gentle-Boy'"—but a serious problem if the name of the author were to be identified with the author himself, because then the man himself would be that commodity. (Hawthorne's later differentiating between "Nathaniel Hawthorne" and the "real human being" in his prefaces indicates at the very least his awareness of this problem.[6] To avoid such an identification, Hawthorne early on adopted various fictive authorial selves and thus avoided both self-exposure and fame until 1837, but in 1837 he attempted a new relation to his audience by way of an author which for the first time would bear his name.

As a sketch of the Puritans, "Endicott and the Red Cross" is representative of Hawthorne's historical sketches of the 1830s and is often read as one of Hawthorne's meditations on Puritan history. It is unique, however, because it is the last Puritan tale Hawthorne would write until "Main Street" and *The Scarlet Letter* twelve years later, and the liberties Hawthorne often takes with his sources in this tale approach travesty. Written toward the end of the first real boom period in American historiography, the tale can also be read as Hawthorne's meditation on the writing of history and particularly on the contemporary use of historical narrative as moral exemplum. In the 1830s, historical writing was also a path to fame, since the character of the historian was often identified with the central figure his narrative celebrated. The "vindication" of the character of a historical figure, then, was at least implicitly a vehicle for self-promotion. In this sense, what is dramatized in "Endicott and the Red Cross" is not so much "one of the boldest exploits which our history records" as it is the bold exploit of writing history, of appropriating materials from the past for some present moral or political purpose through which activity the historian leaves his mark on his world. As Hawthorne was aware, I think, the concept of character as employed in historical narratives confused the realms of personality and society, of authorship and political action. Authorial self-expression and, indeed, the self were understood by his contemporaries as social and political entities while politics was viewed as a clash of personalities. Because this tale is at least partly a parody of historical writing, it is one of the most widely misunderstood of all of Hawthorne's tales, but misunderstood in such a typical way that I think an examination of the tale as rhetoric rather than allegory will help reorient criticism of Hawthorne's other historical writings.[7] It is not merely a story "about" the Puritans or "about" his contemporaries in Puritan dress or "about" his political or historical ideas or values or his desire to make his mark on the world. It is all of these bound up in a use of historical narrative that both enables and questions narrative's constituting of history, politics, moral values, and the self.

The tale of the publication of *Twice-told Tales* has itself often been told, but a few points bear repeating. When Hawthorne returned to Salem in the fall of 1836 after the fiasco as editor of the *American Magazine of Useful and Entertaining Knowledge,* he was apparently despondent and, in the words of his Bowdoin classmate, Horatio Bridge, "in need of all the encouragement his friends could give."[8] From Bridge, that encouragement was considerable. He took it upon himself to rescue Hawthorne by engineering publication of Hawthorne's book and by secretly guaranteeing the publisher against financial losses. Bridge also mobilized other Bowdoin alumni, Congressman Jonathan Cilley and Senator-elect Franklin Pierce, on Hawthorne's behalf. And he counseled Hawthorne to keep writing and remain "independent." Bridge's letters express a fear that Hawthorne would end his "mortal woes on his own responsibility" whether through suicide or, more likely, through marriage. These two forms of giving up seemed equivalent for Bridge, who admitted he too might have married "if I did not love myself too well."[9] Hawthorne's problem, according to Bridge, is his "self-distrust," and as an object lesson Bridge offers Franklin Pierce: "With no very remarkable talents, he, at the age of thirty-four fills one of the highest stations in the nation" (Bridge, p. 74) because, as Bridge elaborates in another letter, "Frank's whole energies have been exerted for years in building up himself" (Julian, 1:49). By contrast, Hawthorne had been characterized facetiously by Cilley as an "aristocratic" artist "who hides himself from his own generation in a study or garret and neglects in the spring-time of his life to plant and maintain that posterity to which he looks for praise and commendation" (Julian, 1:45). For Hawthorne's Democratic friends, the manifestation of "self-love" is the key to success, and success if that "praise and commendation" reflected back on oneself by one's children or an admiring nation. Marriage and death are equivalent figures for stasis, the very opposite of active self-expression. Hidden self-love is a shameful and aristocratic "fiddling," but the expression of self-love—whether in writing, speaking, or fathering—produces visible expressions of the self as it populates the world with potential admirers.

In Bridge's scheme, *Twice-told Tales* was designed to make Hawthorne visible, to bring his name to the attention of publishers and influential politicians. As a literary event in itself, this heterogeneous collection of Hawthorne's previously published writings did not yield immediate "praise and commendation." Indeed, despite a well-orchestrated campaign of friendly reviews, newspaper notices, and reprinted stories, book sales were not impressive. It was the spring of 1837, after all, and Hawthorne's notices were crowded out by articles about bank closings and hard times, mob actions and Andrew Jackson's farewell to the presidency. In the Salem newspapers, for example, a brief review of *Twice-told Tales* appeared alongside Jackson's "Farewell Address," "A Rill from the Town Pump" alongside a Whig denunciation of Jackson, and "A Bell's Biography" with news of bank closings in New Orleans and suspensions in New York.[10] Early in March, the Salem *Gazette* advertised *Twice-told Tales* at the bottom of a page devoted to a long appraisal of Jackson's administration. The following week, "Fancy's Showbox" was printed next to a blast against the "Farewell Address," which the *Gazette* characterized as "the parting Bull fulminated by the political Pope," and as different from the original "Farewell Address" as the respective characters of Jackson and Washington.[11] Three days later, amid news of a mob in Philadelphia and the Flour Riot trial of "loco-focos" in New York, there appeared a small notice to the effect that "Hawthorn [*sic*]" is not a *"nom de guerre,"* no "man of straw, but a taxpayer in Salem, where he and his fathers before him, have lived these two hundred years, supporting an honorable name."[12] Two weeks later, Samuel Goodrich wrote Hawthorne, soliciting tales for the 1838 *Token,* and Hawthorne eventually sent five pieces, the last he would ever write for Goodrich. "Peter Goldthwaite's Treasure" deals with an obsessive desire for wealth and fame, "Slyph Etherege" and "The Shaker Bridal" with a violated intimacy and a celibate marriage, and "Night Sketches" follows a solitary observer of the vanity of city life. "Endicott and the Red Cross" was the other, an ironic celebration of a break with papistry and monarchy in the name of "liberty of conscience."[13]

When he received Goodrich's letter, Hawthorne had in his possession George Bancroft's *History of the United States* and a laudatory review of Charles Wentworth Upham's biography of Sir Henry Vane.[14] Both of these historians would have been of personal and political as well as historiographic interest to Hawthorne. Bancroft would shortly become the collector of the Port of Boston and was already an important conduit for political patronage, the man Bridge and Pierce tried to influence directly and through "loco-foco" intermediaries in New York. Interestingly enough, considering the Spenserian significance of "Red Cross," he would later be nicknamed "The Blatant Beast" by Hawthorne and his wife. Upham, whose biography of Vane Sophia Peabody praised extravagantly and Hawthorne would later cite in *Grandfather's Chair* (1841), would still later be the author of the Whig petition demanding Hawthorne's removal from the Salem Custom-House, and would serve as a model for the unctuous Jaffrey Pyncheon in *The House of the Seven Gables* (1851). At this point, however, he was the junior pastor at the First Church of Salem and a remarkably popular lecturer on Salem history. In the Salem *Gazette*, directly beneath the notice acknowledging Hawthorne's existence is a taxpayer, Upham was praised for having been "received with so much enthusiasm" in Boston for his "industry . . . in the collection of facts and materials, and skill in the use of them."[15] Two years older than Hawthorne, he was already famous for his disputes with other Salem ministers in defense of "liberty of conscience" and for his *Lectures on Witchcraft* (1833), which, incidentally, mentioned Hawthorne's ancestor, witch-trial judge John Hathorne, only twice and then only in passing. In the spring of 1837, Upham introduced his Harvard classmate, Ralph Waldo Emerson, to the Salem Lyceum, and delivered himself a series of biographical and historical lectures in Salem and Boston, speaking in February and again in March on Roger Williams.[16] This is interesting as a context of "Endicott and Red Cross" because the tale suffers more distortion of source material than almost any other of Hawthorne's, particularly with regard to the character of Williams. Interesting, too, since Bridge had just written in his review of Hawthorne's book that no other writer "can so well portray the times and manners of the Puritans" (Bridge, p. 71). Like these two ambitious politicians/historians, Bancroft and Upham, Hawthorne uses Williams as a vehicle for self-presentation. But, unlike them, his presentation of Williams ironically undermines history as a mode of self-presentation.

The outline of Hawthorne's tale, which is a set piece for a political harangue, and as such a typical mix of antiquarianism and melodrama, is not very remarkable.[17] The Puritan community assembles for its "martial exercise," and the features of the settlement are mirrored in the "highly polished breastplate" of Endicott, whose "grizzled beard" gives him away as a type of Jacksonian warrior/politician. At the center of the reflected community is the meeting house with the grim head of a wolf nailed to its porch. In "close vicinity" is the whipping post and nearby the pillory and the stocks. A Royalist and an Anglican are confined there and on the meeting house steps stand a "male and female figure," the former a "wanton gospeller" and the latter a woman who had "wagged her unruly [tongue]" at the church elders. Other Puritans bear the marks of theocratic discipline: slit nostrils, cropped ears, and branded cheeks; a young woman wears a scarlet "A" "on the breast of her gown in the eyes of all the world and her own children." An elderly Roger Williams enters with "black tidings"—news of a governor-general to be sent from England to assume political control of the Puritan colonies. Despite his warning to Endicott that the news not be "suddenly noised abroad," Endicott brushes him aside, takes charge and delivers his speech. He reminds his "fellow exiles" of the "native country" they had left in pursuit of "liberty of conscience," reminds them of the hardships they have suffered in this "howling wilderness," and imagines for them a Salem fallen into the hands of King Charles and Archbishop Laud: "we shall briefly behold a cross on the spire of this tabernacle which we have builded, and a high altar within its walls, with wax tapers burning round it at noonday. We shall hear the sacring-bell, and voices of the Romish priests saying the mass." He then exhorts them to defend their "own soil," which they have "bought" and "won" and "cleared" and "tilled" and "sanctified" through their own efforts, and having filled his auditors with "his own spirit," he "thrusts" his sword through the King's banner to an accompanying "cry of triumph" from the crowd.[18]

What *is* remarkable about the tale are Hawthorne's distortions of source material and his rhetorical undermining of the apparent meaning of the tale. As Michael Davitt Bell and Neal

Frank Doubleday have pointed out, the punishments depicted are exaggerated and anachronistic—the punishment for adultery, for example, was not instituted until some sixty years later and even so the color and location of the letter are Hawthorne's.[19] The "black tidings" were not the cause but one of the consequences of Endicott's action. Roger Williams was not elderly, but rather a man of about thirty, already under suspicion as a heretic and in almost all accounts—including Hawthorne's later version in *Grandfather's Chair*—the instigator of the episode. Although Endicott was censured by the magistracy for his "rash indiscretion," the punishment was mitigated because John Winthrop argued that he had acted out of "tenderness of conscience." According to the magistracy, it was Williams's preaching on graven images—or to those historians less kindly disposed, like Cotton Mather, his "perswasion"—which had influenced Endicott to deface the King's banner and jeopardize the status of the colonies. By splitting these co-conspirators, Hawthorne has opened up an interesting contradiction in his narrative.

The character of Roger Williams was a point of special interest among Hawthorne's sources. Winthrop and Mather had little good to report of his Salem years and Thomas Hutchinson thought him quixotic.[20] When the Reverend William Bentley of Salem attempted to vindicate his character in 1799, he occasioned an unusually heated debate in the Massachusetts Historical Society. An anonymous detractor citing Winthrop, Mather, Hutchinson, and William Hubbard characterized Williams as a "comet blazing in his eccentric orb," and Bentley was forced to reassert his contention that Williams was well loved by his congregation and offered as proof further assertions that Williams revered authority and even circulated his writing privately and destroyed his manuscripts in order to "quiet public fears." Even as the author of a "silent" critique of theocracy, however, his part in the episode of the Red Cross was a difficult one, as it was for any champion of Williams, for Bentley to explain.[21] When Bancroft transformed Williams into an avatar of Jacksonian democracy, he ignored the episode altogether.[22] Bancroft's romantic history required clear conflict and heroic action in defense of the spirit of democracy, and, indeed, if Endicott were his subject, the outline of Hawthorne's story would not have looked out of place in his history. Although Bancroft's Williams carried the cause of "liberty of conscience" into the political arena by demanding a strict separation of church and state, his relation to Endicott's symbolic act was clearly too ambiguous for heroic dramatization.

In Bancroft's account, Massachusetts had already established a "representative government [which] was as perfect two centuries ago as it is today."[23] In order to preserve that democracy, however, certain laws were passed "pregnant with evil and with good . . . [which] narrowed the franchise" (1:362) and thus instituted an "aristocracy"—"not of wealth, but of those who had been ransomed at too high a price to be ruled by polluting passions." Although the "germ of representative government was already visible," the Puritans "shrank from contradiction as from the approach of peril" (1:368). Enter Roger Williams: despite his "gentleness and forebearance," he "condemned" the theocracy because it "plucked up the roots of civil society and brought all the strifes of the state into the garden and paradise of the church." From compulsory worship to the Freeman's oath, Williams fought against each threat to a true representative democracy, which alone could purify the church and liberalize the government. Like the Jacksonians who followed him, he "seemed an ally of a civil faction; to himself he appeared only to make a frank avowal of truth" (1:372). The magistracy sought to isolate him, but like a good Jacksonian, Williams circulated a petition—"in modern terms, he appealed to the people." His isolation increased, however; "even his wife, under a delusive idea of duty, was for a season influenced to disturb the tranquility of his home with ther reproaches. Williams was left alone, absolutely alone" (1:374).

This last point deserves added comment, because Bancroft's version differs markedly from most others. According to Thomas Hutchinson, it was a sign of Williams's eccentricity that he "separated from his wife, and would neither ask a blessing nor give thanks at his meals if his wife were present, because she attended the publick worship in the church of Salem" (1:35). Among Hawthorne's contemporaries, John Quincy Adams thought it a sign of Williams's "conscientious, contentious spirit" that his "war of intolerance" led to a quarrel with his wife. And according to the Salem *Gazette,* the most striking anecdote in Upham's lecture on Williams was that his preaching "discomposed the internal economy of many families."[24] To more conservative historians, the domestic economy of the family is a sign of the essential harmony of natural and civil orders and for

Whigs like Upham, Williams is a tragic example of a breakdown in that harmony which was the result of partisan politics. To a staunch Democrat like Bancroft, however, Williams's isolation justifies his politics. The "germ" of representative democracy cannot be left to develop on its own in its own context, but must be nurtured through the example of foster fathers like Williams. Aristocracies cripple the free natural expression of liberty; theocracies pollute both church and state; laws are "pregnant" with good and evil; and even wives are given to delusions and reproaching. What is at stake in these readings of Williams's character is not so much the principle he fought for, nor even his importance as a historical figure. Rather, by representing Williams's character, historians present their politics as historical romance, and by characterizing Williams's domestic relationships, they present historical romance as family romance, thus conflating political action and personal experience.

For this reason, a favorite rhetorical figure for Jacksonian polemicists was that of "mother." In one aspect, typified by the Indian removal debates, the Eaton affair, and the war against "Mother Bank," this maternal figure typified natural disorder, indifference, or hostility as it withheld nurturance or expressed itself unpredictably. The opposed aspect, the composite figure of "women and children" typified that ideal of democratic natural and civil order which justified "manly" action against the first type.[25] Thus Endicott's "howling wilderness" where savages and wild animals lie in wait, where "stubborn roots . . . break our ploughshares," where "[o]ur children cry for bread, and we must dig in the sands of the seashore to satisfy them." So, too, the need to separate from the offspring of an "adulteress" in England and to punish an adulteress in Salem, and the importance of the Puritan women who hold up their children to look Endicott in the face. So, too, that grotesque image of the woman condemned to wear a cleft-stick on her tongue. As Hawthorne muses in conventionally misogynistic terms, "her countenance and gestures give much cause to apprehend that, the moment the stick should be removed, a repetition of the offence would demand new ingenuity in chastising it." Independence, in the Democratic view, requires ingenious methods for controlling the functions of nurturance and sexual and verbal expression and appropriating them for use by drawing distinctions between wilderness and settlement, between the mothers of Israel and the whores of Babylon, and between noise—e.g., "howling," Royalist toasts, Anglican prayers, profanity, tongue-wagging—and, on the other hand, appropriate speech. It is no idle metaphor Endicott uses in characterizing the threat of a governor-general "in whose breast shall be deposited all the law and equity of the land." Political control is determined by control of the metaphoric maternal functions and, ultimately, by control of the metaphors themselves. Thus Bancroft's insistent use of natural and maternal figures to justify Williams's place as the forefather who attempted to nurture the "germ" of representative democracy but was ultimately defeated by the restrictions of contemporary political (and familial) structures. Williams then becomes an example for Jacksonian politicians and Bancroft as a historian who attempt to foster the spirit of democracy against the conservative politics and historiography of their own time.[26]

For this reason, Bancroft's *History* and particularly his treatment of Williams was correctly read by his supporters and detractors as a declaration of his politics. But while Bancroft's use of historical figures may have been obvious, especially to those who disagreed with his politics, it was a strategy he shared with them. Upham characterized his disputes with other Salem clergy as an unfolding of Williams's arguments for "liberty of conscience." Even the flamboyant Henry Vane—whom Bancroft thought an artistocrat and a dandy—was useful for Upham's identifying himself with the struggle for "liberty of conscience" and his extended dramatization of Vane's execution, when Vane's last words were drowned out by the noise of an Anglican mob, was quoted in full in the conservative *North American Review*.[27] The task of the historian, then, is to give speech back to the forefathers and in so doing make their words come alive again and re-mark their place in history. But of course, like Hawthorne's Endicott, the historian does not so much rediscover the lost significance of the words as fill in the silent marks "with his own spirit." Hawthorne's ironic treatment of Endicott and Williams indicates, I think, his awareness of this implication of the author in the characters whose actions he authorizes and whose heroism authorizes his own activity.

In framing his tale, Hawthorne recalls a time when "our forefathers perceived their danger, but were resolved that their infant country should not fall without a struggle, even beneath the giant strength of the king's right arm." The tale then proceeds with an almost inexorable logic to its conclusion in Endicott's act and the praise bestowed on him by the narrator. Operating against this logic is a series of reservations, chief among them the circumstance that only Endicott's "giant strength" is ever displayed, and the gentle or dependent qualities signified by "infant" are more often threatened than nurtured or protected by Endicott. Although Endicott stands at the center of the tale, describing the community, retelling its history, warning of its precariousness, and exhorting it to action, Hawthorne withholds authority from him at crucial points. His contention that "the savages lieth in wait for us" is belied by the rather innocous "stately savages" with their "childish weapons" who gaze at the spectacle of Endicott's soldiers, each armed like an "individual fortress." Although the community is first seen reflected (metaphorically as well as literally) on Endicott's "highly polished breastplate," Williams arrives later, his shoes "bemired" from his journey, and stoops to drink at a fountain omitted from the previous landscape. Endicott's appeal to "liberty of conscience" is immediately challenged by the wanton gospeller and Endicott is forced to stop and distinguish between "liberty of conscience" and "license to ridicule and profane," a distinction which few readers have found convincing. Instead, readers usually see in the difference between Endicott's menacing sword waving and Williams's "sad and quiet smile" at that point, an indication of Hawthorne's true meaning. Endicott's harangue oversteps the bounds of propriety when he rails against "this grandson of a papistical and adultress Scotchwoman, whose death proved that a golden crown doth not always save an anointed head from the block," and when Williams objects, he too is silenced by Endicott. Despite the narrator's praise of Endicott, Hawthorne has left the unmistakable impression that Endicott's speech has not so much described as created another "howling wilderness." The more power Endicott appropriates for himself, the less authority he is granted, and as a result readers tend to look to the figure of the elderly Williams for the reverent and mild qualities of liberal religion and sentimentalized nature.

Endicott defines the goals of the community: "to make a new world unto ourselves, and painfully seek a path from hence to Heaven"—as if Heaven as a condition of plentitude were a literal place distanced in time—whereas Williams gazes "heavenward" before drinking his simple draught, thus indicating a condition beyond the limits of Endicott's discourse, yet present.

But this is not merely a dispute over providential typologies; it indicates Hawthorne's method of insinuating himself throughout his text as that silent presence beyond the limits of his own narrative. While Endicott's speech, and indeed the whole story, proceeds like a natural unfolding of the conflict presented in his introduction, Hawthorne makes his presence felt by undermining the authority of those who control the language, whether Endicott or his narrator. Hawthorne does not defend the adulteress, but encourages fanciful speculation about her ingenious embroidery that has obscured the significance of her badge of shame. Hawhtorne does not directly confront Endicott's definition of "liberty of conscience," but uses the wanton gospeller's wisecrack as a way of questioning Endicott's authority. Finally, Hawthrone parodies Endicott's fear that the colonies will be "delivered" into the hands of the pope, by his narrator's praising Endicott as the example of those who accomplished the "deliverance" of the colonies "after the bones of the stern Puritan had lain more than a century in the dust." While the narrator exults, "forever honored by the name of Endicott," Hawthorne's final image is not of the stern Puritan in Heaven, but of his "bones . . . in the dust." In the end, only the figure of Williams and the Hawthorne persona that figure represents have survived Hawthorne's dissembling of Endicott's narrow assertions and the narrator's uncritical praise.

Williams is a safe vehicle for Hawthorne's self-presentation. An elderly "father" with no family, an authority whose source of authority is unavailable for criticism and need not be challenged, Williams is a marginal figure who criticizes Endicott's assertions and political assertions in general, without assuming a central position. It is an ingenious strategy: naive readers will read the story as a straightforward celebration of our forefathers and be amused or annoyed at Hawthorne's fanciful interjections; more subtle readers will read in what is omitted or obscured traces of an authorial presence and will identify Hawthorne's character with his representation of Williams's. But this Williams is a character who never was, just like the marginal solitary author Hawthorne dramatized in his letters to Longfellow at this time—the figure who had stepped aside from the "main current of life" and by some witchery could not get back, the figure who felt himself a ghost, the figure who imagined himself an old man with no store of memories.[28] This marginal persona in one guise or another, disturbing but not confronting the main current of life, would serve Hawthorne throughout his career, and here at the beginning of his public career we can see him adopting, not the brassy Democratic self that Bridge had encouraged or that one might expect from a young man declaring himself a serious writer, but a fictional grandfather whose silent critique of an exuberant patriotic voice presents history as the unfolding of a series of other people's memories. Hawthorne's letter to Longfellow presented both personae: one, a young writer eager for favorable notice from an established author, and the other, this marginal observer of life. In the letters, this strategy was only partially successful, for although Longfellow reviewed *Twice-told Tales* very favorably in the *North American Review* and underscored their "national . . . character" and the reader's necessary "personal interest for the author [whose] calm, thoughtful face seems to be looking at you from every page,"[29] he was less receptive to Hawthorne's scheme to collaborate on a series of children's books. After the review appeared—by far the most important review Hawthorne had yet received—the brief correspondence terminated.

With Elizabeth Peabody's encouragement, however, Hawthorne wrote the children's books himself, beginning in 1841 with *Grandfather's Chair*. In this collection of historical sketches, he retold the tale of Endicott and the Red Cross, but this time with instructive differences. In this version, bathed in the conditional, "Roger Williams and John Endicott used to talk about" the graven image and Williams "probably" would say "were it my business to draw a sword, I should reckon it sinful to fight under such a banner." Grandfather suggests that "probably" Endicott addressed the community with a speech which may have concluded: "I have resolved that we will rather be God's soldiers, than soldiers of the Pope of Rome; and in that mood I now cut the Papal Cross out of this banner."[30] Lest there be any mistake about Endicott's motives, one of Grandfather's young auditors asks if Endicott "meant to imply that Massachusetts was independent of England." Truer to historical record than the narrator of the other sketch (who has Endicott shout, "What have we to do with England?"), Grandfather replies, "A sense of the independence of his adopted country, must have been in that bold man's heart . . . but I doubt whether he had given the matter much consideration, except in its religious bearing." Grandfather does not retell "one of the boldest exploits which our history records," but in flattening the language and denying a revolutionary typology, he modestly provides a glimpse of "Puritan character."

Had Hawthorne remained solely a writer of children's books, perhaps this "truer" version would be better known; or more likely, neither it nor the author of *True Stories from History and Biography* (1851) would be known at all. But he wrote *The Scarlet Letter* (1850) and that romance elevated tales like "Endicott and the Red Cross" into a place of prominence in his works. Unlike the single narrative voice of *Grandfather's Chair,* the clash of romantic and realistic voices in *The Scarlet Letter* and of jingoistic cant and moralistic silence in "Endicott and the Red Cross" produces an authorial presence that legitimates itself and the "history" it seems to record. While the voice of the former seems merely conventional, the mutual interference of two no less conventional voices produces the self of the "true" author who seems to express profoundly the spirit of his age. Through this self-ironizing strategy, the fictitious author and a fictitious event compel belief beyond what the modest "facts" would seem to warrant. While Bancroft's *History* has itself become a historical curiosity and few people have heard of Upham, a shy and reclusive "Hawthorne" is still presumed to speak for the Puritans.

## Notes

1. One of the most recent examples of this method in its general form is Larzer Ziff's *Literary Democracy: The Declaration in Cultural Independence in America* (New York: Viking Press, 1981). In his chapter entitled "The Great Conservative," Ziff quotes Hawthorne's apology for revolutionary mobs from *Grandfather's Chair:* "We must forgive what was wrong in their actions, and look into their hearts and minds for the honorable motives that impelled them" (p. 118). From this statement, Ziff reconstructs Hawthorne as alienated moralist: "What Hester embodies fully, many a protagonist in Hawthorne's stories allegorized: an ambition for self-realization commencing in the heart but in its isolated ardor passing over the common feelings of humanity" (p. 121). Rather than taking Hawthorne's statement as a personal insight, I prefer to read it as a conventional platitude and no more nor less conventional than the "sexuality" Ziff sees as Hawthorne's negation of "social conventions." It seems to me that the real value of such a statement is that it provides a clear example of the nineteenth century's replacing of political discourse with a rhetoric of subjectivity—"actions" with "honorable motives." In this perspective, ambition appears driven by a desire for "self-realization" and originates in the "heart" that it isolates from an intersubjective community. From the perspective of a political discourse, however, the situation is reversed: post-revolution-

ary America produces a desire for "Fame" and limits the range of permissible political activity. "Character" replaces "heroism" and symbolic reenactments of the "separation" from England (usually in the form of character assassination) become commonplace by Jackson's time. In contrast to the eighteenth-century notion of character as a public mark, "character" in this new sense is only the outward form of that isolated subject whose political activity has been proscribed, and the community to which the subject looks for "self-realization" is not the polis but its own isolated subjectivity universalized: "the common feelings of humanity."

2. Sacvan Bercovitch, *The Puritan Origins of the American Self* (New Haven, Conn.: Yale University Press, 1975), p. 9. Bercovitch's argument is that the peculiar Puritan fusion of "sainthood" and "nationality" was a necessary consequence of their social position: because they were "visible members of the true church, their social enterprise was aligned with the work of redemption. And because they were so aligned, the spiritual progress of each saint among them was manifest in the progress of their venture" (p. 90). Substituting secular for sacred terms—"republic" for "true church," "liberty" for "redemption," "self-realization" for "spiritual progress," and "individual" for "saint"—yields a statement that would apply equally to what Jacksonians said about themselves. It is not surprising, then, that Bercovitch should find Hawthorne's Endicott a "harbinger of the Revolution" (p. 143) because his own readings of "Endicott and the Red Cross"—"Endicott's Breastplate: Symbolism and Typology in 'Endicott and the Red Cross,'" *Studies in Short Fiction* 4 (1967): 289–99 and "Diabolus in Salem," *English Language Notes* 6 (1969): 280–85—are themselves harbingers of the methodology of *Puritan Origins* and *The American Jeremiad* (Madison, Wis.: University of Wisconsin Press, 1978). While his work has brilliantly diagnosed the importance of naive patriotism, the need for a "mythic mode of cultural continuity" (*Puritan Origins*, p. 143) to satisfy the American craving for a positive "identity," it has also undervalued an equally important skepticism that is the differential side of the American obsession with identity. In portraying Endicott as a "harbinger of the Revolution," Hawthorne is neither recovering Puritan typology nor is he writing a Jacksonian Jeremiad. My argument is that he is indicating that such a narrative is expected in the 1830s and that, as historian, he will be implicated in his narrative. So he lies: "Endicott and the Red Cross" is the *only* version of this event to that time (including Hawthorne's own later version in *Grandfather's Chair*) which figures Endicott as a harbinger of the Revolution.

3. James Mellow sets the tone for his evocatively Victorian biography by beginning in the year 1837 with Hawthorne meeting Sophia Peabody. See *Nathaniel Hawthorne in His Times* (Boston: Houghton, Mifflin, 1980), pp. 3–8, 65–98. See also Arlin Turner, *Nathaniel Hawthorne: A Biography* (New York: Oxford University Press, 1980), pp. 80–90. The sources for both—and indeed for almost all Hawthorne biographies dealing with this period—are Julian Hawthorne, *Nathaniel Hawthorne and His Wife*, 2 vols. (Boston: Houghton, Mifflin, 1885) and Horatio Bridge, *Personal Recollections of Nathaniel Hawthorne* (New York: Harper and Bros., 1893). In most biographies, these sources are supplemented by letters from Hawthorne to his sisters (at the Essex Institute) and to Longfellow (at the Houghton Library), and fleshed out with readings of Hawthorne's fiction. The fairly predictable differences in readings of Hawthorne's "character" arise when biographers and critics favor one or another of Hawthorne's personae—for Mellow it is the isolate in search of intimacy and community. In "A Psychoanalysis of Hawthorne's Style," *Genre* 14 (1981): 383–409, I have explored the difficulties that typically beset biographers who must contend with Hawthorne's self-dramatizing in his letters, his fiction, and his dealings with family and friends.

4. *Hawthorne's Lost Notebook, 1835–1841* (University Park, Penn.: Pennsylvania State

University Press, 1978), p. 25. "Fame," "Ruin," and "a place to fill in the world" are themes that appear regularly throughout the 1836–37 entries.

5. Despite an excess of psychologizing in both cases, George Forgie and Michael Paul Rogin argue well for the importance of "fame," the cult of personality, and the family as political icon in the early nineteenth century. Forgie, *Patricide in the House Divided: A Psychological Interpretation of Lincoln and His Age* (New York: Norton, 1979); Rogin, *Fathers and Children: Andrew Jackson and the Subjugation of the American Indian* (New York: Knopf, 1975).

6. See "The Custom-House" preface to *The Scarlet Letter* and "The Old Manse" preface to *Mosses from an Old Manse,* vols. 1 and 10 of the Centenary Edition of the *Works of Nathaniel Hawthorne* (Columbus: Ohio State University Press, 1963–).

7. See, especially, Richard Harter Fogle, *Hawthorne's Fiction: The Light and the Dark* (Norman, Okla.: University of Oklahoma Press, 1964), p. 9, and Roy Harvey Pearce, "Romance and the Study of History," in Pearce, ed., *Hawthorne Centenary Essays* (Columbus: Ohio State University Press, 1964), pp. 232–33.

8. Bridge, *Personal Recollections,* p. 80; hereafter cited in the text as Bridge.

9. Julian Hawthorne, *Nathaniel Hawthorne,* 1:36; hereafter cited in the text as Julian.

10. Essex *Register,* 23:21 (13 March 1837), 23:22 (16 March 1837), 23:23 (20 March 1837). This last issue also contained news of the Whig State Convention naming Hawthorne's editor, S. G. Goodrich, as the Norfolk County delegate, and advertised Emerson's lecture at the Salem Lyceum sponsored by Charles Upham and the Society for the Diffusion of Useful Knowledge.

11. Salem *Gazette,* n.s. 15:19 (7 March 1837), 15:21 (14 March 1837); "The parting Bull fulminated by the political Pope, the kissing of whose toe made Mr. Van Buren his successor—is pitiful from its now impotent venom, and ludicrous for its mock-heroic tone of Wisdom, Purity and Patriotism." The *Gazette* continued with an editorial reprinted from the New York *American.* It demonstrates that Hawthorne's language in "Endicott and the Red Cross" was fairly commonplace in contemporary polemics:

> In every thing—in topics—in tone—in oblivion of self, and earnest looking forward into the future—in consistency with the character and acts of the signer, as pure solicitude for the interest of the people—and in the manner of reference to his own personal acts—this address of General Jackson is as much in contrast with *the* Farewell Address, as are the character, and will be the fame, of Washington and Jackson.
> Happily it is the last *Humbug* which the mischievous popularity of this illiterate, violent, vain and iron-willed soldier, can impose upon a confiding and credulous people.

12. Salem *Gazette,* n.s. 15:22 (17 March 1837). This notice was a response to an article in the Newburyport *Herald,* which assumed that "Hawthorne" was a pseudonym. In one sense it was, Hawthorne having added the "w" to his surname.

13. An interesting Eriksonian analysis might be pursued by interpreting the combined themes of these five stories and reading them against Erikson's norms of "generativity." Most interesting, I think, is the relentless irony Hawthorne trains on his own materials in these stories: Peter Goldthwaite's virtual self-destruction, the cruelty of the artist's idealizing and disillusioning of "Sylph" Etheredge, the patriarch's envisioning of a glorious future without humans in "The Shaker Bridal." Interesting, too, are the editorial changes Hawthorne made in his previously published stories as they were collected in *Twice-told Tales,* deletions of ironic political commentary from "The Gentle Boy" and an extravagant appeal to a feminine "reader" from "The Vision of the Fountain." See "Historical Collation," *Twice-told Tales,* Centenary Edition, 9:613–18, 623–24.

14. Marion Kesselring, "Hawthorne's Reading, 1828–1850," *Bulletin of the New York Public Library* 53 (1949).

15. Salem *Gazette*, n.s. 15:22 (17 March 1837).

16. Salem *Gazette*, n.s. 15:13 (24 February 1837), 15:24 (24 March 1837). The Salem *Observer* commented on Emerson's lecture, 15:13 (1 April 1837), but noted that Upham was "too well established" to require mention.

In his *Second Century Lecture of the First Church* (Salem, Mass.: Foote and Brown, 1829), Upham placed himself in a line of descent from Williams through Hugh Peters (for his valuing of industry over theology) and Henry Vane (for his "character" as revealed at his execution). As a contemporary of Hawthorne's, it is not surprising to see a similarly theatrical use of anti-Papist typology: "Thus have the churches of New-England, throughout their whole history, been the subjects, and the parishes the victims, of Congregational Cardinals and Presbyterian Popes" (p. 53). By the early 1830s he had succeeded in making himself well known at the expense of the "Cardinals" and "Popes" that were the targets of his frequent broadsides.

In the spring of 1837 he was involved in a minor scandal, having been accused of spreading rumors about his senior pastor's intemperance. Among the consequences of this little tempest was his temporary resignation from the pulpit and a serious breach in his close relationship with the Peabody family, especially with Sophia, who had praised his biography of Henry Vane extravagantly. It seems that in breaking with his senior pastor, Upham had blamed Sophia's father for being the source of the rumors he himself denied spreading. The First Church was also Hawthorne's family's church, and since Hawthorne's mother had always wanted him to be a minister, it might be interesting to speculate about the relation between Upham's supposed breach of decorum and his separation from the Church and Roger Williams's concern that rumors not be "suddenly noised abroad" in Hawthorne's story. See Sophia Peabody to Ann S. Upham, 29 November 1835; Nathaniel Peabody to C. W. Upham, 14 May 1837; and C. W. Upham to Nathaniel Peabody, 15 May 1837, in the Saltonstall Papers, Massachusetts Historical Society.

17. *Twice-told Tales*, Centenary Edition, 9:433–41.

18. It would be misleading to read these rather obvious sexual metaphors as indications of a deep structure of personal conflict that informs the political "manifest content"—as Ziff, Forgie, Rogin and to some extent Bercovitch do. Such gothicisms were an important feature of the political vocabulary of the 1830s and 1840s and were built into the genre of Jacksonian polemic.

19. Michael Davitt Bell, *Hawthorne and the Historical Romance of New England* (Princeton, N.J.: Princeton University Press, 1971), pp. 53–60; Neal Frank Doubleday, *Hawthorne's Early Tales: A Critical Study* (Durham, N.C.: Duke University Press, 1972), pp. 101–8. Bell and Doubleday reorient Bercovitch's assertion that Hawthorne "carefully relies upon recorded fact" ("Breastplate," p. 294) by showing that only by relying on historical records could Hawthorne have distorted those facts so thoroughly. Unlike Bell and Doubleday, I think his distortions have less to do with an interpretation of an obscure event in the 1630s than with the rhetoric of the 1830s.

20. *Winthrop's Journal*, ed. J. K. Hosmer, 2 vols. (New York: Scribner, 1908), especially 1:149–68; Mather, *Magnalia Christi Americana*, 2 vols. (Hartford, Conn.: Silas Andrus, 1820), 2:430: Williams was "a preacher that had less *light* than *fire* in him." Hutchinson, *History of the Colony and Province of Massachusetts-Bay*, ed. Lawrence Shaw Mayo, 2 vols. (Cambridge, Mass.: Harvard University Press, 1936), 1:35–37. William Hubbard, "History of New-England," *Massachusetts Historical Society Collections*, 2d series, 5 (1815), p. 164: Endicott was "supposed, like Barnabus, to be carried away with the notions of rigid Separation, imbibed from Mr. Roger Williams." Rev. John Eliot, "Eccle-

siastical History of Massachusetts," *MHSC,* 1st series, 9 (1804), p. 25: Williams was a religious zealot who "like other partisans of religious controversy . . . [argued] notions, or sentiments of little consequence to good morals."

21. Rev.William Bentley, "A Description and History of Salem," *MHSC,* 1st Series, 6 (1799), pp. 212–88; "Remarks on 'A History of Salem,'" *MHSC,* 1st series, 7 (1800), pp. iii–v: "The protrait of [Williams], drawn in this history, is so unlike that, left by his contemporaries and acquaintances, that were it not for his *name,* no mortal would imagine it designed for the same person"; "Remarks Upon Remarks on the History of Salem," *MHSC,* 1st series, 8 (1802), pp. 1–4: ". . . he is immortal. He was a father of a free colony, and even in this generation his name is blessed." Bentley's version of the tale is remarkable for its waffling: "Endicott ventured to apply [Williams's] doctrine, and cut the cross from the military standard. Endicott did it without advice; but the resentment of the magistrate spent itself upon Williams who, though innocent, was the real cause of it" ("Description," p. 246).

22. George Bancroft, *A History of the United States,* 10 vols. (Boston: Little, Brown, 1861–75), 1:368–75; futher citations appear in the text. Volume 1, the only volume Hawthorne definitely saw, was originally published in 1834.

23. This was a typical formula for maintaining what Bercovitch calls a "mythic mode of cultural continuity." In typically ironic Hawthorne fashion, the formula appears in "Endicott and the Red Cross" as an inversion of the typical: "Let not the reader argue, from any of these evidences of iniquity, that the times of the Puritans were more vicious than our own" (9:435). The main difference, according to Hawthorne, was that, analogous to the fate of politics in his own time, the Puritans made their sins public and exposed them to shame whereas his contemporaries kept them private.

24. Hutchinson, *History of the Colony,* 1:35; John Quincy Adams, "The New England Confederacy of 1643," *MHSC,* 3d series, 9 (1846), p. 209; Salem *Gazette,* n.s. 15:13 (14 February 1837).

25. It is important to remember that figures of maternity do not necessarily refer—especially in political discourse—to people who are mothers. As was seen in the recent debates over Ann Douglas's *The Feminization of American Culture* (1977), there is a good deal of confusion over just this issue. While Douglas herself encouraged a reductive reading that virtually identified the terms feminine/feminized/narcissistic/consumerist, many of her critics were too willing to read "woman" or "mother" literally rather than probing the ways in which the habit of relating words to "experience" or to "the self" positions the reader by way of a particular figure in political discourse. For obvious examples, notice how often welfare is still typified by a black mother despite statistical evidence to the contrary, or the third world by a hungry child or mother and child or a thin peasant hoeing rocky ground. Debates about foreign policy obsessively characterize the United States as the figure who fosters growth when nature cannot or when growth is inhibited by the children of transgression, regardless whether those are the agents of "communism" or "terrorism" (for conservatives) or "oligarchy" or "military despotism" (for liberals). These examples are not misrepresentations of a reality that could be more accurately or fairly represented (although they are that). Primarily they are narrativized political arguments that compel allegiance not by presenting "facts" but by structuring response.

In Hawthorne's time, the figure of women and children was used dramatically in the accusations surrounding the 1834 burning of the Ursuline convent in Charlestown. Anti-Catholic agitators such as Lyman Beecher claimed to be protecting New England women and children from papist outsiders, and when two girls "escaped" from the convent school with tales of gothic terror, the convent was burned and sacked. At the resulting trial, however, the mob leaders were portrayed as paid outsiders who violated a domicile that housed only women and children. Hawthorne himself had made use of such figures in his ironic rendering of the Hannah Duston captivity narrative: framed by swipes at the "old, hard-hearted pedantic bigot Cotton Mather," his source, and a Washington Irving wink to the reader that her husband "had such knowledge of the good lady's character as afforded him a comfortable hope that she would hold her own, even in a contest with a whole tribe of Indians"—the killing of Duston's infant is no match for Duston's butchering of the Indians: mostly women and children, all devout Catholics who prayed three times a day, all killed in their sleep and scalped for bounty. "Mob Law," *North American Review* 43 (1836); "The Duston Family," *American Magazine of Useful and Entertaining Knowledge*, 11:9 (May 1836), pp. 395–97, reprinted in Arlin Turner, *Hawthorne as Editor* (University, La.: Louisiana State University Press, 1941), pp. 131–37.

26. If one were looking for historical analogues for Hawthorne's tale, a more fruitful source than the Puritans might be the loco-foco agitation in New York in the spring of 1837. Bercovitch astutely relates the Williams/Endicott pair to Moses and Aaron and then reads the tale, by way of Williams's later writings and Puritan typology, as Hawthorne's criticism of 1634. Probably of more immediate interest for understanding Hawthorne's attitude toward politics and history, however, are the pair Moses Jaques and Levi Slamm, who were charged with contempt as a result of the February 1837 "Flour Riot." Jaques was an elderly man, and Slamm's bombastic oratorical style had led the New York *Herald* to dub the loco-focos "Slamm Bang & Company." Fitzwilliam Byrdsall, a contemporary chronicler of the loco-foco party, commented on the contempt action: "though we had separated ourselves from British government, we were still slaves to their will." On 3 April, Jaques announced his mayoral candidacy, asking for confidence "upon the altar of liberty," and Slamm exhorted his followers to purge American politics of its repressive British features by reminding them that the British "drove our fathers to the savage wilds of a distant continent." Byrdsall, *History of the Loco-Foco or Equal Rights Party* (1842; reprint ed., New York: Burt Franklin, 1967), pp. 121, 133, 137. Because the loco-focos split the Democratic vote, Tammany Hall lost the mayorality and control of the city council to the Whigs, a circumstance that probably would have amused one side of Hawthorne. Another side of Hawthorne would likely have been interested in New York politics, because Franklin Pierce had been in contact with such loco-focos and sympathizers as Eli Moore and C. C. Cambreleng on his behalf and told him so in a letter of 28 March (Julian, 1:35). My argument, however, is not that Hawthorne was writing about events either in 1837 or 1634, but rather about the way virtually any "facts" infused with political purpose and demonstrating "character" could produce a compelling romance called "history."

27. *North American Review* 42 (1836): 116–48. Fully six pages of this review were devoted to Upham's rendering of Vane's execution. (One of the children in *Grandfather's Chair* cites Upham's biography and exclaims, "what a beautiful death he died, long afterwards! beautiful, though it was on a scaffold." *True Stories from History and Biography*, Centenary Edition, 6:29.) In introducing his topic, the reviewer quoted Sir James Mackintosh's tribute to Vane and Vane's few theological writings as *"the first direct assertion of the liberty of conscience!"* (p. 126). Upham, in his lectures, and Bancroft in his history, accorded that honor to Williams while Eliot did to the Browns (Anglicans). It was, in the 1830s, a fairly loose term that indicated the story's hero, while "Pope" or "King" indicated his antagonist. For Bancroft, "liberty of conscience" signified the goals of the antiaristocratic Jacksonian party, and for Whigs, resistance to "King Andrew."

28. Hawthorne to Longfellow, 4 June 1837; also 7 March 1837; 19 June 1837, in the

Houghton Library. The letter of 4 June is excerpted by Turner, *Hawthorne as Editor,* pp. 89–90, who finds it "one of the most remarkable instances of self-revelation and self-analysis in our literary archives" (p. 88). Mellow, while still considering it a "dramatic glimpse of his life since Bowdoin" (*Nathaniel Hawthorne,* p. 79), is more sensitive to the rhetorical situation and attentive to the work of self-presentation in Hawthorne's letter. Knowing the rhetorical situation, it is especially difficult to overlook the performative character of this "self-revelation." Indeed, Hawthorne's eagerness to direct Longfellow's attention to his "seclusion" leads him to comment in a curiously obtuse way to Longfellow's veiled allusion to recent "troubles" (the death of his wife): "I know not what they may have been; but I can assure you that trouble is the next best thing to enjoyment, and that there is no fate in this world so horrible as to have no share in either its joys or sorrows. For the last ten years, I have not lived, but only dreamed of living. It may be true that there have been some unsubstantial pleasures here in the shade, which I should have missed in the sunshine; but you cannot conceive how utterly devoid of satisfaction all my retrospects are. I have laid up no treasure of pleasant remembrances, against old age; but there is some comfort in thinking that my future years can hardly fail to be more varied, and therefore more tolerable, than the past." Quoted in Turner, p. 89.

29. *North American Review* 42 (1836): 62–63.
30. *True Stories from History and Biography,* Centenary Edition, 6:22–25.

# James, Browning, and the Theatrical Self: *The Wings of the Dove* and *In a Balcony*

## Ross Posnock

*University of Washington*

WRITING in 1913 to H. G. Wells to report his less than enthusiastic reponse to the younger writer's latest work, James explains: "I am of my nature . . . a critical, a non-naif, questioning, worrying reader." With this warning James hopes to justify his remarkable reading habits, which he goes on to describe: "To read a novel at all I perform afresh, to my sense, the act of writing it, that is of rehandling the subject according to my own lights and over-scoring the author's form and pressure with my own vision and understanding of the way." James hastens to add that his attitude, rather than a result of his restless boredom with the text at hand, "is the very measure of my attention and interest." Only on those rare occasions when James "sees a subject" in what that author has done, and "feels its appeal," is he stimulated to rewrite.[1]

James's best-known rewriting is in homage to the writer of whom "the English tongue may be most proud" and whom James rates "high—higher than anyone": Robert Browning.[2] To celebrate the poet's centenary in 1912, James made his first formal public appearance in seventeen years to honor Browning with his ultimate literary tribute: a rewriting (or more precisely the sketch of one) of *The Ring and the Book* as a Jamesian novel. "From my first reading," upon its publication in two volumes in 1868, "the pang of the novel they might have constituted sprang sharply from them."[3] The novelist's rewriting of Browning's masterpiece is based on his audacious belief that the poem is less an "achieved form" than a "mere preparation for one." While James confesses that his "appropriation" is "irreverent," he insists that it is a "restless refinement of homage" to an author whose personality and poetry fascinated, influenced, and disturbed him for over thirty years.

Because Browning's poetry, according to James, "has touched *everything* with a breadth,"[4] the poet creates a "complexity of suggestion" hardly to be exhausted by the novelist's rewriting of *The Ring and the Book*. Thus James concludes by stating: "I have wanted, alas, to say such still other fine, fond things—it being our poet's great nature to prompt them at every step."[5] What follows is concerned with one of the other things James left unsaid: that his impulse to redo the poet's works is not confined to *The Ring and the Book*.[6] In 1912 James merely spins "my dream of the matter"; but ten years before he actually used a Browning text by rewriting the poet's verse play *In a Balcony* as *The Wings of the Dove*. The most significant aspect of James's remarkable "appropriation" of *In a Balcony* is his "rehandling," with his "own vision and understanding," of the "subject" of theatricality, which is a matter of compelling interest to both authors throughout their careers, and especially in the two texts to be examined.

I

The disarmingly personal opening of the novel's preface has had the happy effect, from James's viewpoint, of diverting readers from investigating the work's literary sources. When James speaks of the germinal "idea" of the novel as "that of a young person . . . early stricken and doomed,"[7] critics have rightly inferred that James is alluding to the death of Minny Temple. And it is with her death that discussions of the novel's sources usually begin and end.[8] But James's admission that *The Wings of the Dove* represents "to my memory a very old—if I shouldn't perhaps rather say a very young motive"—directs us back not only to his tragic cousin but to other momentous events of his youth. Among them is his reading, at the age of sixteen, of Browning's *Men and Women*, an experience that James would vividly recall years later as one of the "sudden milestones" of his "inward . . . life."[9] James's discovery of the poet made him "our God," as T. S. Perry described Browning's special prominence in the formation of the "very young" sensibilities of James, Perry, and their friends.[10] In the pages of that volume James doubtless found *In a Balcony*, which he would eventually redo as *The Wings of the Dove*. Although he waited some forty years to use the play, James's preface stresses the novel's youthful origins: "I can scarce remember the time when the situation on which this long-drawn fiction mainly rests was not vividly present to me." While James makes no specific reference to *In a Balcony*, the novelist almost certainly knew the play, since he was a lifelong reader of Browning, who always remained "the author of *Men and Women*."

The plot of *In a Balcony*, consisting as it does of a single scene and only three characters, can easily be summarized. This verse play concerns the efforts of the lovers Constance and Norbert to find a way to marry without offending their Queen. Among the obstacles to their marriage is Constance's conviction that the Queen, who she believes is jealously possessive, will refuse to surrender the trusted and beloved Norbert, the Queen's prime minister, to her poor cousin Constance. Constance's uncertainty about the depth of Norbert's commitment to her is another barrier to their marriage. After dismissing Norbert's insistent demand that they simply ask the Queen at once, the scheming Constance creates a plot, a masquerade that will involve Norbert falsely declaring his love for the Queen. According to Constance, "since none love Queens directly," she will refuse Norbert and will give Constance to him as a substitute. The plot backfires because, after a series of complications, the Queen is discovered to have fully believed Norbert's declaration; the sheltered, lonely ruler has fallen in love with her prime minister. And when the forthright Norbert declares the truth to the Queen—that it is Constance he really loves—she furiously stalks off. Left alone on the balcony, their plan shattered, the lovers are convinced that the Queen plans to punish them, even execute them. Faced with the prospect of death the lovers passionately declare their love. The play ends with the Queen's guard approaching, and the fate of Constance and Norbert left unknown.

Parallels with *The Wings of the Dove* are strikingly obvious. Both works dramatize the relations among a triangle consisting of a young couple and a lonely deprived woman, possessed of enormous power, who can remove the obstacles that prevent the lovers from marrying. The Queen and Milly the "princess" are a peculiar combination of the potent and the powerless; heirs to vast fortunes and emotionally and sexually deprived, vulnerable to the declarations of an attractive "suitor." Cast as suitors in their lovers' schemes, Norbert and Densher are essentially passive, subservient to dynamic, ambitious, shrewdly manipulative women. Because they suffer from a lack of will and the obsessions of unrequited sexual passion, both men are easily entangled in the immoral designs of their partners. The main action in both works is the formation and enacting of a plot—a deliberately fictive stratagem that consists of the man confessing his love to the lonely woman. But the scheme goes awry in both cases when one member of the triangle falls unexpectedly in love: the Queen with Norbert, Densher with Milly's memory. There is a notable congruence in the final movements of both works, as the main characters—Densher and Constance—engage in acts of self-purgation that leave them engulfed in a profound stillness. The marriages that have been impending from the start end in ruin.

Before pursuing the relations between these works we can clarify our understanding of what James took from *In a Balcony* by noting Blackmur's distinction between "real" and "mechanical" plot. The latter is "what the action is about as anecdote," while the "real plot" "reveals the being of the people to whom the action happens and thus reveals the action of the soul in its poetic drama."[11] James, I think, borrows the "mechanical plot" of Browning's play as the scaffolding for his "real plot": the exploration of his main characters' "inward drama," to use James's phrase about Densher. In effect, James rewrites *In a Balcony* by transforming "the guarded objectivity" characteristic of the dramatic genre into the drama of consciousness. Juxtaposing these texts makes particularly vivid the novelist's attempt at a fusion of the "scenic method" he had discovered as he began work on *The Wings of the Dove* in 1895, with the explanations and "amplifications" of narration. This synthesis James calls "dramatic analysis," which defines the representational technique of the three late masterpieces.

But *In a Balcony* provides James with more than a scaffolding; its characterization, formal strategy, and the complicity of author and character make Browning's play a remarkable prefiguration in miniature (as would befit a play of one short scene) of *The Wings of the Dove*. However, the above aspects must be inscribed within the master theme that profoundly links these works: their exploration of the theatrical self. In their lives and art Browning and James are fascinated by theatrical behavior—the masks, roles, and conventions that constitute the self in its experience of social reality. Indeed, their oeuvres provide two of the nineteenth century's most searching examinations of theatricality and the intimately related impulses to aestheticize reality and to treat people as objets d'art.

Browning's dramatic monologues, in their depiction of a speaker's strategic self-dramatizations, reveal how the self represents rather than simply presents itself to others. The poet's adoption of various masks in his monologues defines his artistic role-playing, which finds a counterpart in his own self-representation. The notoriously impenetrable social mask Browning constructed baffled many, but no one was more intrigued than Henry James, who resorted to a theory of "two Brownings" to explain the disparity between the poet's public and private selves. Given James's interest in Browning's own theatricality, it is not surprising that he would find absorbing the work in which self-representation is made the central subject of the poet's literary representation. And theatricality partly accounts for the fact that *In a Balcony* is one of Browning's personal favorites among his works.[12] Because theatricality is deeply involved with representation in life and art, and indeed "derives its interest precisely from the fact that it functions without regard for a sharp distinction between literature and social life," as Stephen Greenblatt points out, it is, perhaps, inevitable that the following will reveal the autobiographical motives in these two texts.[13]

## II

As unabashedly performing selves, Constance and Kate masterfully perform on the social stage, revealing a prodigious energy and skill. But they are not merely gifted dissemblers adept at playing roles; they also create them for themselves and others, as they author plots and fabricate fictions. In so doing, Constance and Kate literally enact Browning's and James's plots, and align themselves with their creators as "delegates"—a function James explicitly sought for his characters.

Constance celebrates indirection as the essential mode of human behavior; pretense and role-playing are for her the groundwork of social interaction. In an effort to instruct Norbert in her view of reality, Constance offers an "example": "I let you kiss me, hold my hands—Why? do you know why? . . . The kiss, because you have a name at court: / This hand and this, that you may shut in each / A jewel, if you please to pick up such."[14] For Constance sincerity seems to have been replaced by the careful management of impressions for the sake of exploiting others. The theatricality of her view of experience is implicit at this point, but comes to the fore in her passionate outpouring to Norbert quoted below, where she urges him to keep their love secret:

> Where are you now? immersed in cares of state—
> Where am I now? intent on festal robes—
> . . . . . . . . . . . . . . .
> What was this thought for, . . .
> Which broke the council up?—to bring about
> One minute's meeting in the corridor!
> And then the sudden sleights, strange secrecies,
> Complots inscrutable, deep telegraphs,
> Long-planned chance-meetings, hazards of a look,
> "Does she know? does she not know? saved or lost?"
> A year of this compression's ecstasy
> All goes for nothing! you would give this up
> For the old way, the open way, the world's, . . .
>
> [Ll. 185–97]

This speech, which constitutes a summation of her perception of reality, reveals that Constance lives her life as if she is an actress in a romantic drama, or more precisely, melodrama. Moreover, in her artful management of her illicit love affair, she can be considered the author of the melodrama that is her life. Indeed, Constance seems to relish the intricate scheming and the "ecstasy" of "compression" it affords, at least as much as her love of Norbert. It is a measure of her theatricality that what so distrubs Constance is the prospect that the clandestine plotting she cherishes must come to an end when she submits to the "old way, the open way" of marriage. Instead of being eager to marry her lover and escape the agitations of a secret romance, Constance seeks only to continue her skilled dissembling in even more ingenious plots. Given her delight in intrigue, it is hardly surprising that Norbert's forthright demand for an "open, easy" love founded on the "truth" of his passion for her is dismissed by Constance. His simple trust in "ourselves being true," causes him to reject Constance's vision of the Queen: "The Queen's the Queen, / I am myself—no picture, but alive / In every nerve and every muscle, here / At the palace window" (ll. 148–51). Norbert's tautologies imply a view of the self as stable and substantial, anchored to the immediate by a commitment to "being true"; such a conception is precisely the opposite of his lover's theatrical self.

Densher's conflict with Kate is akin to the struggle between Norbert and Constance: Densher, like Norbert, seeks to be "true" but eventually becomes enmeshed in his lover's design. Because of a sincere wish not to deceive Milly, Densher tentatively adopts a posture of inaction in order to maintain his moral equilibrium. But "the inevitabilities of the abjection of love"—particularly his acute sense of sexual frustration—finally impel Densher to act in both senses of the word. As in *In a Balcony*, the refusal of sexual union is the means by which the woman coerces her lover into surrendering to her plot. Norbert's impassioned: "Love has been so long-Subdued in / Eating me through and through," is echoed in Densher's intense feeling of deprivation. Sounding like an introspective Norbert, Densher feels "a kind of rage at what he wasn't having; an exasperation, a resentment, begotten truly by the very impatience of desire, in respect of his postponed and relegated, his so extremely manipulated state."[15] Realizing that he has been "perpetually bent to her will," Densher is struck by a "sense almost of shame"; he wonders whether he has "really no will left. How could he know . . . without putting the matter to the test?" He tests his will, of course, by demanding that Kate sleep with him as payment for performing in her scheme. By linking desire and theatricality Browning and James expose the homologous structure of these phenomena—both are activities constituted by a lack or absence. If desire by definition is a desire for some absent thing, theatricality also depends on a "postponed . . . state," a perpetual deferral of the fully present, stable self implicit in Norbert's phrase "ourselves being true," and Densher's plea to Kate: "take me just as I am." Constance's reply—"Not now!" (Her very first words)—and Kate's response—"Let us wait"—signify the deferment these women embody; their identities are founded on the gap that creates, indeed constitutes, desire and the theatrical self. For an absence of self, as we shall see, makes possible the role-playing of Constance and Kate.

Although Densher only grudgingly consents to Kate's plot, he fully recognizes "the heroic ring" of her audacity, which has its source in what Densher admiringly calls "her pure talent for life." Kate's "talent,' which belittles "his own incapacity for action," is never more vivid to Densher than when he observes her "beautiful entrance" on the social stage of Lancaster Gate in book six, chapter 3. This scene gives rise to Densher's most awed and ambivalent response to her "talent," as he defines it as essentially theatrical, and in glimpsing the complexity of Kate's role-playing he finds that her theatrical self has created a distance between them.

Kate's entrance on to the "social scene" of Lancaster Gate, where Aunt Maud presides, strikes Densher as the arrival of a "distinguished actress." "As such a person was to dress the part, to walk, to look, to speak, in every way to express, the part, so all this was what Kate was to do for the character she had undertaken, under her aunt's roof, to represent" (2:34). Because Maud disapproves of the impoverished journalist as a suitor for her niece, Kate fabricates a Kate indifferent to Densher; this is the "character" she has "undertaken" to "represent." As Densher watches Kate's performance in "the glare of the footlights," he explores the theatrical metaphor that her behavior inevitably brings to mind. With characteristic passivity, Densher sees himself "as in his purchases stall at the play" observing the "faultless soldier on parade." He perceives that under Aunt Maud's intense scrutiny Kate's face is "disciplined," her "expression impeccable," and Densher has the sharp sense that "the drama . . . was between *them,* them quite preponderantly; with Merton Densher relegated to mere spectatorship" (2:35). But Densher, far from feeling comfortable in the audience, is acutely uneasy; instead of joining in the "proper round of applause" for Kate, he is "almost too scared to take part in the ovation," and can only stare in anguished silence. Densher feels "the least bit sick . . . his appreciation had turned for the instant to fear—had just turned, as we have said, to sickness" (2:34).

Densher's "sickness" has a deeper cause than his disgust at Maud's "managerial appreciation" of her niece's "tangible value" and dissatisfaction with the minor role he has been assigned. The crucial reason for Densher's unease is that the "game" must be played at all. In his conversation with Kate before the "drama," Densher, as he had done earlier in the novel, makes his hatred of the plot explicit, and reiterates his plea to marry Kate and end their scheme. What Densher craves is simply to be alone with his lover; he savors their rare and precious privacy:

They were alone—it *was* all right: he took in anew the shut doors and the permitted privacy, the solid stillness of the great house. . . . What it amounted to was that he couldn't have her . . . evasive. . . . He didn't want her deeper than himself, fine as it might be as wit or as character; he wanted to keep her where their communication would be straight and easy and their intercourse independent. [2:19]

Densher's anguish stems from his suspicion that he will never be able to "keep" Kate from performing; "she was made for great social uses," as Milly observes in one of the shrewdest assessments of Kate. Milly's insight expresses an essential truth about Kate: in spite of her genuine love of Densher, her theatricalized self rebels not only against his pleas, but is at odds with the very assumptions that form the basis of his thought. Her insistence on a performing self conflicts with Densher's desire to be taken "just as I am," for social performance creates a "represented" self (as Kate is described as representing a character to Maud) in distinct contrast to the private, "natural" self Densher's language implies. From Kate's viewpoint, a space where "their communication would be straight and easy and their intercourse independent" is nonexistent because the theatrical self, being fundamentally social, entails the abnegation of the private self and the intimacy it thrives on.[16]

But to speak of Kate's theatricality as contingent upon a sacrifice of her private self is imprecise, for it assumes that she possesses a substantial, stable identity to sacrifice. In fact, Kate's performing self, like Constance's, depends on the lack of a solid, centered self, which enables her to move easily from role to role in a theatricalized version of the Keatsian "chameleon poet." Strikingly, it is Milly who notes that an absence of self characterizes Kate: "Kate had for her new friend's eyes the extraordinary and attaching property of appearing at a given moment to show as a beautiful stranger, to cut her connexions and lose her identity" (1:223). In appearing to Milly as a "stranger," "more objective," and "other," Kate reveals that her free-floating self is constituted by an essential blankness of selfhood. James makes this conception of the theatrical self explicit in *The Tragic Muse,* where Peter Sherringham defines the source of Miriam's histrionic genius: "What's rare in you is that you have . . . no nature of your own . . . you are always playing something; there are no intervals. It's the absence of intervals, of a *fond* or background."[17]

Kate's need to be "always playing something" finds satisfaction in her prolonging of her clandestine romance; she and Constance are exhilarated by the sheer activity of artful dissembling. Kate tells Densher: "there's fun in it too. We must get our fun where we can . . . our relation's quite beautiful. It's not a bit vulgar. I cling to some saving romance in things" (1:72). Clearly what constitutes "romance" for Kate are secret rendezvous with Densher and her hoodwinking of Maud and Milly. Despite her obstinacy about marriage, Densher remains enthralled not only by Kate's theatrical panache, but by her talents as a dramatist. When, early in the novel, she describes Maud as having "fixed upon me herself, settled on me with her wonderful gilded claws . . . an eagle—with a gilded beak as well, and with wings for great flights" (1:73), her flow of vivid images makes a great impression on Densher: "it had, really, her sketch of the affair, a high color and a great style; at all of which he gazed a minute as at a picture by a master" (1:74).

The "great style" of Kate's "sketch" is founded on her capacity for image-making, which is evident in her effortless transformation of Maud into a wealth of evocative and witty guises. Whether depicting herself as a "trembling kid" about to be "introduced into a cage of the lioness" Maud, or calling her aunt "a great seamed silk balloon," and, most notoriously, dubbing Milly Theale a "dove," the fertility of Kate's metaphoric imagination defines her view of reality as aesthetic. Deep in Kate's sensibility is the artistic propensity for imposing fictive constructs upon reality by recasting experience into symbols. Inevitably her symbol-making reduces the human actuality of those she perceives by imprisoning them in constructions of language. But the impulse to aestheticize reality is not confined to Kate; indeed, it is the most characteristic and frequent mode of perception in *The Wings of the Dove,* affecting all the major figures, and significantly James himself.

### III

The aesthetic activity that pervades James's novel is made vivid by focusing on Milly's reaction to Kate's declaration that she is a "dove." The effect of Kate's announcement is to make Milly feel "herself ever so delicately, so considerately embraced; not with familiarity or as a liberty taken, but almost ceremonially and in the manner of an *accolade;* partly as if, though a dove who could perch on a finger, one were also a princess with whom forms were to be observed" (1:283). Milly's train of thought here is significant: she feels like a "princess," for Kate's benediction inevitably recalls to her mind another "accolade"—Susie's oft-repeated image of Milly, which is, of course, "princess."

"Mrs. Stringham was a woman of the world, but Milly Theale was a princess, the only one she had yet to deal with" (1:120). Susie's princess embodies the "romantic life itself" to her rather saccharine imagination, and Milly is aware of her friend "always suspiciously sparing her"; "to treat her as a princess was a positive need of her companion's mind" (1:255). But if Milly is Susie's "princess," she is first of all James's "princess," as he makes explicit in the final section of the preface. James admits to approaching Milly "circuitously," "at second hand, as an unspotted princess is ever dealt with; the pressure all around her kept easy for her, the sounds, the movements regulated." The congruity between James's and Susie's attitude toward Milly is the product of the novelist's effort to establish an intimacy between himself and his characters, whom he conceives of as the "impersonal author's concrete deputy or delegate, a convenient substitute or apologist for the creative power."[18]

Apart from their wish to "spare" and protect Milly, Mrs. Stringham's and her creator's solicitude is simultaneously insidious, for in treating Milly as a "princess" they muffle her actuality and particularly her imminent doom. To be "merciful" to the vulnerable Milly, and to express this feeling in imagery—"princess," "dove," "American girl"—is to transform her into a fictive construct. And once her symbolic identity eclipses her personal identity one is free to manipulate the symbol and weave it into a plot. This process of dehumanization is precisely the activity of the novel's central figures, as their compulsion to use Milly is nearly inextricable from their sympathy for her. James himself is not exempt from aestheticizing Milly, for in his method of "merciful indirection"—which also describes the behavior of his characters toward Milly—James enacts an aesthetic attitude as he dramatizes it.

Susie's view of Milly as "effete and overtutored . . . infinitely refined," could serve as a summation of Constance's image of the Queen. Both Susie and Constance see them in rather cliché terms, as stage princesses, an image Susie makes explicit when she calls Milly a "princess in a conventional tragedy" (1:120). Constance's romanticized perception of reality leads her to dismiss Norbert's view of the Queen as "just" and "generous" because it is far too prosaic. In casting her in a more colorful role, Constance portrays the Queen as leading a "life / Better than life, and yet no life at all, / Conceive her born in such a magic dome, / Pictures all around her!" (ll. 104–7). Cloistered in her fabulous palace, the "sole spectator" of the works of art that surround her, the lonely ruler gains all her knowledge of life from the "silent gallery," never daring to venture outside. Constance's vision of the Queen's rarefied existence "more grandiose than life" is pointedly ironic since it is most apt as a self-portrait, for the blight of aestheticism she thinks has infected the Queen has, in fact, victimized Constance.

As soon as the Queen comes on stage it becomes obvious that Constance's image of her is distorted; rather than wholly aestheticized, the Queen is also forthright and compassionate, eager to convince Constance of the morally redemptive power of love. Her belief is founded on an absolute trust in God, to whom she has committed her "will and power." In remaining "mute, passive and acquiescent," as she describes herself (l. 563), the Queen is directly opposed to Constance's mobile self that depends on performing and plotting as a means of deferring the consummation of desire and insuring the "compression's ecstasy" of subtle masquerades. In her refusal to come to rest in the stasis of marriage, Constance, like Kate, gains a continual infusion of energy that permits her to act. In contrast is the Queen's submission to God's will, which has granted her serenity: "I will not play . . . deceive," she tells Constance, as if deliberately distinguishing herself from her cousin. Stillness, mental and physical, is as foreign to Constance as it is to Kate, the "panther" who stalks Milly. The famous tableau in which James freezes his two heroines echoes the tense confrontation of Constance and the Queen: "figures so associated and yet so opposed, so mutually watchful; that of the angular pale princess . . . Mainly seated, mainly still, and that of the upright restless slow-circling lady of the court" (2:139). James's allusion here to "some dim scene in a Maeterlinck play" is not the only relevant dramatic analogue, for James's scene precisely frames the essential agon of *In a Balcony.*

If "life in these four walls" has left the Queen deprived, as she confesses it has, Milly seeks to make the best of her imprisonment within her palace. Milly's description of her life within the Palazzo Leporelli is strikingly similar to the Queen's existence: "She insisted that her palace—with all its romance and art and history—had set up round her a whirlwind of suggestion that never dropped for an hour. It wasn't, therefore, within such walls, confinement, it was the freedom of all the centuries" (2:174). In this passage Milly's image and her reality coincide; in Venice she becomes "a princess in a palace," as she describes herself at one point. Milly enacts the role of the "dove" and gives it a measure of reality; she joins with Kate, Susie, Densher, and James in the aestheticizing process. After receiving Kate's accolade, Milly muses: "she would have to be clear on how a dove would act." Milly, then, cannot be seen simply as a passive victim of aestheticization; not only does she participate in the process of transforming herself into the images people create for her, but she proves skillful in her role-playing.[19] In her Venetian palace Milly gives her triumphant social performance, in which she eclipses even the beautiful Kate, who seems "somehow—for Kate—wanting in lustre." Awed by Milly's luminous presence, Densher realizes she is "acquitting herself tonight as a hostess . . . under some supreme idea"—namely of portraying the role of the "American girl as he had originally found her" (2:216, 203).

As my discussion of Milly should suggest, there are no characters in James whose experience is free from the use of roles, manners, and conventions. Because reality is fundamentally, if not exclusively, social for James, these mediators are not barriers or sources of inauthenticity. For theatricality, or what in *The Tragic Muse* is named the "affectation" of a "personal manner," "must have begun, long ago, with the first act of reflective expression—the substitution of the few placed articulate words for the cry or the thump or the hug."[20] This remarkable passage, inserted into the New York edition of *The Tragic Muse*, presents a "myth of origins" dramatizing man's entry into what Lacan calls the Symbolic Order—the code of language and custom—which is simultaneous, according to James, with his adoption of a "personal manner." Language and theatricality originate as the primal "substitution"—the imposition of an alien, impersonal symbol system in place of the unmediated "cry or thump." This "substitution," which permanently defers direct communication, forcing it to be expressed through the mediation of language and "manner," is estranging to the self, which, paradoxically, experiences a sense of absence or loss in the very process of being transformed into a representation of itself in social reality.[21] And this absence or lack in the self is most acute, as we have seen, in the flamboyantly theatrical self. Thus, for James, all self-representation is founded on a gap in the subject, which widens according to how elaborate the representation.[22] Only with the renunciation of theatricality and language is the lack of being filled; but, as the endings of both works make clear, such fulfillment is inseparable from death.

The Queen of *In a Balcony* also discovers the inevitability of role-playing, and we see in Browning's character the same complex merging of fiction and reality that defines Milly's experience. Like Milly, she not only accepts the images of herself created by others, but permits these imposed fictions to have reality. The Queen by her own admission exists upon a "pedestal" where she leads an exquisitely dehumanized existence, forced to "stand and see men come and go." Abandoned upon this pedestal, the Queen has felt herself "grow marble"; what "young man" would be attracted to "my marble stateliness?" she asks Constance. The Queen is painfully aware that as a living art work she has hardened into the cold beauty of a "marble statue . . . / They praise and point at as preferred to life. / Yet leave for the first breathing woman's smile" (ll. 409–11). The implicit meaning in the Queen's speech—that to be perceived as a human work of art is ultimately to be dead—reveals the most extreme dimension of the aestheticizing process, which is acutely grasped by Milly in her famous encounter with the Bronzino portrait. Seeing the "face of a young woman," "splendidly dressed," Milly thinks she is a "very great personage— only unaccompanied by a joy." In her shock of recognition at her physical likeness to this young woman, Milly realizes, through tears, that the Bronzino woman is "dead, dead, dead. Milly recognized her in words that had nothing to do with her" (1:231). She then utters: "I shall never be better than this," revealing in this moment of tormented communion with the portrait her acknowledgment of the deathly "apotheosis" of her imprisonment in art.

My insistence on the aesthetic impulse and the essential theatricality of James's and Browning's heroines, seeks to clarify these complex and elusive women, who have at times been described too broadly. Critics have been contented with bland remarks about Kate's "self-command"[23] or Constance being "peculiarly wily."[24] Sallie Sears correctly observes that James's novel has "manipulation" as its "real subject," but her sense of manipulation as the regarding of a "fellow human being not as a person but as an object for use" should be refined.[25] For James, as well as Browning, is interested in a particular aspect of manipulation—aestheticization, the manipulation of reality into fictive patterns. Significantly, this phenomenon is explicitly named by James in a crucial passage in which he reflects upon its implications. James confronts the aestheticizing process through his delegate Densher, who has been left alone in Venice with Milly and Susie; he is there to enact his role in Kate's plot. Alone in his rooms, awaiting in anxious anticipation the latest word on Milly's health, Densher at last faces "the truth about Milly," "the facts of her condition":

> He hadn't only never been near the facts of her condition . . . he hadn't only, with all the world, hovered outside an impenetrable ring fence, within which there reigned a kind of expensive vagueness made up of smiles and silences and beautiful fictions and priceless arrangements, all strained to breaking; but he had also, with everyone else, as he now felt, actively fostered suppressions which were in the direct interest of every one's good manner, every one's pity, every one's really quite generous ideal. It was a conspiracy of silence, as the cliché went, to which no one had made an exception, the great smudge of mortality across the picture, the shadow of pain and horror, finding in no quarter a surface of spirit or of speech that consented to reflect it. "The mere aesthetic instinct of mankind—!" our young man had more than once said to himself; letting the rest of the proposition drop. [2:298–99]

In this passage James lets no one off; "every one" is indicted in the "conspiracy" against Milly. Not only does Densher, having exhausted his rationalizations, confront the facts of his entanglement, but James reveals his own complicity, as he charges his "beautiful fiction" with responsibility for Milly's imprisonment inside the "impenetrable" fence of silence. For in speaking of "vagueness," "silences," "suppressions," James describes his formal strategies, especially in the novel's "false and deformed" second half, which "bristles with dodges," as he admits.[26]

Densher's acknowledgment that he has deliberately avoided the "facts" of Milly's "condition," that the "specified had been chased like a dangerous animal," seems to him a momentous breakthrough, for now "the facts of physical suffering, of incurable pain . . . had been made at a stroke intense, and this was to be the way he was now to feel them" (2:299). But this unmediated view of the "facts," a "vision" Densher now thinks "not only possible but inevitable," is compromised by the persistence of the "aesthetic instinct," which will come to dominate Densher as he moves toward an increasing isolation. After his return from Venice, where Milly has died, Densher repudiates his role-playing—"we've played our dreadful game and we've lost," he tells Kate—and yearns to "escape everything" by seeking refuge in a purely inward life where he can think of Milly; he becomes a "man haunted with a memory." Like Susanna's music in Stevens's poem, in remembering Milly, Densher's imagination "plays on the clear viol of her memory, / And makes a constant sacrament of praise." On the Christmas morning when Milly's letter arrives, Densher's "intelligence and his imagination, his soul and his sense had never on the whole *been* so intensely engaged," as he sits alone in the dark contemplating the possible "turns" Milly "would have given her act" of "splendid generosity." Thus Densher's rejection of theatricality ironically results in his absorption in aestheticization, and of the most rarefied kind, since the subject of his imaginative musings is dead (2:251–52). Instead of feeling the "facts," Densher indulges in an endless process of refining the "might have been," of Milly's memory. In his indifference to reality, his imagination is liberated from the constraints of the referential, and Densher becomes the reductio ad absurdum of the Jamesian center of consciousness, a parody of the "supersubtle" reflector.[27]

Densher's withdrawal from Kate, whose prodigious "talent" for life ceased to matter in the "deepened," "sacred hush" of his rooms (2:396), amounts to a refusal to act—to represent himself on the social stage. But he is not only socially unrepresentable; his retreat into a purely contemplative existence makes him no longer representable novelistically. Because "something had happened to him too beautiful and sacred to describe," Densher becomes as illegible as Milly in James's form. As there is no "surface of spirit or of speech that consented to reflect" the sheer actuality of Milly's dying agony, Densher's inner allegiance to her, which grows steadily throughout book ten, goes beyond representation and becomes another gap in James's text. The "conspiracy of silence" that betrays Milly finally victimizes Densher; they both end engulfed by an "expensive vagueness." In a less direct sense Kate is betrayed by the novel's form, for in the last book we are shut up wholly within Densher's consciousness, and can only glimpse her as she is refracted through his mind.

## IV

The final movement of *In a Balcony* is remarkably congruent to *The Wings of the Dove:* both works conclude in an uneasy stillness engendered by the renunciation of theatricality. Constance, like Densher, abandons performance; "Enough, my part is played," she says, putting an end to her scheme (l. 766). The marriages that have loomed from the start are left "hanging unfinished," as they dissolve in the silence of "no words nor any notes at all," as Kate early in the novel described the "ravaged" history of her "house" in terms of a dying musical phrase (1:4). Densher's refusal to perform coincides with the apparent extinction of his desire for Kate, who tells him that Milly's "memory's your love. You want no other."

James presents, in Densher's silent worship of Milly, a pseudoreligious devotion. Densher's isolation by the end of book ten has often been regarded as a profound spiritual conversion; one critic, expressing a popular viewpoint, argues that Densher's meditations "partake of the religious," providing "a glimpse of the divine."[28] Although there are legitimate grounds for it in the text, a religious reading must ignore what is most crucial: the tenacity of the "aesthetic instinct" and its importance as a source of irony and parody. Densher does indeed undergo a conversion, but we have seen that his absorption in Milly is more aesthetic than religious, a celebration of an "intensely engaged" imagination rather than a kenetic act of religious surrender. Because for James the "aesthetic instinct," as the phrase suggests, is inherent in human sensibility, he regards with suspicion the effort to transcend the aesthetic. The primacy of the aesthetic is also reflected in his conception of the "canvas of life." While James does not deny authentic or unmediated experience, it is inscribed within the prior artistic perception of reality.

The endings of both works witness the writers, in effect, forcing their main characters to atone by leaving them in a state of passivity. As one would expect when the complicity between such characters as Constance and Densher and their authors is so marked, these acts of atonement reverberate beyond the text to involve personal motives of Browning and James. But before pursuing these implications it would be useful to consider how the form of these texts permits, even demands, entanglement with life. Browning and James employ strikingly similar formal strategies, founded on a shared conception of literary representation as deformed, imperfect because incomplete, resisting the carefully unified stability of fixed meaning.[29] This deformation is enacted on two levels: both works conclude with the failure of a plot, which is left "hanging unfinished," a problem in closure reflecting the "palpable voids," "missing links," and "dodges" James confesses to, and the open ending of Browning's play, where the lovers' fate is left suspended. These gaps create in the reader (as they did in Norbert and Densher) a desire to participate, to make an imaginative commitment to the text. Because the cessation of desire, the closing of gaps, creates a deathly inertness, as the fates of Constance and Densher attest, by avoiding the stasis of full representation, Browning and James prolong their plots in the play of the reader's imagination. But to permit texts to flaunt their "deformities" (James's word) is morally risky for both reader and writer. In denying the reader the comforts of a more stable, closed form, *In a Balcony* and *The Wings of the Dove* solicit the reader's active engagement, which leads inevitably to his implication in the characters' moral dilemmas. We, like Densher, ponder the "might-have-been" of Milly. But the moral hazards involved in the relation of reader and character are minor when compared to the more intimate and complex complicity between Browning, James, and their delegates.

So profoundly involved are both authors in their characters' acts of purgation that the endings of these works are dictated in part by the psychological needs of Browning and James. In other words, their "delegates" are not simply atoning for themselves, so to speak, but indirectly are redeeming their creators, who share an impulse to purge themselves. The relation of Constance's renunciation to Browning's own needs can be illuminated by briefly returning to the play's last scene. Constance's purification recalls the "ceremonies of expulsion" Leo Bersani has identified as society's punishment of many of the major figures of nineteenth-century fiction—those characters whose lack of a "coherent wholeness of personality" threatens the central foundation of bourgeois realism, namely an "ideology of the self as a fundamentally intelligible structure unaffected by a history of fragmented, discontinuous desires."[30] The pattern Bersani notes informs Constance's final moments, where she is, if not punished, forced to surrender her unstable, mobile self. But the question remains as to why Browning is compelled to purify the theatrical self. One significant reason emerges when we focus on Browning's own theatricality—his dependence on elaborate social masks. In discussing the relation between Browning's personal and artistic selves, Hillis Miller has written:

> his selfhood must be defined as the failure to have any one definite self, and as the need to enact, in the imagination, the roles of the most diverse people in order to satisfy all the impulses of his being. To be such a self was, in Victorian England, a shameful and reprehensible thing.[31]

As the novel depended on a portrayal of the self as, in Bersani's words, "fundamentally intelligible," society likewise demanded a coherent self of its writers.

I agree with Miller's view of Browning's selfhood, but I would like to probe further to examine precisely *how* Browning, in his art, manages "to satisfy all the impulses of his being." In the case of *In a Balcony* we can locate with some precision the relation of Browning's selfhood to his art. In this play the poet has created a "deputy" in Constance, who shares his theatrical self and enacts his plot. By then converting her into a passive and God-loving person, Browning is able to vicariously experience his heroine's conversion. In other words, Browning forces Constance to experience the purification that he feels he himself needs because of his sense of "shame" at his "failure" to have a stable self. Perhaps the fact that Browning called *In a Balcony* his personal favorite among the works can be explained in that it allowed him this vicarious, mediated purgation of his "failure," and thereby liberated his imagination to enter, with renewed vitality, the lives of a great array of men and women.

If Constance is, in a sense, purified "for" Browning, this pattern of sacrifice is explicit in *The Wings of the Dove*. In their final conversation Kate insists that Milly "died for" Densher; he, in turn, leads a death-in-life existence that is "for" Milly: an expression of worship and an act of expiation for having manipulated the "dove." But, like Constance in relation to Browning, Densher must be purified "for" James as well. Because of his intimate involvement in the betrayal of Milly, James forces his deputy to enact a sacrificial homage to her, an act of atonement that soothes the creator as much as Densher. But James's need for purgation, like Browning's, is prompted not only by what has occurred in his text; he is impelled by guilt of a more personal nature. I am alluding to his "use" of his cousin Minny as a model for Milly.

Although James speaks reverentially of "wrapping" her "tragedy" in the "beauty and dignity of art," art, for James, as his final preface reveals, is profoundly impure; it is as pervaded by manipulation, exploitation, compromise, and sacrifice as the life it represents. James avoids any suggestion of the negative aspect of art in his remarks about Minny quoted above by displacing it onto his description of what "life" did to her: "Life claimed her and used her and beset her."[32] In his intention to represent her life in art, James discovers that it is inevitable that he too will "claim" and "use" and "beset" her as a stimulus to his imagination. So inescapable is the fact of the artist's manipulations and exploitations, that the novel which will commemorate his beloved cousin will be about the uses made of a doomed American girl.

But in *The Wings of the Dove,* James makes use of another hero of his youth, as his splendidly creative "rehandling" of *In a Balcony* reveals. In the conclusion of his centenary tribute, James implicitly links the poet to Minny and Milly as a muse of the imagination: "I feel that Browning's great generous wings are over us still and . . . that they shake down on us his blessing."[33] This is a remarkable echo of Kate's final image of Milly, who in her "stupendous" bequest has "stretched out her wings" until "they cover" the lovers. In these last words of James's homage Browning takes his place with the other sacrificial doves whose fate is to inspire and bless (Densher in book ten describes himself as "blessed" by Milly) those who plot. And James's 1912 tribute to Browning constitutes, in part, his attempt to atone for his "irreverent" use of *In a Balcony.* It is the privilege and the burden of the "man of imagination"[34] to both celebrate and "work over"[35] Browning's play, Minny's life, Milly's memory, with the transforming power of the "aesthetic instinct."

## Notes

1. *The Letters of Henry James,* ed. Percy Lubbock (New York: Scribner's 1920), 2:334.
2. Quoted in Maisie Ward, *Two Robert Brownings?* (New York: Holt, Rinehart, 1969), p. 175. Ward is quoting from an unpublished James letter of 1888.

3. Henry James, *Notes on Novelists* (London: Dent, 1914), p. 387.

4. Ward, *Two Brownings*, p. 176.

5. James, *Notes*, p. 411.

6. Significantly, a similar "pang" to rewrite Browning occurs in James's one other public encounter with a Browning text—his 1875 review of *The Inn Album*—where in the midst of a harsh dismissal of the work James asserts that "a great poem might perhaps have been made of it." He concludes by calling it "a series of rough notes for a poem," a response that anticipates his reaction to *The Ring and the Book*. James's review can be found in "On a Drama of Mr. Browning," *Views and Reviews* (Boston: Ball, 1908).

7. Henry James, *The Art of the Novel*, ed. R. P. Blackmur (New York: Scribner's, 1962), p. 288.

8. There are exceptions, of course: Bewley's labored comparison of *The Marble Faun* and James's novel; more recently *Hedda Gabler* has been put forth as a source. See Marius Bewley, *The Complex Fate* (New York: Grove Press, 1954), and Michael Egan, *Henry James: The Ibsen Years* (New York: Barnes and Noble, 1972), pp. 115–48. A recent discussion of the preface's opening is admirable in its attempt to loosen the hold Minny Temple has had on the preface. In their commentary to the Norton critical edition of the novel, Crowley and Hocks suggest a variety of plausible meanings in James's remarks. They correctly argue that "James's conception is indeed a matrix of things at once 'very old' and 'very young.'" Among James's "pressing old memories and associations from his youthful past," the editors cite "his sense of beginning of his own career as a writer; the influence of Hawthorne; the development of his early literary idiom and method." Although this interpretation is commendable in its scope of reference, it neglects to probe deeply into the implications of its own findings, for Browning is a crucial figure in James's sense of his literary beginnings. See *The Wings of the Dove*, ed. J. Donald Crowley and Richard Hocks (New York: Norton, 1978), p. 439.

9. Henry James, *Autobiography*, ed. F. W. Dupee (New York: Criterion, 1956), p. 292.

10. Perry's remark is quoted in Louise Greer, *Browning and America* (Chapel Hill, N.C.: University of North Carolina Press, 1952), p. 84.

11. Crowley and Hocks, eds., *Wings of the Dove*, p. 506.

12. Browning's fondness for the play has not been shared by critics, most of whom have largely neglected the work, perhaps because the great monologues of *Men and Women* have overshadowed *In a Balcony*. E. E. Stoll and Morse Peckham have been among the very few modern critics to have discerned the work's importance. See E. E. Stoll, "Browning's *In a Balcony*," *Modern Language Quarterly* 3 (1942): 407–17; and Morse Peckham, *Beyond the Tragic Vision* (New York: Braziller, 1962), p. 275. Peckham provides only a brief assessment of the play. In his *Victorian Revolutionaries* (New York: Braziller, 1970) Peckham makes equally brief but suggestive remarks.

13. Stephen J. Greenblatt, *Renaissance Self-Fashioning* (Chicago: University of Chicago Press, 1980), p. 3.

14. *In a Balcony*, in vol. 4, *The Works of Robert Browning*, ed. F. G. Kenyon, Centenary Edition in 10 vols. (London: Smith & Elder, 1912), ll. 79–83. Subsequent references in the text.

15. *The Wings of the Dove*, vols. 19, 20, *The Novels and Tales of Henry James*, 26 vols. (New York: Scribner's, 1907–17), 2:175–76. Subsequent references in the text. All citations below to Jame's fiction refer to the Scribner's edition.

16. The tension between theatricality and intimacy has been noted by Richard Sennett in *The Fall of Public Man* (New York: Random House, 1978), p. 37.

17. Henry James, *The Tragic Muse*, 2:210. In *The Tragic Muse*, James's most sustained and explicit exploration of the theatrical self, Peter's relation to Miriam recalls the conflicts in the two works under discussion. Like Densher and Norbert, Peter is

attempting to force an inveterate performer off the stage (in this case literally so) to exist in the private realm of marriage.

18. James, *The Art of the Novel*, p. 327.

19. Too often Milly's theatricality is slighted by critics in an effort to maintain a valid but superficial dichotomy between Kate the performer and Milly the doomed innocent. Even as acute a critic as Leo Bersani enforces this dichotomy when he writes of Milly (in company with Fanny Price and Maggie Verver) that she has "no talent for representing the self in the world." See *A Future for Astyanax* (Boston: Little, Brown, 1976), p. 81.

20. *The Tragic Muse*, 2:173.

21. My rhetoric here is borrowed from Lacan by way of Fredric Jameson's discussion of the alienating effect of the Symbolic Order in "Imaginary and Symbolic in Lacan," *Yale French Studies*, no. 55–56 (1977), p. 363.

22. This conception of theatricality as a radical gap explains James's "whimsical" but oft-repeated belief in Browning's split into two selves—"esoteric" and "exoteric"; the former is his private identity and the latter his public one. James's remarks about Browning are in a letter to Alice James, quoted by Leon Edel in *Henry James: The Conquest of London* (Philadephia: Lippincott, 1962), p. 330. James's fictional exploration of the "puzzle" of Browning's double identity is titled "The Private Life," in vol. 17 of Scribner's edition.

23. Dorothea Krook, *The Ordeal of Consciousness in Henry James* (Cambridge: Cambridge University Press, 1962), p. 215.

24. The remark is Arthur Symons's; quoted in Stoll, "Browning's *In a Balcony*."

25. Crowley and Hocks, eds., *Wings of the Dove*, p. 553. Sears's view is echoed in a recent work on James, Nicola Bradbury's *Henry James: The Later Novels* (New York: Oxford University Press, 1979). Bradbury makes correct, but broad and unfocused, remarks concerning Kate's "manipulative vigour" (p. 121) and the "myth-making process" and "manipulative categorization of other people" in the novel (p. 86), and ignores James's participation.

26. James, *The Art of the Novel*, p. 202. James's complicity with his characters, and the fusion of moral and formal problems this creates, figures prominently in Laurence Holland's seminal *The Expense of Vision* (Princeton, N.J.: Princeton University Press, 1964). The present analysis of this aspect of *The Wings of the Dove* is indebted to Holland.

27. For a few of Densher directly opposing the one argued here, see Robert Caserio, *Plot, Story, and the Novel* (Princeton, N.J.: Princeton University Press, 1979), pp. 198–231; this is a provocative, if unconvincing, reading.

28. R. W. B. Lewis, *The Trials of the Word* (New Haven, Conn.: Yale University Press, 1964), pp. 113, 123.

29. Herbert Tucker, in his penetrating study of Browning, also emphasizes Browning's incomplete and imperfect poetic forms. In his belief that "Browning's moral doctrine of incompleteness finds a clear aesthetic analogue in his poetics," Tucker stresses the poet's strategies of deferment. While agreeing with Tucker's view of the importance of deferral in Browning's work, I view it as also partly a reflection of the poet's preoccupation with the theatrical self, which is necessarily unstable and deferring. See *Browning's Beginnings* (Minneapolis: University of Minnesota Press, 1980), p. 5.

30. Bersani, *A Future for Astyanax*, pp. 55–56.

31. J. Hillis Miller, *The Disappearance of God* (New York: Schocken, 1965), p. 105.

32. James, *Autobiography*, p. 509.

33. James, *Notes on Novelists*, p. 411.

34. James, *The Art of the Novel*, p. 313.

35. James, *Notes on Novelists*, p. 406.

# Eliot, Burglary, and Musical Order

## Michael Beehler
*Montana State University*

> Without music life would be a mistake.
> —*Twilight of the Idols*

THE concluding talk in Eliot's series of lectures given at Harvard during the winter of 1932–33 contains within it an extraordinary image of the "use" of meaning in a poem. Toward the end of his talk, Eliot compares poetry to burglary and meaning to a diversionary piece of meat: "The chief use of the 'meaning' of a poem, in the ordinary sense, may be (for here again I am speaking of some kinds of poetry and not all) to satisfy one habit of the reader, to keep his mind diverted and quiet, while the poem does its work upon him: much as the imaginary burglar is always provided with a bit of nice meat for the house-dog. This is a normal situation of which I approve" (*UPUC*, p. 151).[1] The image does not make clear the precise nature of poetic "work" other than to define it as, apparently, a particular type of theft, but it does underscore a certain subreption that allows this theft to take place, a subreption fundamental to poetry and poetic meaning "in the ordinary sense." According to this image, poetry works only through the mediation of a clever diversion or detour, a rerouting of the reader's attention away from the transgression that the poem is actually accomplishing and toward a gift, the "meat" of the poem, that it freely gives the reader. This meaty gift is meaningful to poetry, however, only because it misrepresents poetry's transgressive theft. Here, meaning subreptitiously protects the transgression that is poetry's true work, a burglarizing of property, by hiding it in an illusion through which it appears to be a giving rather than a taking away. The subreptitious relationship between meat and theft, meaning and the poem, thus dramatizes what Eliot calls the "normal situation" of poetry.

This subreptitious relationship can be traced in Eliot's many considerations of poetic meaning and particularly in his efforts to untangle the problematic connections between the meaning of poetry and the music of poetry. His emphasis upon the originary role of music in poetry—in one essay he notes that "a poem . . . may tend to realize itself first as a particular rhythm before it reaches its expression in words, and . . . this rhythm may bring to birth the idea and the image" (*OPP*, p. 32)—recalls a similar emphasis upon music developed in Nietzsche's first book, *The Birth of Tragedy from the Spirit of Music*. Indeed, it is the Apollo/Dionysus relationship elaborated in that book, and Nietzsche's particular understanding of originary, Dionysiac music, that shadow Eliot's later discussions of meaning, music, and theft.

Eliot knew Nietzsche well from his Harvard studies in philosophy, a knowledge evident in his review of Wolf's critical work, *The Philosophy of Nietzsche*. In this review, published in the April, 1916, issue of *International Journal of Ethics* (and signed T. Stearns Eliot), Eliot expresses his disappointment with Wolf's book for its "omission of any account of Nietzsche's views on art," and suggests that "we should have liked to see Nietzsche's views on evolution and change compared with those of Bergson and James, and to hear more of his attitude toward Darwinism, and something of his affinities with Butler." On the subject of the will to power, Eliot agrees with Wolf that "Nietzsche's view of nature [is] essentially Schopenhauerian."[2] It is Nietzsche's voice that resonates in *The Waste Land,* although it is a voice suppressed by Eliot's explanatory notes. Both Eliot and Nietzsche refer, for example, to the same passage from *Tristan and Isolde,* Eliot in "The Burial of the Dead" with the four-line quotation that introduces the hyacinth girl and in the single response, "Oed' und leer das Meer," that closes that scene, and Nietzsche toward the end of *The Birth of Tragedy,* where he describes the third act of Wagner's opera: "But now the Apollonian power, bent upon reconstituting the nearly shattered individual, asserts itself, proffering the balm of a delightful illusion. Suddenly we see only Tristan, lying motionless and torpid, and hear him ask, 'Why does that familiar strain waken me?' And what before had seemed a hollow sigh echoing from the womb of things now says to us simply, 'Waste and empty the sea.' "[3]

Of greater interest, however, is the question asked just before the Wagner section of "The Burial of the Dead": "What are the roots that clutch, what branches grow / Out of this stony rubbish?" The sense of European culture's hunger to remember its roots, and the poet's desire to redeem the "heap of broken images" in a new myth of unity and significance, echo both imagistically and emotionally a passage from the twenty-third section of *The Birth of Tragedy*, where Nietzsche writes:

> Every culture that has lost myth has lost, by the same token, its natural, healthy creativity. . . . let us consider . . . a culture without any fixed and consecrated place of origin, condemned to exhaust all possibilities and feed miserably and parasitically on every culture under the sun. Here we have our present age, the result of a Socratism bent on the extermination of myth. Man today, stripped of myth, stands famished among all pasts and must dig frantically for roots, be it among the most remote antiquities. What does our great historical hunger signify, our clutching about us of countless other cultures, our consuming desire for knowledge, if not the loss of myth, of a mythic home, the mythic womb? [*BT*, pp. 136–37]

Nietzsche's reflections read as a virtual gloss of Eliot's later poem.

In a 1967 monograph on *Wagner, the King, and "The Waste Land,"* Herbert Knust comments upon Nietzsche's sense of the relationship between myth and culture, derived from *The Birth of Tragedy*, and Eliot's critical notions of the "objective correlative" and the "mythical method." He refers to a passage from Nietzsche's first book that "stipulates that myth needs an 'adequate objectification' in the spoken word (one translator actually uses the term 'objective correlative') and—like Eliot—he points to the deficiency of this objective equivalence in Hamlet."[4] This is the relevant passage:

> [Greek] heroes seem to us always more superficial in their speeches than in their actions: the myth, we might say, never finds an adequate objective correlative in the spoken word [we recall here Eliot's complaint that "Hamlet's bafflement at the absence of objective equivalent to his feelings is a prolongation of the bafflement of his creator in the face of his artistic problem" (*SW*, p. 101)] . . . (The same may be claimed for Shakespeare, whose Hamlet speaks more superficially than he acts, so that the interpretation of *Hamlet* given earlier had to be based on a deeper investigation of the whole texture of the play.) [*BT*, p. 103]

As in the first section of *The Waste Land*, it is Nietzsche's suppressed voice that resounds in Eliot's "Hamlet and His Problems." Knust goes on to point out the "double effect" of Eliot's mythical method, a doubled irony that not only plays out "the vitality of myths against a dead society, but . . . also implies a criticism of [certain] myths themselves."[5] Here Knust finds in Eliot a critique of "sensuous and seductive"—but decadently mystical—myths that repeats Nietzsche's condemnation of Wagner.

But it is Nietzsche's elaboration of the specular relationship between Dionysus and Apollo that, in a highly circumspect manner, most profoundly informs Eliot's criticism, particularly when that criticism explores the place of meaning in poetry and music. In *The Birth of Tragedy* Apollo appears, of course, as the figurative "god of all plastic powers and the soothsaying god" (*BT*, p. 21). The lucent "god of light," reason, and truth, it is Apollo who supports and expresses the *"principium individuationis"* (*BT*, p. 22), and it is as the embodiment of this principle that he stands as the god of spatial resolution. His realm is that of the plastic, spatial arts, and his mastery of space renders him the "god of individuation and just boundaries" (*BT*, p. 65). Apollo "draw[s] boundary lines" and by so doing organizes space into a pattern, apportioning each constituent of this spatial figure to its proper place. By thus enforcing limits and boundaries, Apollo allows for individuation, and acts to protect the simple and the individual from duplicity and disarray. Through the clarifying lucidity afforded by the god of light, the Hellenic cosmos, Nietzsche asserts, resolves itself into a figure of organized space, a pattern in which all the parts remain in their proper places. Apollo is, in this sense, the god of the proper, of propriety, and of property—of that which reflects the mastery of ownership and one's own place.

But this mastering resolution, with its proper, spatial boundaries, is for Nietzsche only an illusionary and protective compensation for the Greek's earlier, horrifying look into "the abyss" of nature. He draws his image, naturally enough, from the sun: "After an energetic attempt to focus on the sun, we have, by way of remedy almost, dark spots before our eyes when we turn away. Conversely, the luminous images of the Sophoclean heroes—those Apollonian masks—are the necessary productions of a deep look into the horror of nature: luminous spots, as it were, designed to cure an eye hurt by the ghastly night" (*BT*, pp. 59–60). Apollo, and the spatial propriety he stands for, thus appear as a fictive light, a hallucinatory radiance that protects the Greeks from the truly blinding light of abysmal nature. Where lucidity and propriety appear—

where Apollo, the lucent one, presents himself—there, for Nietzsche, is the diversionary and protective illusion: there the insight and truths that arise only as "the luminous afterimage which kind nature provides our eyes after a look into the abyss" (*BT*, p. 61).

In "fierce opposition" to the spatializing figure of Apollo stands Dionysus, who for Nietzsche represents the creative tendency toward the "nonvisual art of music" (*BT*, p. 19). Where Apollo embodies the desire for the propriety of just boundaries, Dionysus, Nietzsche's image of the "ecstatic artist," figures an ex-static "wandering apart" that refuses the confines of boundaries and thereby explodes the illusion of propriety (*BT*, p. 24): "lest the Apollonian tendency freeze all form into Egyptian rigidity, and in attempting to prescribe its orbit to each particular wave inhibit the movement of the lake, the Dionysiac flood tide periodically destroys all the little circles in which the Apollonian will would confine Hellenism" (*BT*, p. 65). It is Dionysiac music—the temporal, pro-cessional creative tendency—that breaks into the rigid spatial pattern that is Apollo's domain: breaks open the pattern and transgresses its boundaries, thereby disclosing its artificiality and robbing it of its proprietory "truth." It is, for Nietzsche, music alone that "allows us to understand the delight felt at the annihilation of the individual" (*BT*, p. 101): at the ecstatic demolition of the precise and lucid clarity that results from the Apollonian imposition of the *principium individuationis*. In this principle "the eternal goal of the original Oneness, namely its redemption through illusion, accomplishes itself," but this unity, the "ground of Being," is "itself" ex-statically doubled. "Ever-suffering and contradictory," perpetually differing from itself as original contradiction, it "time and again has need of rapt vision and delightful illusion" to redeem and resolve itself (*BT*, p. 32). Such resolution, however, is only the provisional illusion of Apollo recurrently broken into by the iterating temporality of Dionysus, by the primordially necessary "time and again" of repetition.

Thus for Nietzsche, Dionysiac music, by repeatedly breaking into the bounds of propriety established by the illusionary Apollonian patterning of space, most directly reflects the "pain and contradiction" of the "ground of Being." This perpetual transgression cannot be mastered by the images of Apollonian language, for it "resists any adequate treatment by language, for the simple reason that music, in referring to primordial contradiction and pain, symbolizes a sphere which is both earlier than appearance and beyond it. Once we set it over against music, all appearance becomes mere analogy. So it happens that language, the organ and symbol of appearance, can never succeed in bringing the innermost core of music to the surface" (*BT*, p. 46). Through its *principium individuationis*, Apollonian imagery—language—creates the hallucination of appearance, of the individual existing properly to itself, and determinately marked off by "just boundaries" from other individuals that are properly themselves. Through this illusion, then, Apollo "masters" or resolves the original contradiction of "Being." It is within this illusion that truth—as noncontradiction, non-self-difference—first arises,[6] but only as a figurative non-self-difference annihilated by the original contradiction reflected in Dionysiac music. Thus Nietzsche's emphasis upon the "supreme significance of *musical dissonance*" (*BT*, p. 143), upon the primordial nature of a self-difference that discloses the metaphoricity of all "just boundaries" and of the proper—of property—itself. Musical dissonance is a multivocality that is never proper to itself, but is always differing from itself, stealing away its "proper" self by transgressing the boundaries that would hold it to "itself": "musical dissonance . . . makes us need to hear and at the same time to go beyond that hearing" (*BT*, p. 143). It is the contradiction that breaks into the rigid calm of a harmonic pattern, and it is Dionysiac music that is the "incarnation" of this original dissonance and difference (*BT*, p. 145).

There is, then, a fraternal and specular relationship between Apollo and Dionysus, for each god speaks only through the detour of the other: Apollo to interpret and resolve, through the subreption of his illusory boundaries, the dissonance of Dionysus, which appears only in the transgression of those boundaries. Thus the Greek drama presents the "coming and going of the shuttle as it weaves the tissue":

> In the final effect of tragedy the Dionysiac element triumphs once again: its closing sounds are such as were never heard in the Apollonian realm. The Apollonian illusion reveals its identity as the veil thrown over the Dionysiac meanings for the duration of the play, and yet the illusion is so potent that at its close the Apollonian drama is projected into a sphere where it begins to speak with Dionysiac wisdom, thereby denying itself and its Apollonian concreteness. The difficult relations between the two elements in tragedy may be symbolized by a fraternal union between the two deities:

> Dionysos speaks the language of Apollo, but Apollo, finally, the language of Dionysos. [*BT*, p. 131]

Since neither god can speak in his own, proper language, the "forward propulsion" of Greek drama derives from the necessity of this original detour, of this primordial theft of the other's language: a continual transgression that repeats, "time and again," the ex-static, contradictory dissonance Nietzsche names "Being." This pro-cessional temporality of the drama "reminds us that conditions are aspects of one and the same Dionysiac phenomenon, of that spirit which playfully shatters and rebuilds the teeming world of individuals—much as, in Heracleitus, the plastic power of the universe is compared to a child tossing pebbles or building a sand pile and then destroying what he has built" (*BT*, pp. 143–44).

Nietzsche's reference to Heracleitus points prospectively toward Eliot's use of the Greek philosopher in his epigraph to *Four Quartets*, but the entire Apollo/Dionysus discussion throws light upon Eliot's burglary image and its disclosure of the relationship between meaning and poetic work. Just as Apollo presents subreptitious images of the original, contradictory difference figured by Dionysus, so the "meaning" of a poem—the "meat," substance, truth, or subject sought by the house-dog reader—is a subreption of the poem's actual work: a calming diversion that allows the burglary to take place. Such meaning is meaty and substantial—it is the determinable aspect of the poem that the reader can ingest or devour, and thereby master or make his own—but since that meat is only ever the illusion of the poem's proper work, its mastery is only ever the mastery of an illusion and, therefore, the illusion of mastery. Meaning is thus an Apollonian staging of meaning, a subreption that throws the reader off the poem's scent, hiding from view the poem's burglary that is always in progress whenever the meaty meaning appears. And what is burglary but a transgression of "just boundaries," a breaking into, opening up, and stealing away of property? In Eliot's image, however, such transgression of the proper is not an aberration of bad poetry, not an occasional criminality that befalls poetry from some depraved outside, but it is rather the approved and "normal" "work" that "the poem does." Like the musical dissonance that is for Nietzsche the incarnation of contradictory self-difference, and therefore the disruptive doubling of every Apollonian illusion of just boundaries, every figure of the proper, the "work" of the poem is a perpetual burglary, a raid on property and a transgression of the boundaries that would hold the proper to itself. Poetic meaning—like the "Apollonian mask"—is only the "veil thrown over" the Dionysiac ex-stasis that is the poem's law-breaking work.

When Eliot writes directly about music, however, he often does so in an effort to affirm music and rhythm as the privileged expressions of truth and meaning—an Apollonian affirmation that, nevertheless, finally destructs itself in Dionysiac duplicity. In "Poetry and Drama," for example, Eliot asserts that "beyond the nameable, classifiable emotions and motives of our conscious life when directed towards action . . . there is a fringe of indefinite extent, of feeling which we can only detect, so to speak, out of the corner of the eye and can never completely focus." Words and names—the symbols of language, in other words—can only take us so far toward this significant fringe, which, however, "music can express" (*OPP*, p. 93). Harry Antrim notes that for Eliot, "language may inherently possess structures which in their rhythm and music bear correspondence to the ground of human emotion,"[7] an observation consistent with Eliot's privileging of music and rhythm, cited earlier, in which he points out that a "particular rhythm" may reflect the origin or ground of a poem, giving "birth to the idea and the image" (*OPP*, p. 32). Where language fails—where it is enclosed by the borders of the "nameable"—music succeeds, transcending those borders and taking us, apparently, back to poetry's origin. This, for Eliot, is the role of the "auditory imagination," a faculty that, through musical rhythm, provides access to the origin: "what I call the 'auditory imagination' is the feeling for syllable and rhythm, penetrating far below the conscious levels of thought and feeling, invigorating every word; sinking to the most primitive and forgotten, returning to the origin and bringing something back, seeking the beginning and the end" (*UPUC*, p. 119).

For Eliot, then, music is apparently able to transcend the limitations of words, limitations that forever hold words away from the origin, rendering them incapable of expressing it. Rhythm "invigorates" words by reaching beyond them toward an "unattainable timelessness," a "stillness of painting or sculpture" that appears as the unnameable fringe beyond the pale of words from which words nevertheless draw sustenance.[8] It is toward this "most primitive," most original "stillness" that Eliot writes his poetry, a poetry that he desires to be "so transparent that in reading it we are intent on what the poem *points at,* and not on the poetry itself." Such poetry seeks to "get *beyond poetry,* as Beethoven, in his later works, strove to get *beyond music.*"[9] Thus Eliot draws a continual analogy between the goal of music and the goal of poetry, while at the same time marking poetry's origin and sustenance in musical rhythm itself.

But although poetry may originate in music, and although music is able to express the "border of . . . feelings" that always lie beyond poetry's words, music is at the same time poetry's death: "We can never emulate music, because to arrive at the condition of music would be the annihilation of poetry" (*OPP,* p. 93). It is the dangerous origin from which poetry must always swerve: for Eliot, poetry must always detour away from its musical origin in order to be other than its own annihilation. The problem with Milton, for example, is that his poetry is too musical—"the arrangement is for the sake of musical value, not for significance"—and thus it leads nowhere "outside of the mazes of sound" (*OPP,* pp. 161, 163): "The emphasis is on the sound, not the vision, upon the word, not the idea" (*OPP,* p. 179). The result is a labyrinthine maze of sound in which one wanders without a map, without an Ariadne's thread to follow to the maze's reconciling outside. To check this abysmal maze of sound, to arrange it into a determinate spatial figure (a map over which can be traced the thread of a journey that resolves the turnings of the maze) is, for Eliot, the job of "meaning," and thus Milton should have learned that "the music of verse is strongest in poetry which has a definite meaning expressed in the properest words" (*OPP,* p. 183). The maze of sound—the labyrinth from which poetry springs, the place in which all paths are doubled and contradictory—calls forth the reconciling thread of definition and propriety, of determinate and visible meaning. To avoid losing itself—annihilating itself—to the layrinthine indeterminacy of its origin, poetry must make this detour toward a meaningful clarity.

Between music and meaning in poetry, then, Eliot posits a specular relationship similar to the one Nietzsche outlines between Dionysus and Apollo in Greek drama. In order to be itself at all—in order to stand out from its originating, rhythmic maze of sound, in which all is lost and annihilated—poetry must speak with a language other than music, a language of "vision," "idea," and "intellectual meaning" that "supplements the music by another means" (*OPP*, p. 179; *SW*, p. 146). This supplementary language adds to poetry's musical maze the thread of determinate meaning that lifts the poem out of the annihilatory "condition of music," stealing away its sound toward vision, its rhythm toward idea, in a move that distances and protects the poem from the dangers of its origin: "it is not quite so commonplace to observe that the meaning of the poem may be . . . something remote from its origins" (*OPP*, p. 22). Like the Apollonian subreption of Dionysus, meaning establishes "just boundaries" of sense within the originating but dangerous rhythms of poetry, and thus, as Eliot often asserts, "the music of poetry is not something which exists apart from the meaning," since such a separation, such an emulation or unswerving representation of poetry's rhythmic origins, would mark the death of poetry (*OPP*, p. 21). The language of meaning, however, patterns the musical maze into an organized figure, translating sound into sight, hearing into vision, time—since it is only in time that music unfolds itself—into bounded space.

Such a translation repeats Apollo's interpretation of the abyss of original contradiction figured by Dionysus, the spatializing of musical dissonance into the resolved pattern of the image. But where in Nietzsche this reconciling pattern is only a provisional and protective illusion—a figurative lucidity or "luminous afterimage"—that veils contradiction, dissonance, and difference, in Eliot it often appears as a sign of meaningful presence, as the eternal still point and center of the turning world of time. The problem with *Hamlet*, in other words, is that it has no such central lucidity, no meaningful "objective equivalent" to pattern and resolve Hamlet's excessive actions. For Eliot, what lies at the center of *Hamlet* is darkness, not light, and this is why the feeling of the play is "very difficult to localize": "The subject might conceivably have expanded into a tragedy like [*Othello, Coriolanus*, etc.], intelligible, self-complete, in the sunlight. *Hamlet*, like the sonnets, is full of some stuff that the writer could not drag to light" (*SW*, p. 100). *Hamlet* is contradictory, a scandal to the just boundaries of propriety that would allow the critic to resolve it into a determinable figure like, for example, the "suspicion of Othello, the infatuation of Antony, or the pride of Coriolanus" (*SW*, p. 100). It transgresses the properly "intelligible," the "self-complete," and thus refuses to stand "in the sunlight" of meaningfulness and noncontradiction.

*Hamlet*, in other words, fails exactly where the plays of John Marston succeed. Where Hamlet's excessive actions transgress the propriety of any determinably lucid and originating motivation or meaning, Marston's plays always give us "the sense of something behind, more real than any of his personages and their action," and it is for this reason that Marston "establishes himself among the writers of genius" (*EE*, p. 190). This "more real" is an "underlying serenity" that reconciles the "tumultuousness of the action, and the ferocity and horror of certain parts of the play," into a meaningful "pattern" or "under-pattern . . . behind the pattern into which the characters deliberately involve themselves" (*EE*, pp. 194, 190). Eliot equates this under-pattern or resolving, spatial figure to the "Fate" of the "ancient world," to the "delicate theology" of Christianity, and to the "crudities of psychological or economic necessity" characteristic of the "modern world" (*EE*, p. 194). In each temporal epoch, the under-pattern is the higher reality, the still point of "underlying serenity," that organizes time and renders it intelligible. In Marston's plays, the under-pattern is the non-self-contradictory and referential center that organizes the plays' actions into a meaningful figure. Like the "still point of the turning world," the under-pattern is a figure of transcendent and reconciling meaning, of an Apollonian-like propriety and truth.

But the essay on Marston, while putting forth the new-critical metaphysics of the under-pattern, nevertheless inaugurates a critique of that metaphysics which recalls Nietzsche's critique of Apollonian truth. Eliot's text discloses the under-pattern—that transcendently meaningful "more real"—to be a problematic dark spot, a luminous afterimage similar to the illusionary truths of Apollo. In a brief qualification, Eliot describes the under-pattern as "the kind of pattern which we perceive in our own lives only at rare moments of inattention and detachment, *drowsing in sunlight*" (*EE*, pp. 194; my italics). As in Nietzsche, it is in Eliot only when the sun is turned from, when it is veiled by the eyelid in a drowsing slumber, that the under-pattern appears at all, and thus the under-pattern is not simply a sign of meaning and revelation, but also a sign of veiling and detour: a contradiction that undoes the "underlying serenity" with which

Eliot invests the figure. It is only by turning away from—by forgetting through detached "inattention"—this dissonant contradiction that the figure can be taken to be the sign of reconciliation, of self-complete lucidity and meaning. The moment of this lucid insight is a moment of protective, diversionary blindness, a moment of illusion and—more specifically—of storytelling. This is particularly apparent in *Murder in the Cathedral*, during which Thomas councils the chorus that their sufferings will be turned to "sudden painful joy / When the figure of God's purpose is made complete": when, that is, the meaningful under-pattern of the eternal resolves the patternless mazes of contradictory time. Then,

> You shall forget these things, toiling in the household,
> You shall remember them, *drowsing by the fire,*
> When age and forgetfulness sweeten memory
> Only like a dream that has often been told
> And often been changed in the telling.
> [*CPP*, pp. 208–9; my italics]

It is only through the detour of time, through the forgetfulness of memory, and through the repeated telling of the dream as a story (told while "drowsing by the fire")—in short, through a variety of illusion-creating mediations—that the "figure of God's purpose" ever reveals itself as "complete." But the mediations disclose the figurativeness of the figure, marking it as a "luminous afterimage which kind nature provides our eyes after a look into the abyss" (*BT*, p. 61). Thomas's final line echoes the diversionary property of the Apollonian—and Eliotic—illusion of pattern, of propriety, and meaning: "Human kind cannot bear very much reality" (*CP*, p. 209). Like the meat thrown to the house-dog, the under-pattern of serene, complete, and proper meaning—privileged by Eliot as "most real"—is finally a subreptitious ruse.

And like Apollo finally speaking with the language of Dionysus, meaning—which is both most real and most illusionary, both meaty substance and mere slight-of-hand trickery—ultimately repeats the annihilating indeterminacy—characteristic, for Eliot, of the rhythmic "mazes of sound" from which poetry springs—it supplies with a supplementary pattern. By being originally doubled in this manner, meaning in Eliot always appears to exceed its boundaries, to break into itself by an internal contradiction that is always stealing away its privileged serenity, its self-complete propriety. Meaning, then, is the trace or evidence of a burglary, of a primordial transgression that is nothing less than the theft of the proper "itself"—for meaning always already burgles its own propriety by disclosing the originality of its dissonant contradiction. The "normal situation" of poetry—like the normal project of Greek drama—is the repetitive playing out of this self-burglary: of the resolving of dissonance in a diverting meaning that ultimately recalls the contradiction of its origin. Eliot's discussions of music and meaning show that, in order for poetry to exist, its rhythmic origins must speak with the language of meaning—music must be spatialized into an orderly pattern—but that that meaning finally comes to speak the transgressive, annihilatory language of music.

## Notes

1. This paper uses the following abbreviations for works by Eliot that will be cited in the text: *UPUC: The Use of Poetry and the Use of Criticism* (London: Faber & Faber, 1933); *OPP: On Poetry and Poets* (London: Farrar, Straus, & Giroux, 1943); *SW: The Sacred Wood* (London: Methuen, 1920); *EE: Elizabethan Essays* (London: Faber & Faber, 1934); *CPP: The Complete Poems and Plays, 1909–1950* (New York: Harcourt, Brace, 1971).

2. *International Journal of Ethics* 29, no. 3 (April 1916): 427.

3. Friedrich Nietzsche, *The Birth of Tragedy* and *The Genealogy of Morals*, trans. Francis Golffing (Garden City, N.Y.: Doubleday, 1956), pp. 127–28. This text will hereafter be cited as *BT*.

4. Herbert Knust, *Wagner, the King, and "The Waste Land"* (University Park, Penn.: Pennsylvania State University Press, 1967), p. 69.

5. Ibid., p. 69. Knust explains that it is "highly relevant for Eliot's case [in *The Waste Land*] that Nietzsche, in his own pronouncements on Wagner, condemned the fallacy of Wagner's mythical world" (p. 67).

6. "The legislature of language also gives the first laws of truth: since here, for the first time, originates the contrast between truth and falsity." It is language that constructs and enforces the illusionary "contrasts" of "just boundaries." Friedrich Nietzsche, "Truth and Falsity in an Ultramoral Sense," *The Philosophy of Nietzsche*, ed. Geoffrey Clive (New York: New American Library, 1965), p. 506.

7. Harry T. Antrim, *T. S. Eliot's Concept of Language: A Study of its Development* (Gainesville, Fla.: University of Florida Press, 1971), pp. 45–46.

8. T. S. Eliot, introduction to "The Art of Poetry," in *Collected Works of Paul Valery*, vol. 7 (New York: Pantheon, 1958), p. xiv.

9. William Harmon, "T. S. Eliot's Raid on the Inarticulate," *PMLA* 91, no. 3 (May 1976): 459 n.22.

# The Dynamics of Vision in William Carlos Williams and Charles Sheeler

## William Marling

*Case Western Reserve University*

IN the 1910s both William Carlos Williams and Charles Sheeler belonged to an artistic coterie called the Arensberg Circle, but curiously, they did not meet until afterward when both were mature artists. At that point, Sheeler said, "Here is the man I've been looking for all my life." And Williams felt Sheeler "looked at things directly, truly. . . . as we talked we found that we both meant to lead a life which meant direct association and communication with immediate things."[1]

They became friends quickly. References to "visiting the Sheelers" in Connecticut and New York are common in Williams's correspondence after 1919. He even told his publisher to drop in on them. Sheeler read Williams's *In the American Grain* as it appeared chapter by chapter in *Broom* and "was warmly enthusiastic." Occasionally they collaborated, as in their 1925 attack on H. L. Mencken in *Aesthetic*.[2]

The relationship was more than a social one. The backdrop of Williams's development as a poet is a pattern of collaboration with painters in whom he found an echo of his interests. Friendships with Charles Demuth and Marsden Hartley expanded his thematic and technical range; the presence of Marcel Duchamp led him to numerous poetic experiments. Sheeler would seem a different case, however, since both men were mature artists when they met. Yet they looked to one another for help in promoting "the American scene," and they shared a common belief in the visual nature of the creative process. They confirmed each other, personally and artistically, in a way that Williams hinted at in his *Autobiography*, when he used Sheeler's renovated gatehouse as an analogue by which to explain the importance of "projective verse." "It is ourselves we organize" Williams concluded, "to *give the mind its stay*."[3]

This phrase calls to mind the comment of Martin Friedman, the eminent Sheeler scholar, that "the precisionist painting process is one of the continual editing." Both remarks emphasize the process of putting art into final form; both acknowledge the distinction that art gains in cooling and shaping. In attending to this final form, Williams and Sheeler were guided by knowledge of the actual mechanics of visions, but they used that knowledge to disrupt our customary ways of seeing things. In actual vision, Rudolph Arnheim writes, the "conflict between the intruding outer world and the order of the inner world creates a tension, which is eliminated when a movement of the eyeball makes the centers coincide, thus adapting the inner order to the outer."[4] Williams and Sheeler, in their art, control the coincidence of the two centers, placing at this convergence something viewers would customarily ignore, or off-centering their audiences deliberately.

In the process of "editing" for final form, Sheeler and Williams shared much in common. "When I paint," Sheeler said, "my object is to show what I have found, not what I am looking for." The forms he discovered, wrote a biographer, were "*urformen*—forms which for us are source forms." The same emphasis on vision and form typified Williams's work when he met Sheeler; he was on guard against a "poetic looseness" that led to "little impact upon the mind."[5] His lines were tightly cast, his stanzas minimal. Yet, as Williams said, he and Sheeler were also interested in the "direct relation of reality." How could they have reconciled with their focus on form, necessarily a kind of abstraction, with "direct relation"?

The answer lies in their "visual editing." Both understood that they had an *acquired* way of seeing. Sheeler said that when he studied with William Merrit Chase he was ordered to complete each painting in a single sitting. "We didn't have the eyes to see beyond what a single sitting could reveal," he said. He implied that most of the picture appeared to him only after attentive, disciplined contemplation. The vision he sought was not in appearance per se. He wrote in his Black Book, a kind of personal Bible, that "we may only discern the thing when it is on the horizon—either in advance or retreat—in the moment that we pass the edges are blurred and the form unrecognized."[6]

In the same book he copied a Zen parable by Ch'ing-yuan that is revealing: "To a man who knows nothing, Mountains are Mountains, Waters are Waters, and Trees are Trees. But when he has studied and knows a little, Mountains are no longer Mountains, Waters no longer Waters, and Trees no longer Trees. But when he has thoroughly understood, Mountains are again Mountains, Waters are Waters, and Trees are Trees." Beside this Sheeler wrote "I like."[7]

Other painters who applied Eastern philosophy to their work moved in Sheeler's circle. He was a close friend of Marcel Duchamp, who had been influenced by Oriental philosophy, and he worked for and exhibited with Marius De Zayas, who "expounded the Quietist philosophy of Lao-tse with its many corollaries for art and life."[8]

Sheeler's work first attracted Williams for its "bewildering directness of vision, without blur, through the fantastic overlay with which our lives so vastly are concerned." He claimed that Sheeler's vision was related to his own. "Not ideas about the thing, but the thing itself," counseled Williams.[9]

How did this poet and painter imbue their theoretic concerns with this quality? Why do the mountains become mountains again? Koryu Osaka, a contemporary Zen master, commented on Sheeler's favorite parable that the student, after extensive meditation, understood that the world was fundamentally united as matter: "In the state of oneness, the mountain is no longer high, the water no longer deep." The world becomes undifferentiated. Osaka noted, however, that "when you work hard and do not become attached to this highly desirable state of oneness . . . you also perceive distinctions, but the distinctions are now viewed through the wisdom of subtle observation . . . the colors become subtle colors, the sounds subtle sounds, taste, subtle taste."[10] Everything becomes individuated and unique, the "magic reality" typical of Sheeler's painting and Williams's poetry.

In *Visual Thinking* Rudolph Arnheim gives an Occidental explanation of this process: "There appear to be three attitudes. One kind of observer perceives the contribution of the context as an attribute of the object itself." Another type "seek[s] to peel off the influence of the context in order to obtain the local object in its pure unimpaired state." Arnheim notes the same third state as the Zen master: "The third approach fully appreciates and enjoys the infinite and often profound and puzzling changes the object undergoes as it moves from situation to situation." Arnheim calls this "the aesthetic attitude."[11] Whether we choose the Eastern or Western version, we can note this visual dynamic in both Sheeler and Williams.

Sheeler's "aesthetic attitude" began with close attention to his own vision:

> It is inevitable that the eye of the artist should see not one but a succession of images . . . the eye is roving, and includes at one time only a very small area that is sharply defined. Moving on, it performs the same function within another area, so that the total vision of a landscape, for instance, is really a mosaic of small fragments separately seen, which become united in our memory. This composite image creates the illusion that we have seen at one time everything within the landscape sharply defined, from the rocks at our feet to the distant blue hills, but we have not.

An unexpressed part of this process is time. "Perception takes time," notes Arnheim. Time is the realm in which this accretive, meditative dynamic of seeing accumulates. There mountains become mountains again, having been dissolved and reassembled again in what Sheeler calls a "mosaic." This mosaic is guided by the primal knowledge gained in the initial dissolution. In that stage Sheeler learned, said Williams, that "every hair on every body anywhere, now or then, in its minute distinctiveness is the same hair, on every body, anywhere, at any time, changed as it may be to feather, quill or scale."[12] Amid this oneness, Sheeler explains that "something seen keeps recurring in memory with an insistence increasingly vivid with attributes added which escape observation on first acquaintance. Gradually a mental image is built up," Sheeler said, "which takes on a personal identity."[13]

Unlike other painters, Sheeler experienced neither a flash of perception nor a commanding impression, and sought neither personal expression nor analytic dissection. His vision was reductive; it sought common denominators, general conditions of experience. But it was also cumulative and diverse; he waited for initially unnoticed attributes and those subjective qualities that gave a sense of "personal identity." "To cipher his widest reaches of understanding," wrote Williams, he "used characters of intensely local bearing."[14]

As he began his canvases, Sheeler concerned himself with mass and form; the degree to which his work is dominated by monochromatic color schemes, or open unmodulated expanses of water, sky, or field has been unappreciated. In the background of most of his work is this suggestion of undifferentiated flux, a primal ground in which mountains are no longer mountains.

Against this background of oneness he composed the particulars masterfully. Sheeler said that he "endeavored to combine the memory and *the present* in any given painting."[15] For a painter this means the closure of masses, the arrangement of forms, and the use of such rhythmic elements as lines and points.

At this point meditative art can move in two ways. One emphasizes discipline and excludes expression of the self; it insists on a high degree of finish and understatement in the handling of materials. The other, especially in sumi-e painting and Zen poetry, encourages the use of the accidental and personal as notes of the differentiation present in unity.

Sheeler's proclivity, always toward the disciplined branch, was encouraged by Duchamp, with whom he talked about "suppressing the flamboyancy of personality in art." In his work, Sheeler said, he took care that "no embellishment meets the eye."[16] Friedman noted that Sheeler's pictures "are brought to an icily defined and flawless finish, with virtually no evidence of the brushstrokes or the trials and hesitations of arriving at the finished stage . . . there is little reveling in the sensuous qualities of pigment."[17]

During this period of friendship, Williams arrived at a poetically similar technique, though by a different process. Williams's personal demon was formlessness. His friend Marsden Hartley expressed the situation in a letter to Alfred Stieglitz:

> Williams you know is a very lovely fellow for himself and he certainly has made a splendid struggle to plasticize all his various selves and he is perhaps more people at once than anyone I've ever known—not vague persons but he's a small town of serious citizens in one being.[18]

Since childhood Williams had felt a lack of personal coherence in the face of strong emotion, particularly when dealing with women or sex. His brother Ed had counseled restraint, and had guided Williams toward a highly defined, intractable classicism in both personality and art.

Thus, until 1914 Williams wrote a traditional, neo-Keatsian poetry; emotional qualities were smothered in meter, rhyme, and archaisms. But in the Arensberg Circle he met artists such as Demuth, Hartley, and Sheeler, who encouraged him to combine his earlier interest in painting with his poetry. This gave Williams the outline of a solution to his personal conflict:

> My failure to work inside a pattern—a positive sin—is the cause of my virtues . . . I cannot work inside a pattern because I can't find a pattern that will have me. My whole effort . . . is to find a pattern large enough, modern enough, flexible enough to include my desires.[19]

The personal "pattern" that he eventually arrived at was so important that Williams deleted it from the final draft of the *Autobiography:*

> I have had several but not many intimate friendships with men during my life, patterned I suppose, on my youthful experience with my brother . . . all artists [here he mentions Pound, Demuth, and McAlmon] . . . On the other hand, there is Flossie, my wife, who is the rock on which I have built.
> Men have given the direction to my life and women have always supplied the energy.[20]

This clue provided, an association of masculinity with form and line, of femininity with color and mass, gradually reveals itself in Williams's work. From Demuth and Hartley, Williams had learned to use these associations as a way of working out and balancing his personal inner turbulance. In Sheeler he discovered the confirmation of his method.

The language with which Williams described his "aesthetic" is more lineal. He thought that two opposed forces ran through all art: "One is closely clipt with ascertained bounds while the other runs away, going along from point to point, like a child picking flowers under a hedge." He recognized the second, "romantic" impulse as the basis and final justification of art. But if he gave himself over to this impulse, a paralyzing personal muteness resulted. For Williams the state of "oneness" was abandonment of form. It was solitary, wordless, certain, obsessive and unproductive—a state of blankness preparatory to something else.[21]

Williams moved on to the reconstitution of the "mosaic" as soon as possible, though he tried to keep classic forms at a distance. "Sit down blind and start to fling the words around like pigments—try to see what nature would do under the same circumstances," he wrote.[22] He believed that the impulse contained its own principles, an idea he derived from Kandinsky's writings and study of Matisse. Williams learned to consider the approach and passing of his sensual impulses, in particular, as closely as Sheeler had considered objects on the horizon. When he wrote to Pound "I can't write fiction. All I do is try to understand something in its natural colors and shapes," Williams was indicating his first intimation of how to form his feelings. Color and shape were the first important modes of control that painting revealed to him.

For Williams color was an almost chemical reaction to experience. Color, he wrote, was "something in any case ponderable in the experience of other men." "Color is light," he wrote in a review of American naive painting. "Color is what most distinguished the artist: color was what these people wanted to brighten the walls of their houses, color to the last inch of the canvas." In color lay their admirable vitality and also their error, for it "ran, mostly, to the very edge of the canvas as if they were afraid that something would be left out, covered the whole of their surface."[23] Covering all, Williams learned, it diminished all.

Color is bound by the forms that it fills, and Williams learned that although form was primarily a stop on the romantic impulse, it could also be approached from the inside—employed in the putting down to create rhythm or measure:

> there is a tendency expressed in all the masters when their early and later works are compared to become more simple or as I believe more abstract, more general. That is he sees not trees and fence rails but horizontal and perpendicular lines, not an apple and a human face but crimson and a faint green shadow. But beyond that there are laws, even more abstract, that one rarely discovers, which may, in general, be classed as of that rhythm which bespeaks life.[24]

Williams found he could best achieve this rhythm through contraction, a kind of visual or poetic shorthand: "Picking out a flower or a bird in detail that becomes an abstract term of enlightenment." These highly defined details, often in the foreground of the work of Sheeler and Williams, act as visual avatars of an implied primal or "contextual" unity. This was one of the parallels in Williams's mind when he said, "A design in the poem and a design in the picture should make them more or less the same thing."[25]

After the initial ferment occurred, Williams said, a "calming" took place, and the recalcitrant impulse was put into form: "the grossly active agent of the moment . . . tries to break the artist from his complete position to make him serve an incomplete function":

> This is very bad, this looseness, according to one of the major tenets of art, conscious restriction of prescribed form, and very good according to another—unconfined acceptance of experience. Close order makes for penetration. Looseness is likely to prove weakness, having too little impact upon the mind.[26]

Thus the classical force that keeps art "closely clipt" within ascertained bounds came to the fore. It prevented the "looseness" that led to "little impact upon the mind."

Williams devised a number of limiting devices; the ways in which the triadic line and his punctuation check the grammatical flow of his verse have been much discussed. But his purely visual means have gone unnoticed.

In Williams's early poetry the shapes of things are of particular importance. "The young doctor is dancing with happiness . . . alone at the prow of the ferry," he wrote of himself in "January Suite." The shape of the prow—the V-shape—is Williams's most frequent sign for something ineffable temporarily caught and held. In "A Solitary Disciple" the shape appears in the steeple of the church. The title of "The Attic which Is Desire" makes the meaning of the sign explicit. That poem describes "the unused tent / of / bare beams / beyond which / directly wait / the night / and day"—an empty form awaiting a noumenal infusion. Williams pinions to this a flashing soda sign that represents the present and the particular.[27]

The use of visual shapes in Williams's poetry is not limited to the acute angle, which he learned from Kandinsky. In "The Red Lily," when Williams addressed the spirit he wished to evoke, he stated, "the crossroads is your home." In other poems he used densely cross-hatched masses that call attention, as Osaka Roshi might say, to their "suchness." The "reddish / purplish, forked, upstanding, twiggy / stuff of bushes" in "Spring and All" is famous, as is "the alphabet of / the trees" in "The Botticellian Trees."[28] Williams's genius at visual "signing" reached a pinnacle in "Flowers by the Sea," in which he made the objects exchange forms and natures within eight lines.

Tracing the careers of Sheeler and Williams in tandem reveals several interesting linkages. Sheeler discovered his "visual aesthetic" several years before Williams, beginning with *Lhasa* (1916). The subject, the holy city of Tibetan Buddhism, is linked to Marcel Duchamp's *Nude Descending the Staircase* in its emphasis on the stairlike structure of the mountain; the spiraling motion replicates the revolutions of the nude's legs. Reviewing the picture, Williams wrote, "The monasteries of our thoughts have walls like any others for painting to carry us beyond them to reality. Lucky the man who can dispel them with a Sheeler."[29] In *Flower Forms* (1917), Sheeler established the primacy of form as his meditative tool. His color is luminous but premeditated; his modulations lack the spontaneity and vibrance that mark a colorist. His shading establishes edge and mass. A calm, accretive vision begins to guide his composition, and leads logically to *Church St. El* (1920). In this view of the elevated track and buildings, Sheeler borrows again from Eastern art. He compared his spatial handling here with that found in Oriental painting, noting that he "placed the point of greatest concern close to the position of the spectator, well down in front, rather than at some distant point on the horizon."[30] This was also his most complex and emphatically planar canvas to date, the impression of three dimensions owing only to the receding diagonals. He shows, for the first time, the mountain as mountain again.

At a corresponding point in his career, Williams was laying out the elements in such poetic landscapes as "The Tulip Bed" (1921) with the precision of a Canaletto.

> The May sun - whom
> all things imitate -
> that glues small leaves to
> the wooden trees
> shone from the sky
> through bluegauze clouds
> upon the ground.
> Under the leafy trees
> where the suburban streets
> lay crossed
> with houses on each corner,
> tangled shadows had begun
> to join
> the roadway and the lawns.
> With excellent precision

> the tulip bed
> inside the iron fence
> upreared its gaudy
> yellow, white and red,
> rimmed round with grass,
> reposedly.[31]

Notice that Williams, like a painter, first decides on the source of light, then paints from the background to the foreground, from the top to the bottom. He leafs out his trees and paints in the skyscape: "shone from the sky / through bluegauze clouds." He drops down under the "leafy trees" and fills in details closer to the viewer. There are crossed streets, houses on each corner, and shadows that blur the edges of lawn and roadway. In the foreground and at the bottom of his canvas, unexpectedly, is "the tulip bed / inside the iron fence" where the tulips thrust up their "gaudy / yellow, white and red." But Williams has learned not to let his color run off the canvas. The tulips must be "rimmed round with grass / reposedly."

Around 1920 both artists adopted urban settings. *Church St. El* began an interest in the city for Sheeler that he continued in *Offices* (1922), which generated much the same effect except that he loosened his line somewhat. The formal patterns are loosely cast, and light bathes everything in a softer ambience. Color is more muted. The monochromatic color scheme suggests a fundamental unity to the highly reticulated masses.

Williams also kept the point of view in his urban scenes well above the rooftops. In "Fine Work with Pitch and Copper" (1935) we can imagine the men at work on the rooftops of Sheeler's canvases.

> Now they are resting
> in the fleckless light
> separately in unison
>
> like the sacks
> of sifted stone stacked
> regularly by twos
>
> about the flat roof
> ready after lunch
> to be opened and strewn
>
> The copper in eight
> foot strips has been
> beaten lengthwise

> down the center at right
> angles and lies ready
> to edge the coping
>
> One still chewing
> picks up a copper strip
> and runs his eye along it.[32]

As Peter Schmidt noted, an important feature this poem shares with Sheeler's work is its confident identification of men with their jobs. The roofers are artists in industrial Arcadia and see in their materials the potential for formal order that Brancusi saw in stone.

*Upper Deck* (1929) is cited by most scholars as the turning point in Scheeler's art. The emergence of a magic reality in his painting seems at first the result of a fortuitous selection of subject, but Sheeler spoke of it as an accretive, evolving vision. He said of *Upper Deck*, "I never get over the differences between a landscape under clouds with every form receding into a common mass, and the same landscape when light falls upon it, bringing out form after form." The mechanical particulars of Sheeler's ship emerge from a skyscape with which they share a limited tonal range. In fact, if the lines defining the forms were removed, the masses would hardly be differentiated, save the extreme blacks and whites. "This" said Sheeler, "is what I have been getting ready for . . . the structural design implied in abstraction . . . presented in a wholly realistic manner."[33] Yet what Sheeler really discovered in this painting was the power of *line*. Long attracted to edges as his building blocks in the reconstitutive stage of his vision, Sheeler here employed them with subtlety and precision. In mastering edges, he managed to imbue them with a noumenal quality. Dangerous, mysterious, holy, and radiant edges will slash across the best of Sheeler's mature work. They speak of the abyss under the object, the space behind the scene, a slight madness in an exact light. In human experience, after all, edges are so denotative that we overlook their phenomenology: they define walls, blades, streets, cliffs, and cracks. Yet at its edge each object is connected to everything else in the world.

"The edge cuts without cutting," noted Williams in "The Rose." In 1923 he was condensing his newfound aesthetics in the combative prose and intermittent poems of *Spring and All*. In "The Rose" he looked at a painting by Juan Gris and contemplated the sentimental value of the flower: "The rose carried weight of love / but love is at an end—of roses"—and the dynamic involved in defining it freshly: "It is at the edge of the / petal that love waits." For Williams, as for Sheeler, the act of creating the edge was at this point *the* creative act. Edges created the object and related it to all other objects:

> From the petal's edge a line starts
> that being of steel
> infinitely fine, infinitely
> rigid penetrates
> the Milky Way
> without contact . . .[34]

Williams liked to keep his edges in motion (in the swirling shapes of "Ogre") or to change his vantage on them (as in "Young Housewife"). He liked to *arrive* at them, as he did with the attic or V-shape. He was working toward, but perhaps feared arriving at, the completely "defined" edge that dominated Sheeler's work. Sheeler had brought to culmination the aesthetic of definition/dissolution in which they were both working. Williams wanted to keep his means flexible, and an interesting parting of paths occurred about 1930, of which Williams's poem "The Yachts" and Sheeler's *Yachts* and *Pertaining to Yachts and Yachting* are a fine example.

Sheeler's *Yachts* (1924) is a lithograph, of which Williams could have seen copies; it resulted from studies for the earlier *Pertaining to Yachts and Yachting* (1922), a painting uncharacteristic of Sheeler, who was not a sportsman and had little knowledge of sailboats. The latter painting is intended to be a representation of motion, and it shows the influence in the Arensberg Circle of Futurism. The sail edges are overlaid and intersecting, conveying a dynamic quality. The waves are treated as blocky masses, suggesting faces to an imaginative viewer. Sheeler called the picture a "study in polyphonic form," a term drawn from Imagist poetry. The canvas is not typical of Sheeler's color, but its ochre to cobalt-blue range is common in Futurist paintings. Reviewing a show that included the canvas, Williams used the phrase "bellying sails," which he later included in his poem.

"The Yachts" appeared in 1935. It describes the movements of yachts in a harbor as they make several attempts to race. Williams captures the atmospheric effects of Sheeler's painting when he describes the boats as "moth-like in mists, scintillant in the minute / brilliance of cloudless days."[35] Through several stanzas he appears to consider Sheeler's themes: the craftsmanship and definition of the yachts, which are "the best man knows to pit against" the ocean; the beauty of their motion; and the ubiquity of the sea. Sheeler's men are insignificant—Williams also calls them "ant-like."

Williams's first considerations are compositional, the relation of the large boats to the smaller "sycophant" ones. But after eight of the poem's eleven verses a change occurs. Williams sees that his real subject lies in his personified images. "The horror of the race dawns staggering the mind," he writes. The yachts, objects of craft and edge, cut through a sea of human faces. Williams's focus had excluded human concerns; it was too "closely clipt." But Williams does not give over the poem to his discovery; he notes that the "skillful yachts pass over" human, emotional concerns, and he draws the conclusion back into the meditative frame. The yachts *pass over,* period. Once defined as yachts, they can hardly do otherwise.

The friendship between Williams and Sheeler continued into the fifties, but they shared less in common. Sheeler's canvases were more and more the carefully drafted, impeccably finished pictures that resulted from his study of the urban scene. Assessing the same scene, Williams would be impressed by its fecundity. In "The Poor" he wrote, "It's the anarchy of poverty / delights me."[36] Sheeler was an artist attending a disciplined vision, while Williams was turning, as he would write later, to the "covered, swaddled, pinched and saved, shrivelled, broken" things of life.[37]

In later years Williams became convinced that Sheeler was "stuck," a victim of his own technique. He asked what Sheeler had done in his painting that he had not done in photography. Williams supplied no answer, but his own conclusion was clear. The disciplined, understated, highly finished school of meditative vision offered the artist a practicum, but not an end. The ceaseless innovation that Williams sought and enjoyed fed on the rough, the personal, the flamboyant, the fortuitous accident. They split irreconcilably. But their paths separated only after a long, common focus on the world as it dissolved and reestablished itself in an unmoving, patient eye.

## Notes

1. Quoted in Constance Rourke, *Charles Sheeler: Artist in the American Tradition* (New York: Da Capo Press, 1969), pp. 49–50.
2. Ibid.

3. William Carlos Williams, *The Autobiography* (New York: Random House, 1951), p. 333; emphasis added.

4. Rudolph Arnheim, *Visual Thinking* (Berkeley, Calif.: University of California Press, 1969), p. 24.

5. Sheeler, in Rourke, pp. 40, 69. Williams in *Imaginations* (New York: New Directions, 1963), pp. 198, 203.

6. Quoted in Martin Friedman, *Charles Sheeler* (New York: Watson-Guptill, 1975), pp. 15, 95.

7. Ibid., p. 97.

8. Rourke, p. 86.

9. William Carlos Williams, introduction, *Charles Sheeler* (New York: The Museum of Modern Art, 1939), p. 6. Williams's maxim appears variously; see "A Sort of a Song," *Selected Poems* (New York: New Directions, 1969), p. 109.

10. Koryu Osaka Roshi, *On Zen Practice II*, ed. Hakuyu Taizan Maezumi and Bernard Tetsegen Glassman (Los Angeles, Calif.: Zen Center of Los Angeles, 1977), pp. 76–77.

11. Arnheim, p. 45.

12. Williams, introduction, *Sheeler*, p. 8.

13. Sheeler, in Rourke, longer passage pp. 119–20, shorter passage, p. 168.

14. Williams, unpublished draft of the introduction, *Sheeler*. Draft is ms. C-75 (a through aa, bb, and cc) at State University of New York at Buffalo.

15. Sheeler, in Friedman, *Sheeler*, p. 99.

16. Sheeler, in Rourke, p. 136.

17. Martin Friedman, *The Precisionist View in American Art* (Minneapolis: Walker Art Center, 1960), p. 13.

18. Marsden Hartley, letter to Alfred Stieglitz, 9 October 1923, Stieglitz Archive, Beinecke Library, Yale University.

19. Williams, letter to John Riordan, 13 October 1926, Barrett Library, University of Virginia, Charlottesville.

20. Williams, unpublished version of *The Autobiography*, at Beinecke Library (Yale Za Williams Autobiography), Yale University.

21. William Carlos Williams, *The Embodiment of Knowledge* (New York: New Directions, 1974), p. 95.

22. William Carlos Williams, *Selected Essays* (New York: New Directions, 1969), p. 305.

23. William Carlos Williams, *Selected Letters* (New York: McDowell, Obolensky, 1957), p. 104; and *Selected Essays*, pp. 34, 330, 334.

24. Williams, *Embodiment*, p. 176.

25. Williams, *Speaking Straight Ahead: Interviews with William Carlos Williams* (Middletown, Conn.: Wesleyan University Press, 1975), p. 53.

26. Williams, *Essays*, p. 203.

27. Williams, *Selected Poems*, pp. 3, 10, 47.

28. Ibid., pp. 24, 48.

29. Williams, introduction, *Sheeler*, p. 7.

30. Sheeler, in Friedman, *Sheeler*, p. 36.

31. William Carlos Williams, *The Collected Earlier Poems* (New York: New Directions, 1951), p. 221.

32. Ibid., p. 368.

33. Sheeler, in Rourke, pp. 109, 143.

34. Williams, *Collected Earlier Poems*.

35. Ibid., p. 106.

36. Ibid., p. 415.

37. Ibid., p. 396.

# The Joy of Textualizing Japan: A Metacommentary on Roland Barthes's *Empire of Signs*

## Hwa Yol Jung
*Moravian College*

*Kogo tokitsukusazare*
—A Zen *jakugo*

L'écriture est . . . un *satori*.
—Roland Barthes

Nowadays the way of educating as well as the way of learning is wrong. True knowledge is not in the written word. Books are always "translations." The "original" is what *is* by its own nature.
—Okada Torajiro (Zen Master)

I

ALONG with Claude Lévi-Strauss, Jacques Lacan, and Michel Foucault, Roland Barthes is a major architect of French structuralism. More specifically, he is one of the most inventive masters of contemporary literary theory who fashioned its directions, modes, and trends. He is indeed, as the Japanese would say, a *meijin* of literary theory. He is called by Jonathan Culler "a cultural institution."[1] In this sense, interdisciplinarity is for Barthes not just a slogan or a theoretical speculation but is practiced in his own writings. Rather than confining himself to a particular discipline or subject matter—such as literature, anthropology, psychoanalysis, history of ideas—his intellectual taste is vast, versatile, and catholic. His versatile inventiveness as well as his *Japonisme* are evidenced in the gem of an essay, *L'Empire des signes* (1970)[2] which is thoroughly Gallic in taking delight in the dillydally of a myriad of things in Japan. Barthes speaks fondly of Japan or "a system of signs called Japan." Versatility, however, does not mean the lack or absence of intellectual focus or unity. *Empire of Signs* is in itself the mosaic scanning by an itinerant eye of the tantalizing parade of signs each of which counts and falls in its proper place—its ordered randomness accentuates the carefree and spontaneous sense of natural balance and unity with no privileged center. It is called a "luxurious and eclectic album."[3] *Empire of Signs* is the cultural landscape or, better, the geography, of itinerant cultural topics.

There is indeed some truth in saying that a great thinker thinks only one single thought. Barthes is no exception. His decentered center is semiology, whose neutral center is language and particularly "literature" as writing *(écriture)*. In his Inaugural Lecture at the Collège de France in 1977, he enunciated clearly and decisively: "I cannot function *outside* language, treating it as a target, and *within* language, treating it as a weapon."[4] And he called contemporary literature a permanent revolution of language and made it synonymous with writing or text. Writing makes knowledge festive or full of *asobi* (joyous play)—to use the expression of Japanese *geisha* culture. It is, in short, the gaiety of language in the manner of *geisha asobi*. The rhetoricity of Barthes's *Empire of Signs* is, without question, of *donjuanesque* quality: it is a seductive exercise in semiological *donjuanisme*.[5] Barthes is indeed a writer *(écrivain)* who is the homo ludens par excellence. Knowledge *(savoir)*, too, is the flavoring *(saveur)* of language or words. No wonder there is a close diatactics between the knowledge of culture and that of cooking.

Barthes's *Empire of Signs* describes Japan as the vast network of signs or a galaxy of signifiers. It is, as Susan Sontag puts it, "the ultimate accolade" of semiology.[6] As fashion is the language of fashion and the city is an ideogram, the country Japan is an "empire of signs" or an ideographic "city." Ludwig Wittgenstein wittingly likens language to a city: "Our language can be seen as an ancient city: a maze of little streets and squares, of old and new houses, and of houses with additions from various periods; and these surrounded by a multitude of new boroughs with straight and regular streets and uniform houses"[7]—and much more, more complex with, say, narrow zigzagging alleys and sometimes with unpassable subterranean tunnels which are even intriguing and befuddling to the native dwellers.

Moreover, *Empire of Signs* is inevitably an intellectual autobiography as well as *Gedankenexperiment* of his deconstructive semiology as a universal science in which Japan is one of its laboratories.[8] Barthes is indeed a *maiko*—to use the *geisha* language—in performing the semiotics of Japanese culture. Every serious endeavor is in part autobiographical—the self becoming the material subject of writing for itself as well as for others. I am here reminded of Raymond Savignac's *Astral* in which "de haut en bas" and "de bas en haut" are dialectically interchangeable. Autobiography or self-indulgence, it should be remembered, is not necessarily navel-gazing and thus acrimonious or opprobrious. For, on the contrary, radical observation is an *interrogation* for—to paraphrase Maurice Merleau-Ponty—a set of observations wherein he who observes is himself implicated by the observation. In other words, radical observation is a "metacommentary" in the sense that Fredric Jameson uses it: "every individual interpretation must include an interpretation of its own existence, must show its own credentials and justify itself: every commentary must be at the same time a metacommentary as well."[9] In this regard, *Empire of Signs* is an exotic subtext or "supplement" to Barthes's structural semiology: at least it adds colors and flavors to the texture and fabric of his written corpus as a whole. Without it the main text itself would be incomplete. The exotic in- and ex-cites his intellectual acumen. It elicits an inciting and exciting reading as well. It would be wrong to say, however, that Barthes intended to write a scholarly text on Japan and make a scholarly contribution to Oriental studies in the tradition of his countrymen Paul Masson-Oursel, Marcel Granet, Henri Maspero, and René Sieffert. Rather, he is an enthusiastic and observant amateur. Precisely because he is an amateur, he is able to pump in an air of fresh insight. Barthes's *Empire of Signs,* as Culler characterizes it judiciously, is a combination of "touristic commentary on Japan with a reflection on signs in everyday life and their ethical implications."[10] It is indeed a discerning, abecedarian account of Japanese culture as a system of signs.

In European history, Orientalism has been like a pendulum that cyclically swings back and forth from the likings and dislikings of the Orient. In French history, it fluctuates from Voltaire to Montesquieu. It is certainly a pathological swing. In an imaginary dialogue with a Japanese scholar, Martin Heidegger once expressed his puzzlement and bemusement that the Japanese forget the beginnings of their own thinking and rush to and chase after anything latest and newest in European thought. In modern history, the Oriental or Japanese love for things Occidental needs no documentation. Particularly because of the Japanese success in industrial development, now the Occidental love for the Orient—Japan in particular—abounds. In 1974 the French *Tel Quel* group including Phillippe Sollers, Julia Kristeva, and Barthes visited China. As a result, Kristeva, for example, published in 1977 *Des Chinoises* which is destined to become an important chapter in the annals of women's liberation. Before his China trip, Barthes visited and toured Japan in 1966 to lecture on structural semiology. According to the account of the French scholar who was President of the Franco-Japanese Institute in Tokyo—Maurice Pinguet to whom *Empire of Signs* was dedicated—Barthes's love for Japan was genuine and deep. In this, I might add, he followed the footsteps of his compatriot Paul Claudel who, more than anyone else, opened up intercultural exchanges between France and Japan in the twentieth century. The Japanese, in turn, responded to Barthes by translating his *L'Empire des signes* four years after its original publication: *Shirushi no Teikoku* (1974).[11] And they celebrated or, better, commemorated Barthes's *oeuvre* in the June, 1980 special issue of *Gendai Shiso* which has the French subtitle— *Revue de la pensée d'aujourd'hui*.

The present essay is a commentary on Barthes's commentary on Japan. I think no apology, however, is necessary to the incomparable essayist Michel de Montaigne, with all due respect and seriousness, who complained about the profusion of commentaries instead of writing about the order of things *(les choses)*, that is, "interpreting *interpretations*" instead of "interpreting *things*" themselves. Montaigne's old but familiar complaint is no doubt a sober reflection on our age of "commentaries," "criticism," and "scholarship." On the other hand, however, we should not forget that, in the first place, as human thought is coextensive with language, the *verbum* is not the surrogate or disguise of the *res* (or *les choses*). Rather, the *verbum* is also the *res*. So "interpreting interpretations" is willy-nilly "interpreting things" themselves. In the second place, since—following the lead of Nietzsche or Harold Bloom's disputation—interpretation is, and will always be, misinterpretation, the interpreted things or words remain to be reinterpreted. Finally, as we will see more clearly later, phenomenological reading turns and returns to the experiential to honor its validity, that is to say, it not only does not bifurcate "interpreting interpretations" and "interpreting things" but actually makes the bifurcation unnecessary and superfluous because in it, as in Zen, "things" themselves are the homestead of all "interpretations."

Be that as it may, the present metacommentary will focus on Barthes's semiological observation of significant Japanese cultural signs and symbols as manifested and surfaced particuarly in Zen, *haiku* and calligraphy (Section II) and then it will critically evaluate the limits of his view of the Japanese empire of signs from the phenomenology of lived experience (Section III). It should be noted from the outset that the question of how a given text is to be read is a controversial question in the contemporary hermeneutics of literature. No matter. I only intend to follow Barthes's own deconstructionist injunction that as there is nothing outside it, the text has an autochthonous status whose fate depends on readership rather than authorship. As, according to Barthes, there is an ineluctable dialectic or even paradox between reading and writing, the only explicit reading *is* writing. The only proper response to writing is another writing which is a metacommentary. By all means, Barthes intended to record in *Empire of Signs* his fascination with Japan as "the country of writing"—Japan's grammatology which is heavily pictographic or ideographic. As the tidal waves of deconstructive grammatology have been sweeping the contemporary literary scene, the tendency is rushing toward Chinese ideography as pure, anti-phonocentric writing.[12] Barthes is by no means the first and will not be the last Occidental who has been mesmerized by things traditionally Japanese. Nevertheless, there is a uniqueness in his *oeuvre:* unlike the other Occidental students, he *textualizes* everything in Japanese culture through deconstructive grammatology whose grand goal is to dismantle logocentrism which allegedly coincides with Western ethnocentrism. Like Igor Stravinsky who confessed that he enjoyed the activity of composing (writing) better than the music itself, deconstructive grammatologists have made writing intransitive: writing is writing is writing.

## II

The title of Barthes's work is, as it were, the wrapper of the content of Japanese culture as a system of signs. To decipher or zero in on the content, we must unwrap the wrapper. The content is packaged with a decorous plethora of cultural *bonsai* cultivated as miniaturized texts. If, however, the wrapper were the gift itself, the title would be the content: there would be no inner soul separate from the textual flesh. For Barthes, Japan displays an epicurean menu of exotic icons: Zen, *satori, mu, haiku, sumotori, pachinko, ikebana, Kabuki, Bunraku, Zengakuren, hashi, miso, sashimi, sukiyaki, tempura,* etc. It would be wrong to conclude that Barthes attends only to the "wrapping" of Japanese culture while dispensing with its "contents." What is to be recognized here is the need to deconstruct the all-too-commonplace dichotomy between the visible and the invisible, outside and inside, appearance and reality, wrapping and content, surface and depth, manifest and latent, concrete and abstract, ritual and choice, text and intention, style and form, deed and word, etc. Where there is no dichotomizing doublet, there is indeed "sincerity."[13] Since the visible body initiates the rite of passage to the invisible soul of an alien culture by a foreign observer or tourist, let's look closer at the outer appearance. It is doubly important in understanding Japanese culture and Barthes's Japan because of the extraordinary attention paid to it by the Japanese themselves and consequently Barthes himself in *Empire of Signs*. From a semiological perspective, too, the outer is as important as, if not more than, the inner.

What is a sign? It is, according to Barthes, the union of the signifier and the signified. The term is translated in Japanese as *shirushi* (or *kigo*) which means any visible *marking*—particularly nonlinguistic marking. It is interesting to see the unusual Japanese deference to the content is indicated immediately in the outer appearance of the translated copy of Barthes's *Empire of Signs*—in addition to its addenda inside (more pictures, extra explanatory notes and the translator's introduction). The translation is boxed and wrapped with wax paper. The cover of the book is clothed with the printing paper of excellent quality. Whether or not one can read Japanese, the external appearance gives one the impression that this is an important work, indeed.

If Barthes's work is to be judged by its cover, we should attend to it. The outer box has a separate wrapper with the photograph of a traditional, aristocratic, anonymous courtly woman which could easily depict a scene from the *Genji monogatari*. The picture is explained in the French original simply as "Fragment d'une carte postale" reminding us of Derrida's recent work on Freud. Without doubt the woman *is* the sur/facial *centerfold* of *Empire of Signs* which is consonant with Barthes's own semiological approach. As a picture is worth a thousand words, the woman is the *"studium"* where Barthes displays the multicolored galaxy of signifiers in Japanese culture. First, it is a picture. As such it *de/sign/ates* the presence of Japan in absence. In photography, according to Barthes, form and content coincide. The literal message of the woman (denotation) is not clear, but its symbolic message (connotation) is worth exploring. Clearly, Barthes is interested in signifying the traditional depth of Japanese culture. Second, the courtly woman is wearing a colorful, long garment that befits her long black hair. This garment is ingrained, as it were, in the fabric of Barthes's text. Interestingly enough, Barthes in *The Fashion System* discusses clothing as protecting, covering, and masking. He quotes Hegel's aesthetics approvingly: "as pure sentience, the body cannot signify; clothing guarantees the passage from sentience to meaning; it is, we might say, *the signified* par excellence."[14] What then does the garment of the courtly woman signify in relation to her pure sentience? The absolute privacy of sex? Speaking about the absence of sex in *pachinko*, Barthes observes that in Japan "sex is in sexuality, not elsewhere," whereas in the United States, on the contrary, "sex is everywhere, except in sexuality."[15]

Third and the most important is the *activity* engaged in by the courtly woman. In traditional Japan, there was a gender gap between man and woman in the activity of writing. What Barthes describes as the country of writing, *kanji* or ideographic calligraphy, whether or not he is aware of it, is typically a male activity, whereas for women it was an irreverent activity. Although there is no definite assurance that she is writing in *kanji* rather than *(hira)kana*—which is highly improbable—the importance of writing is accentuated by the woman in the act of (letter-) writing. Man in the act of writing is normal and usual, whereas woman in the act of writing is rare. As sexuality and textuality coincide in the portrayal of the woman in the act of writing, the bridging of the gender gap signifies anti-phallocentrism as well as anti-logocentrism. If, however, Barthes was only interested in portraying sexuality alone, the more appropriate *centerfold* of his work would have been the "courtesan *(yugo)* with a dog" in the book, a *geisha* girl, or a *shunga* to satisfy the lascivious eye.[16]

Now, so much for the outer cover.

Zen is the inner soul of Japanese culture, and writing is for Barthes Zen's *satori*—an inner awakening or enlightenment. He is fascinated with and celebrates the graphism of all things Japanese. As a nation of ideograms or pictograms, Japan is a graphic bliss or nirvana. Barthes has a tremendous proclivity to describe nonlinguistic signs in linguistic terms: every human face—including his own shown in the *Kobe Shinbun* during his tour in Japan and that of a corpulent *sumotori*—as a written text, an inscription, or a citation; *miso* as adding "a touch of clarity"; *sukiyaki* as becoming "decentered, like an uninterrupted text"; *tempura* as a "grammar" or visibly graphic; the city as an "ideogram"; *Zengakuren* as "a syntax of actions"; the stationary store as an "ideographic marquetry," etc. In the context of his deconstructive grammatology, in short, Barthes's discovery of Japan as a nation of ideographic inscriptions may be likened to the famous wooden statue in Kyoto of the enlightened Zen monk Hoshi where the visage of divinity is emerging through a crevice of his face.

Barthes declares that writing is a *satori:* Zen and *satori* are signified by the void or empty *(le vide).*[17] There is the *kanji* (ideogram) "void" calligraphed for Barthes by a female student. Underneath the *kanji* is the Japanese pronunciation *mu* and *le vide*. In Japan, in the country of writing whose inner soul coincides with Zen, *mu* is the abysmal "ground" or *Urgrund* of everything or everything is a metaphor of *mu*. Barthes writes:

> Writing is after all, in its way, a *satori; satori* (the Zen occurrence) is a more or less powerful (though in no way formal) seism which causes knowledge or the subject, to vacillate: it creates *an emptiness of language*. And it is also an emptiness of language which constitutes writing; it is from this emptiness that derive the features with which Zen, in the exemption from all meaning, writes gardens, gestures, houses, flower arrangements, faces, violence.[18]

The key expression to understand Barthes's Japan—and his deconstructive semiology—is "an emptiness of language." In the first place, however, there is an ambiguity in Barthes's own description of the *kanji "mu"* as *le vide*. *Mu* is *sunyata* in Sanskrit. When a Mahayana text was introduced to the Chinese in the second century, they were not able to grasp with ease the idea of *sunyata* [emptiness, *k'ung* (Chinese) and *ku* (Japanese)] as they did many other "abstract" Buddhist concepts, although they found it akin to the Taoist idea of *wu* (nothingness) as in the famous *wu-wei* (no-action) in the *Tao Te Ching*.[19] Ideogrammatically, *mu* and *ku* are two different characters. *Mu* (Japanese) or *wu* (Chinese) is *le néant*, whereas *ku* is *le vide*. The Japanese translation clearly indicates this difference.

In the second place, the expression "an emptiness of language" is "un *vide de parole*" in Barthes's original French text. Therefore, the English translation of *parole* as "language" is rather misleading inasmuch as it makes little sense to speak of writing as an emptiness of language itself. In the tradition of Saussurean linguistics, *langage* consists of *parole* and *langue*. If writing is "un vide de parole," it is contrasted with speech as event within the (Japanese) language as a system. For it, too, is an integral part of language *(langage)*. The passage cannot be understood otherwise. Writing as a *satori* is anti-phonocentric resonating with the general aim of deconstructive grammatology. The dialectical opposite of writing is not language but speech. The Japanese translation of *parole* as *kotoba* [spoken word(s)] is aware of this fundamental distinction between language as speech and language as writing. Moreover, deeply rooted in Chinese and Japanese thought is the tradition that the dialectical opposite of speech is not writing but rather silence or the "unsayable." There is, however, no glaring contradiction here because writing is always a silent transgression of verbal acts. In the Zen tradition, there is a diatactics of speech and silence: speech is the *yang* of silence and silence the *yin* of speech. Just as in John Cage's compositional techniques sound and silence are posed as complementary, Sontag considers silence not as an "incineration of consciousness" but, on the contrary, as a *pharmakon* for the pollution of language.[20] Silence may be invoked as a copula, hyphen, punctuation, or even rupture in the dialectical flow of human communication. As such its communicative value exceeds and surpasses that of "empty talk" *(parole vide)*.[21] To Zen, as the tradition goes, silence is more suitable than eloquence.

According to D. T. Suzuki, whose name in the West is synonymous with Zen, Zen's *satori* is realized in *performance* which may be (1) verbal (speaking) or (2) actional.[22] In the first place, since Zen is an everyday occurrence in our social life, we need to communicate with one another through the medium of language. Unlike the rules of linguistics as the science of language (presumably including semiology), however, Suzuki insists that Zen verbalism is intuitive and experiential, that is, nonconceptual and lived. Cutting through the conceptual or intellectual sedimentations, Zen attempts to reach directly or im-mediately *konomama* (thisness) or *sonomama* (thatness)—i.e., "isness" the attainment of which is called *satori*. Thus the attainment of *satori* avoids conceptual detours. According to Barthes:

> if this state of *a-language* is a liberation, it is because, for the Buddhist experiment, the proliferation of secondary thoughts (the thought of thought), or what might be called the infinite supplement of supernumerary signifieds—a circle of which language itself is the depository and the model—appears as a jamming: it is on the contrary the abolition of secondary thought which breaks the vicious infinity of language. In all these experiments, apparently, it is not a matter of crushing language beneath the mystic silence of the ineffable, but of *measuring* it, of halting that verbal top which sweeps into the gyration the obsessional play of symbolic substitutions. In short, it is the symbol as semantic operation which is attacked.[23]

In the second place, *satori* is a moral emancipation, that is, moral fulfillment *by doing* which is deeply Sinistic[24] (i.e., both Confucian and Taoist). Consider the famous Confucian idea of the "rectification of names" *(cheng ming)* that is addressed to the performative power of speech in human conduct *qua moral*. The only way to bridge verbalism with moral fulfillment by doing is to regard speaking itself as the act of doing (i.e., the theory of language both as speech acts and as moral acts). The Japanese as well as the Chinese consider "sincerity"—literally meaning the "completion" of "spoken words"—as the acme of moral virtue. Nishida Kitaro—the greatest Japanese philosopher of the twentieth century—regards intuition as the basis of artistic creativity as well as moral conduct. Intuition rather than the intellect is the *élan vital* of artistic and moral creativity. Mencius, too, considered "intuitive knowledge" (*liang chih* or, literally, "good knowledge") as the basis of everyday moral conduct. Culler is right, as noted earlier, that Barthes's commentary on Japan as empire of signs *is* also an ethical one.

In the Japanese as well as the Chinese tradition, painting and writing are inseparable—the fact of which has not failed Barthes's own attention. In calligraphy, writing reaches the status of an art. In it, to inscribe is to paint. As Guillaume Apollinaire "painted" his poetry as *"calligrammes,"* so does the contemporary Japanese painter Hiro Kamimura exemplify an attempt to synthesize painting with ideograms: his "Water and Ice" is a homonymous blending of painting and writing. The *Obaku* sect of Zen excels in *kanji* calligraphy which approximates painting. Painting, moreover, is invariably accompanied by ideographic inscriptions. *Sumiye* painting is an example of how painting approaches writing.[25] Japanese "photocracy"—the craze for pictograms—is too well-known to elaborate. Barthes's own 1970 painting after the Italian futurism (which is used on the front cover jacket of the recent American anthology *A Barthes Reader* edited by Susan Sontag) looks like vertiginous Chinese calligraphy. His own hand-written French transcription of a few Japanese expressions in *Empire of Signs* resembles calligraphy. Calligraphy may be characterized as a choreography of gestures. It is a ballet of ideograms in *rite* order—to paraphrase Marshall McLuhan and Harley Parker.[26] Like Picasso's *Swimmer* and *Acrobat,* calligraphy is a kinetic art: it is the human body in motion or a conversation of gestures. Although he did not have in mind Chinese ideography in particular, R. G. Collingwood is perceptive in observing that every language is a specialized form of bodily gesture and thus the dance is the mother of all languages.[27]

*Haiku* is a polyglot

*La vieille mare:*
*Une grenouille saute dedans:*
*Oh! le bruit de l'eau.*

*Furu ike ya!*
*Kawazu tobikomu,*
*Mizu no oto.*

*The old pond:*
*A frog jumps in:*
*Oh! the sound of the water.*

Barthes's unabated enthusiasm for *haiku* as the elixir of Japanese literature—indeed, all literature—cannot be doubted. *S/Z* which was published in the same year as *Empire of Signs* should perhaps be read as "Semiology/Zen" that celebrates the Japanese tradition.[28] Each of 561 lexias in *S/Z*, as noted earlier by Leitch, is a *haiku* of criticism whose packaged notation equals a cultivated *bonsai*. For Barthes, *haiku* is merely the literary branch of Zen.[29] There is indeed a three-way interfusion of writing, Zen *(satori),* and *haiku*. Barthes, too, notices the ineluctable blending of painting and *haiku* writing in the following two examples. The first is the picture of one cucumber and two eggplants on a *kakemono* by an anonymous sixteenth-century (?) author which is unfortunately omitted from the English translation. It is found in the midst of Barthes's discussion of *haiku*. The three vegetables symbolize or parallel three short lines of a *haiku*. The second is a more suggestive and seductive example than the first. It is the "mushroom picking" by the eighteenth-century Japanese artist Yokoi: three raw mushrooms are pierced through a wisp of straw above which is the following three-line *haiku (poème bref en trois vers):*

> Il se fait cupide        He becomes greedy
> aussi, le regard baissé  his eyes lowered
> sur les champignons      on the mushrooms

If "rawness" *(crudité)* is the kind of a "floating signifier," the painting and the *haiku* are in the state of a sexual, chiasmic invagination. The *kakemono* signifies—to use a mycophilial expression—the "bemushroomed" state of *ekstasis:* the symbolic, spiritual flight of the *haiku* and the pictured mushrooms from the body of the *kakemono*. This may explain why the composer John Cage is interested in fusing Zen and mycology, that is, in ethno-mycology. Be that as it may, Barthes goes on to ask (in handwriting) rhetorically about the "mushroom picking": "Where does the writing begin? Where does the painting begin?" Set aside the rhetoricity of the questions, one might point out that they can be raised only by those for whom Chinese ideography is an unknown art, although the pictured sketch of the three raw mushrooms pierced through a straw resembles, and may thus be mistaken easily for, a polygamous ideogram.

### III

*Empire of Signs* is the testimonial of an itinerant pilgrim—not unlike the Zen monk Hoshi who, too, travelled to China in the beginning of the T'ang period in search of Zen *(satori)*—in search of semiological markings *(shirushi)* in all things Japanese whose epicenter is writing *(écriture).* For Barthes, we may say, Japan was a semiological *geisha* house where the freeplay *(asobi)* of signs takes place.[30] Although Barthes succeeds in "intellectual deprovincialization" and thus must be applauded for his intention and effort to overcome the conceptual "sound barriers" of Western narcissism, we cannot answer with certainty whether or not he succeeds in instituting an exagamous link between semiology and Japanese culture. To be universally valid, his semiology as the *science* of *all* signs must encompass different galaxies of markings of which Japan is only one.

To discover Japan as the country of writing is not at all contrary to the affluent exhibition of the Japanese photocracy we have all come to know so very well in recent years—the photocracy which, in an extended sense of the term, could include photography, painting, dramaturgy, fashions, packaging, gastronomy, and above all calligraphy. *Empire of Signs* is a belletrism of Japan at its best: as Barthes himself admitted, he enjoyed writing it more than any other book. No doubt the most revealing and original formulation of Barthes's work is: writing is a *satori*. As Zen is the inner soul of Japanese culture, there is all the more reason why the *écrivain* Barthes is interested in *haiku* which he views as the privileged monument of Zen. The most significant question is not how many cultural trophies Barthes gathered but whether or not *Empire of Signs*—the "ultimate accolade" of Japanese culture in the eye of a semiologist—is the insemination and dissemination of his semiology. Although every intellectual endeavor for a *savant* is, to some extent, autobiographical and Barthes's *Empire of Signs* is no exception to this rule, one hopes that it is ideally a reciprocation, as in the spirit of exchanging gifts, of the *insemination* (taking) of Zen and the *dissemination* (giving) of his semiology.

The idea of writing as *satori* already involves a semiological strategy. By strategy I mean a chosen set of calculated moves in order to "win" a conceptual game. Part of this strategy is the very selection of what signs are to be taken as significant indicators of Japanese culture. There is, however, a serious problem in relating Zen and *satori* to semiology. It is in essence the problem of reconciling the French cult of writing (*écriture*) and the Japanese cult of inner tranquility, unless, of course, writing like Zen calligraphy is the carnal "enjoyment" (*jouissance* or *asobi*) of a person as a non-utilitarian activity undertaken solely for serenity or what Martin Heidegger calls *Gelassenheit* which has been identified as the common denominator of such Zen specialists as Suzuki, Eugen Herrigel, and Karl von Dürckheim.

It is also the clash between semiology as a conceptual, linguistic system and Zen as intuitive, actional experience, which is correlated with the question of the unity or duality of the inner and the outer, depth and surface, the content and the wrapping, gastronomic look and actual taste, and meaning and sign.[31] The conception of writing as *satori* raises the unresolved paradox of Zen as an *inner* awakening and writing as an *outer* ex/pression. This paradox is accentuated in Barthes's Japan because structural semiology as a method of cultural interpretation has a built-in conceptual propensity to disregard the inner in favor of the outer or, in the case of Japan, to wrap Zen with semiology. Barthes is certainly not unaware of the problem when he defines the sign as the union of the signifier and the signified, and when he acknowledges that Zen wages a war against the prevarication of meaning *(sens)* and that the meaning of a sign is polygamous, not monogamous. John Sturrock thus observes that "In Japanese culture, or at any rate Barthes's version of it, the exterior of a thing *is* the thing, there is no informing but invisible agency within. Japan is a country full of rich and intriguing signifiers whose charm is that they have no signifieds."[32]

For Barthes, there is no inner soul or privileged center in Zen's *satori* because it is *mu* or the void which is contradictory to dominant Western metaphysics. The denial of the inner or depth in favor of the outer or surface may well be a conceptual trapping of structural semiology rather than the understanding of Zen from *within*. Thus Sturrock speculates that "the opposition deep-set/flush is itself a Western not a Japanese one, and the Japanese might very well employ a different code in order to locate the Oriental soul."[33] There is always the latent danger of catching Zen with a semiological net. It is for this reason that in his important article the Chinese philosopher Chang Tung-sun identifies Western reasoning with the logic of identity, while Eastern reasoning with the logic of correlation which is neither monistic, nor dualistic, nor reductionistic.[34] As clothing is to the body, so is the sign to culture. As pure sentience without clothing, the body too cannot signify or at least cannot signify sufficiently. By the same logic, culture cannot signify without signs as external "markings" *(shirushi)*. However, a marking is only an external indication, not a meaning. There is a famous saying by the Chinese Taoist Chuang Tzu that words exist for meaning and once the meaning has been gotten, the words can be forgotten. Culture or language is not like a white onion—a subject of Basho's *haiku* of which Barthes seems fond—every layer of which is a surface without an inner core or center. Even in Zen there is mention of "the mind of no-mind" *(mushin no shin)*. It may very well be true that surface is as telling as depth, but in language the signifier without the signified is "babbling" or "doodling." Culture is like language: to understand it, we must understand the diatactics of the subjective and the objective without a facile reductionism. Cultural interpretation is the navigation of the stormy channel between the Scylla of subjectivity and the Charybdis of objectivity.

What is lacking in Barthes's structural semiology as a method of cultural interpretation, therefore, is, and is compensated for by, a phenomenology of lived experience *(l'expérience vécu)* or the life-world *(le monde vécu: Lebenswelt)*. In Barthes's case of Japan as the country of writing as well as Zen, we need to *hear* Zen's *voice* of invisibility as a prerequisite to *see* its visible surface. There is a lesson to be learned from Ralph Ellison's "invisible man" who struggles for his visibility by lighting up his basement with 1369 light bulbs. The message to be gotten here is not to disregard the outer, but rather to encourage the dialectical coupling of the inner and the outer or the invisible and the visible, that is, to abandon the facile monism, dualism, or reductionism.[35]

Without the benefit of a phenomenology of lived experience as the founding and funding matrix of *all* conceptualization, there is in cultural interpretation the ever-present danger of conceptual "entrapment" or the prevarication of meaning—especially in the interpretation of a culture, including its own linguistic system, which is unfamiliar or dissimilar to the observer's own.[36] It is not to suggest "Go native" or "Think Japanese" here, but only to intimate that a phenomenology of lived experience is the prerequisite for any cultural interpretation. Cultural interpretation is necessarily an echo of the original voice of culture as a network of intersubjective meanings—those meanings which are not just in the minds of the individual actors but rooted in their social and institutional practices including their language. More significantly, to ignore a network of intersubjective meanings is to open—often inadvertently—the safety valve, as it were, that prevents the spillage of ethnocentrism or, as Barthes himself calls it, "Western narcissism."[37] To attend to intersubjective meanings is to respect "a local turn of mind" and not to miss the cultural contextualization of indigenous signifiers. Barthes himself observes that in the Occident the mirror is a narcissistic object for man to look at himself, whereas in the Orient it is *empty* and symbolizes the *emptiness (ku* or *le vide)* of all symbols. To be "enlightened" or to attain a *satori,* Barthes's writing on Japan must be *emptied* of the preemptive strategies of his semiology. To deconstruct (phenomenologically) Barthes's *Empire of Signs* is simply to trace the *presence* of semiological reflection in the mirror of his Japan.

There is no intimation here that Barthes is an ethnocentrist. Nor is it implied that his understanding of Japanese culture is shallow, superficial, or surfacial. What is pointed out is simply the potential danger of the categorial grid of structural semiology or, for that matter, any conceptual system that ignores consciously or unconsciously a system of intersubjective meanings. Barthes himself noted that in Japan sex is in sexuality, not anywhere else. This observation assumes, to be sure, the knowledge of the *inner* working of sexuality in Japan. Parallel to the problematic of the content of wrapping is *Kabuki*'s *onnagata* which is in actuality the male actor playing the staged role of the female (i.e., the transvestite actor). Without knowing the *inner* working of *Kabuki,* here again, he might be easily mistaken for an actress. Let us make no mistake: a mask is *never* a real face, although the former tells on occasion a lot about the latter. Moreover, there is nothing wrong with the good looks of often decorous gastronomic Japanese dishes pleasing to our (hungry) eye, but they do not always or necessarily guarantee good taste. Taste, good or bad, is to be known only in the eating.[38] In brief, when chained to the categorial grid of structural semiology, cultural interpretation courts conceptual reification, that is to say, falsification. As, in Zen, the written is only a copy or translation of something original or real, to *textualize* the real is to *fabricate* it or, at best, to reduce it to a confessional autobiography or a cultural narcissism. In the Japanese language, not in its written but only its spoken form, there is the triple, playful distinction between *hashi-ga* (chopsticks), *haSHI-ga* (bridge), *haSHI-GA* (edge). To wit: with the slightest slip *(lapsus)* of the tongue—not a pen or brush—one can stand at the "bridge" of understanding or at the "edge" of misunderstanding, or when one means to ask for a pair of "chopsticks" at the gastronomic table, he may end up with getting a "bridge"! After having said all this, it is not altogether impossible for anyone to have missed or been "off-side" *(hors jeu)* in the *staging* of the *Bunraku* or *Kabuki* of Barthes's semiology in *Empire of Signs,* that is, the real semiological face or character behind the mask.[39] In that case, he can confess that at least he enjoyed a brief *geisha asobi* (disciplined, not promiscuous, "playfulness") of and in Barthes's house of signs without perhaps knowing its inner workings. By so doing he "supplements" the Nietzschean "freeplay" for "truth." Ultimately, perhaps we are all playing the labyrinthine game of "truth-telling" in the *Rashomon.* As the poem of the thirteenth-century Chinese Master Mumon reads:

> Gateless is the Great Tao,
> There are thousands of ways to it.
> If you pass through this barrier,
> You may walk freely in the universe.[40]

## Notes

1. Jonathan Culler, *Roland Barthes* (New York: Oxford University Press, 1983), p. 9. Among the American literary notables, Susan Sontag is the most enthusiastic admirer of Barthes's literary genius. Recently she writes: "Teacher, man of letters, moralist, philosopher of culture, connoisseur of strong ideas, protean autobiographer . . . of all the intellectual notables who have emerged since World War II in France, Roland Barthes is the one whose work I am most certain will endure." ("Writing Itself: On Roland Barthes," in *A Barthes Reader,* ed. Susan Sontag [New York: Hill and Wang, 1982], p. vii.)

2. Roland Barthes, *L'Empire des signes* (Geneva: Skira, 1970); *Empire of Signs,* trans. Richard Howard (New York: Hill and Wang, 1982).

3. Guy de Mallac, "Métaphores du vide: *L'Empire des signes* de Roland Barthes," *Sub-Stance* 1 (1971): 31.

4. *A Barthes Reader,* p. 473. For Barthes, *l'homme, c'est le langage:* "A . . . principle, particularly important in regard to literature, is that language cannot be considered as a simple instrument, whether utilitarian or decorative, of thought. Man does not exist prior to language, either as a species or as an individual. We never find a state where man is separated from language, which he then creates in order to 'express' what is taking place within him: it is language which teaches the definition of man, not the reverse." ("To Write: An Intransitive Verb?" in Richard Macksey and Eugenio Donato, eds., *The Structuralist Controversy* [Baltimore: Johns Hopkins University Press, 1972], p. 135.) Cf. the American semiotician Charles Sanders Peirce who writes that "it is sufficient to say that there is no element whatever of man's consciousness which has not something corresponding to it in the world; and the reason is obvious. It is that the word or sign which man uses *is* the man himself. For, as the fact that every thought is a sign, taken in conjunction with the fact that life is a train of thought, proves that man is a sign; so, that everything thought is an *external* sign, proves that man is an external sign. That is to say, the man and the external sign are identical, in the same sense in which the words *homo* and *man* are identical. Thus my language is the sum total of myself; for the man is the thought." (*Collected Papers,* vol. 5, *Pragmatism and Prag-*

*maticism,* ed. Charles Hartshorne and Paul Weiss [Cambridge, Mass.: Harvard University Press, 1960], p. 189.)

5. The terms *donjuanesqe* and *donjuanisme* are borrowed from Shoshana Felman, *Le Scandale du corps parlant* (Paris: Editions du Seuil, 1980). If Felman is able to dramatize John Austin's philosophy of language as *donjuanisme* and impregnate *connaissance* with *jouissance,* we should be allowed to invent the hybrid neologism *jouinaissance* after the fashion of James Joyce. The slightest allusion of language to corporeality as hinted at by Felman—"la parole est une promesse corporelle"—elicits a filiality of the philosophy of language with (Lacanian) psychoanalysis. In *Roland Barthes: A Conservative Estimate* (Chicago: University of Chicago Press, 1983), Philip Thody observes that Barthes's *Empire of Signs* is "one of the most hedonistic of all his books, and the one in which he writes with the most enthusiasm about his subject-matter" (p. 121). Another observer comments that Barthes's thinking shifted from the themes of culture, the sign and the text to the notion of pleasure (see ibid., p. 181). Steven Ungar, too, aptly characterizes Barthes as "the professor of desire" in his recent book *Roland Barthes: The Professor of Desire* (Lincoln, Neb.: University of Nebraska Press, 1983). More specifically, John O'Neill coined the term *homotextuality* to intimate the corporeal kinship between the reader and the text in Barthes's work. See "Homotextuality": Barthes on Barthes, Fragments (RB), with a Footnote," in *Hermeneutics,* ed. Gary Shapiro and Alan Sica (Amherst, Mass.: University of Massachusetts Press, 1984), pp. 165–82.

6. "Writing Itself," p. xxiv. Speaking of *Empire of Signs,* Vincent B. Leitsch describes: "Barthes admires the Japanese custom of attending to wrapping while disregarding contents. The surface of the present, not its hidden gift, elicits appreciation. The preparations and the requisites of meaning, ritual and arbitrary, hold more interest and importance than the impatient possession of its truth. Whether the volume is ultimately empty or overfull seems less pressing than that its packaging be enjoyed. The writing of *S/Z* celebrates this non-Western tradition. Thus the lexia, a haiku of criticism, a delicacy of *S/Z,* is less violent manhandling than frail handiwork in miniature. A package of notation. Without hidden truth. A ritual of reading. Bonsai cultivated." (*Deconstructive Criticism* [New York: Columbia University Press, 1983], p. 204.)

7. *Philosophical Investigations,* trans. G. E. M. Anscombe (Oxford: Blackwell, 1953), p. 84.

8. In discussing the legacy of Saussure's linguistics, Jonathan Culler observes that "if everything which has meaning within a culture is a sign and therefore an object of semiological investigation, semiology would come to include most disciplines of the humanities and the social sciences. Any domain of human activity—be it music, architecture, cooking, etiquette, advertising, fashion, literature—could be approached in semiological terms." (*Ferdinand de Saussure* [New York: Penguin Books, 1977], p. 103. See also pp. 95 and 110–11). From a perspective of semiology, language is only one system of signs, though it is a special or privileged one. Thus, semiology broadens its jurisdiction to include all conceivable cultural objects. Barthes's *Empire of Signs* should be read in the broad sense of semiology as a cultural science.

9. Fredric Jameson, "Metacommentary," PMLA 86 (January 1971): 10.

10. *Roland Barthes,* p. 11. Of course, we should not take Culler's use of the term *touristic* as nonserious or supercilious. Rather, he seems to use it after a study fashioned by Dean MacCannell, *The Tourist: A New Theory of the Leisure Class* (New York: Schocken Books, 1976).

11. Roland Barthes, *Shirushi no Teikoku,* trans. So Sacon (Tokyo: Shincho, 1974). Judging from the description of the cover of the Japanese translation, the Japanese consider the work as the "cultural criticism" of Japan. I am indebted to my friend

Kazuhiko Okuda of the International University of Japan for sending me a copy of the Japanese translation of Barthes's *Empire of Signs—Shirushi no Teikoku*. At the conference on "The Languages of Criticism and the Sciences of Man" held under the auspices of the Johns Hopkins Humanities Center in 1966 (the same year in which he visited Japan), Barthes spoke of a homology between language and culture and of the intersection between literature and linguistics as "semio-criticism." (See "To Write: An Intransitive Verb?" p. 135.)

12. See the author's paper "Misreading the Ideogram: From Fenollosa to Derrida and McLuhan," *Paideuma* (forthcoming). In this connection, we should single out the following two important recent works on Japan. One is Noël Burch, *To the Distant Observer*, rev. and ed. Annette Michelson (Berkeley: Unviersity of California Press, 1979). Burch admires Barthes's *Empire of Signs* as "a pioneer text": "it is the first attempt by any Western writer to *read* the Japanese 'text' in the light of contemporary semiotics, . . ." (p. 13). After the fashion of Barthes, Burch treats the Japanese cinema as a system of signs, that is to say, he *textualizes* it. The other is William R. LaFleur, *The Karma of Words* (Berkeley: University of California Press, 1983). LaFleur's work is concerned with the interconnection between Buddhism and the literary arts in medieval Japan. Although his methodology is self-professedly one of the Foucauldian *episteme*, the intertextuality of the religious and the literary in terms of the Japanese concept of *funi* ("nondualism") in his analysis may be likened to the interdisciplinary spirit of Barthes. I am grateful to David Pollack of the University of Rochester for suggesting these two works to me.

13. There is another Confucian ethical term that is inseparably related to sincerity: it is *fidelity* that literally means "man standing by his word." It refers to the responsibility of the speaker to his word as ethical performance. The American poet and essayist Wendell Berry dwells on the ethics of fidelity in *Standing by Words* (San Francisco: North Point Press, 1983), pp. 24–63. Ivan Morris writes about the "tragic heroes in the history of Japan" from ancient times to the time of the *kamikaze* pilots based on this single idea of "sincerity" *(makoto)* which has its origin in Confucian philosophy. (See *The Nobility of Failure* [New York: Holt, Rinehart, and Winston, 1962.]) One would immediately recognize, therefore, that I am using the notion of sincerity in an extended sense. It is preeminently that moral concept which refers to the "unity of knowledge and action" *(chih hsing ho yi)* in Confucian thought: knowledge is the beginning of action and action is the completion of knowledge.

14. *The Fashion System*, trans. Matthew Ward and Richard Howard (New York: Hill and Wang, 1973), p. 258.

15. *Empire of Signs*, p. 29.

16. From the vantage point of Barthes's own semiology, one can say that the cover "fashions" or "dresses" the text of a book. However, when he was introducing the drawings of the fashion designer Erté in 1972, Barthes commented that fashion only seeks "clarity" (not "voluptuousness") and the cover girl is not a good erotic object because she is too preoccupied with becoming a sign. (See Thody, *Roland Barthes*, pp. 99 and 192.)

17. Cf. Isshu Miura and Ruth Fuller Sasaki, *The Zen Koan: Its History and Use in Rinzai Zen* (New York: Harcourt, Brace and World, 1965), p. 3: "The living heart of all Buddhism is enlightenment or satori, and it is upon satori that Zen Buddhism is based. But Zen is not satori, nor is a satori Zen. Satori is the goal of Zen. Moreover, the satori that is the goal of Zen is not merely the satori experience; it is the satori experience deepened through training and directed to a definite end." It would be of some interest to note that "France" and "Buddhism" begin with the same ideogram—an accidental

connection between Barthes the Frenchman and his interest in (Zen) Buddhism. In the most recent collection of critical essays, *L'Obvie et l'obtus* (Paris: Editions du Seuil, 1982), Barthes declares that "Distinguons . . . le *message*, qui veut produire une information, le *signe*, qui veut produire une intellection, et le *geste*, qui produit tout le reste (le 'supplément'), sans forcément vouloir produire quelque chose" (p. 148). *Le geste* is also a *satori* presumably because it produces without being forced to produce anything at all.

18. *Empire of Signs*, p. 4. A Zen master pondered for six years on the *koan* on *mu*. Then he suddenly achieved *satori* and composed the following "Dadaist" poem:

> Mu! Mu! Mu! Mu! Mu!
> Mu! Mu! Mu! Mu! Mu!
> Mu! Mu! Mu! Mu! Mu!
> Mu! Mu! Mu! Mu! Mu!

(See Ben-Ami Scharfstein, "Introduction/Zen: The Tactics of Emptiness," in Yoel Hoffman, trans., *The Sound of the One Hand* [New York: Basic Books, 1975], p. 26.) This book is a compilation of Zen *koan*(s) with answers. To fashion a semiological *koan:* If a semiological package is made of the wrapping ("sign") and the content ("message"), what is the "content" when the "wrapping" is all peeled off? (The answer, of course, is: *mu* or the void!). In *Mind and Nature* (New York: Dutton, 1979), Gregory Bateson emphasizes zero as a message when he writes: "the deep partial truth that 'nothing will come of nothing' in the world of information and organization encounters an interesting contradiction in the circumstance that *zero*, the complete absence of any indicative event, can be a message. . . . The letter that you do not write, the apology you do not offer, the food that you do not put out for the cat—all these can be sufficient and effective messages because zero, *in context*, can be meaningful; and it is the recipient of the message who creates the context" (pp. 46–47).

19. In recounting *Empire of Signs* to Guy Scarpetta in 1971, Barthes commented that "le zen est apparemment bouddhique, mais il n'est pas du côté du bouddhisme; le clivage dont je parle n'est pas celui de l'histoire des religions; c'est précisément celui des langues, du langage." (Roland Barthes, *Le Grain de la voix: Entretiens 1962–1980* [Paris: Editions du Seuil, 1981], p. 115.)

20. See "The Aesthetics of Silence," in *Styles of Radical Will* (New York: Farrar, Straus and Giroux, 1966), pp. 3–34. For Zen all verbalism essentially represents the pollution of reality. See Miura and Sasaki, *The Zen Koan*, p. 35: "Zen is 'without words, without explanations, without instruction, without knowledge.' Zen is self-awakening only. Yet if we want to communicate something about it to others, we are forced to fall back upon words." The positive role of silence in human communication as an ontological issue is explored extensively in Bernard P. Dauenhauer, *Silence: The Phenomenon and Its Ontological Significance* (Bloomington, Ind: Indiana University Press, 1980).

21. In speaking of psychoanalysis as the "talking cure," Jacques Lacan regards "empty speech" as an impediment to the realization of the truth of the subject: "I have tackled the function of speech in analysis from its least rewarding angle, that of 'empty' speech, where the subject seems to be talking in vain about someone who, even if he were his spitting image, can never become one with the assumption of his desire. I have pointed out the source of the growing devaluation of which speech has been the object in both theory and technique." (*Ecrits: A Selection*, trans. Alan Sheridan [New York: W. W. Norton, 1977], pp. 45–46.) In *Love's Body* (New York: Vintage Books, 1968), Norman O. Brown speaks eloquently of the metaphysics of silence in the following passages: "The ego is loquacity, the interior monologue, the soliloquy which isolates. The way of silence leads to the extinction of the ego, mortification. To become empty, to

become nothing; to be free from the constrictions of the self, to have no self, to be of no mind, to be a dead man. . . . The matrix in which the word is sown is silence. Silence is the mother tongue. . . . The meaning is not in the words but between the words, in the silence. . . . The virgin womb of the imagination in which the word becomes flesh is silence; and she remains a virgin. . . . The word is made flesh. To recover the world of silence, of symbolism, is to recover the human body. . . . The true meanings of words are bodily meanings, carnal knowledge; and the bodily meanings are the unspoken meanings. What is always speaking silently is the body" (pp. 264–65).

22. Daisetz Teitaro Suzuki, *Zen and Japanese Culture* (New York: Pantheon Books, 1959).

23. *Empire of Signs*, p. 75.

24. Barthes's own term would be "Sinic." The popular French "myth" of China as a "peculiar mixture of bells, rickshaws and opium dens" is referred to by Barthes as "Sininess" or "Sinity." (*Mythologies*, trans. Annette Lavers [New York: Hill and Wang, 1972], p. 121.)

25. "Calligraphy," Bernard Karlgren writes, "is the mother of Chinese pictorial art and always its intimate ally, and an expert calligrapher has always been just as much esteemed in China as a painter of the first rank. . . . From this close connexion between script and painting it follows that the Chinese artist, who often is both calligrapher and painter, loves to insert in his picture some lines of writing, which he employs with decorative effect in a masterly way." (*Sound and Symbol in Chinese* [London: Oxford University Press, 1923], p. 67.) Another unique, interesting side of Chinese ideography is the invention of a kind of the Rorschach test based on *tsukuriji* ("made-up words") to test the attitudes of the Japanese youth. (See George Fields, *From Bonsai to Levi's* [New York: Macmillan, 1982], pp. 102–5.)

26. Marshall McLuhan and Harley Parker, *Through the Vanishing Point: Space in Poetry and Painting* (New York: Harper and Row, 1968), p. 187.

27. R. G. Collingwood, *The Principles of Art* (Oxford: Clarendon Press, 1938), pp. 243–44.

28. See Barthes, *Le Grain de la voix*, "Sur 'S/Z' et 'l'Empire des signes,'" pp. 69–86.

29. The reason for Barthes's liking for *haiku* lies in the fact that it enables the signified to "evaporate" or disappear, and what is left is only a thin cloud of signifier (il ne reste plus qu'un mince nuage de significant). (*Le Grain de la voix*, p. 114.) The writing of *haiku* appears to be an act of *kenosis* or even "semioclasty." It should be noted, however, that Barthes seems to have been carried away with his enthusiasm of *haiku*, that is, his assertion that *haiku* is merely the literary branch of Zen is a little hyperbolic. According to Suzuki, for example, although they are exquisitely interfused, "*Haiku* and Zen . . . are not to be confused. *Haiku* is *haiku* and Zen is Zen. *Haiku* has its own field, it is poetry, but it also partakes of something of Zen, at the point where a *haiku* gets related to Zen." (*Zen and Japanese Culture*, p. 229.)

30. In relation to the importance of the surfacial, the following description by Liza Crihfield Dalby on *geisha* is relevant and appropriate: "Customers are expected to give a geisha an honorarium, but the cash (preferably a stiffly virgin 5,000-yen note or two) must first be folded into a decorative envelope. A crumpled bill fished from a pocket would hardly do." ("The Art of the Geisha," *Natural History* 92 [February 1983]: 49.) For her complete treatment of Japanese *geisha* culture based on her anthropological field work and personal experience as a *geisha*, see *Geisha* (Berkeley: University of California Press, 1983). The "sociological," "cultural," and "psychoanalytical" approaches to the role of play or playing in relation to human reality is proposed by George Herbert Mead's *Mind, Self and Society*, ed. Charles W. Morris (Chicago: University of Chicago

Press, 1934), Johan Huizinga's *Homo Ludens* (Boston: Beacon Press, 1955), and Donald Woods Winnicott's *Playing and Reality* (London: Tavistock, 1971). Notwithstanding their differences, they all treat playing as a universal element of human reality. Strictly speaking, *geisha asobi* as a nightly activity which began as a male entertainment for males is close structurally to Huizinga's conception of play as an intermezzo in the flow of normal, workaday life. However, I wish to use *asobi* in Winnicott's sense of *playing as doing*. He writes that *"Psychotherapy takes place in the overlap of two areas of playing, that of the patient and that of the therapist. Psychotherapy has to do with two people playing together. The corollary of this is that where playing is not possible then the work done by the therapist is directed towards bringing the patient from a state of not being able to play into a state of being able to play,"* and that *"it is play that is the universal,* and that belongs to health: playing facilitates growth and therefore health; playing leads into group relationships; playing can be a form of communication in psychotherapy; and, lastly, psychoanalysis has been developed as a highly specialized form of playing in the service of communication with oneself and others" (*Playing and Reality*, pp. 38 and 41). I can see no reason why what is true with playing in psychoanalysis and psychotherapy cannot be true in (Barthes's) semiology.

31. In "Maoism, Psychoanalysis, and Hermeneutics: A Methodological Critique of the Interpretation of Cultures," *Asian Thought and Society* (forthcoming), I and Petee Jung challenge shallow cultural hermeneutics and conceptual overkill that ignore a cultural phenomenology of lived experience: we point to the facile trappings of cultural interpretation in relation to Maosim as the Sinicization of Marxism.

32. John Sturrock, "Roland Barthes," in *Structuralism and Since: From Lévi-Strauss to Derrida*, ed. John Sturrock (New York: Oxford University Press, 1979), p. 77.

33. Ibid., p. 78.

34. Chang Tung-sun, "A Chinese Philosopher's Theory of Knowledge," in *Our Language and Our World*, ed. S. I. Hayakawa (New York: Harper, 1959), pp. 299–324. During the course of modernization in the Meiji Restoration whose acceleration was sloganized by a group of Japanese intellectuals as "America our mother, France our father," the Japanese unity of the inner (indigenous) and the outer (foreign) was expressed as "Eastern morality" and "Western science and technology." There may indeed be the difference here between the Eastern "logic of correlation" and the Western "logic of identity."

35. An interesting contrast can be made between the eighteenth-century anatomical sketch of the *vena cava* cited by Barthes and the nineteenth-century Japanese acupuncture figure. The contrast between the two may be depicted as that of the *universal* "semiological" man and the *particular* "Japanese" man. The *vena cava* supplements Barthes's notion of how "to write the body"—"Neither the skin, nor the muscles, nor the bones, nor the nerves, but the rest: an awkward, fibrous, shaggy, raveled thing, a clown's coat." (See Roland Barthes, *Roland Barthes*, trans. Richard Howard [New York: Hill and Wang, 1977], p. 180.) Ironically, however, Barthes's *vena cava* reveals more of the inside "depth" of the body than its counterpart, the "surfacial" body of the Japanese acupuncture figure.

36. Cf. Dean MacCannel and Juliet Flower MacCannel who writes that "we have adopted the stance that comparative cultural studies cannot make sense except as a contribution to a general semiotics of culture." (*The Time of the Sign* [Bloomington, Ind.: Indiana University Press, 1982], p. 3.) This semiotic Procrusteanism might easily, I am afraid, invite conceptual hypostatization that reverse the thesis that language and culture are the masters of linguistics and anthropology. One of the anecdotes of Zen monks published around the turn of this century is an instructive parable for con-

ceptual hypostatization or eutrophication. The edited story begins with the ideogram "emptiness" *(ku, le vide)* which is followed by the title caption "A Cup of Tea." The Zen master Nan-in served tea to a university professor who was visiting him to inquire about Zen. Nan-in poured the visitor's cup full and then kept on pouring. Watching the overflow, the professor could no longer restrain himelf and said: "It is overfull. No more will go in!" Thereupon Nan-in replied: "Like this cup, you are full of your own opinions and speculations. How can I show you Zen unless you first *empty* your cup?" (Paul Reps, *Zen Flesh, Zen Bones* [Rutland, Vt.: Tuttle, 1957], p. 19, italics mine.) Zen "emptying" to which Barthes himself is so attracted should serve as a deconstructive lesson for his semiological method. If by "metacommentary" we mean the piling of conceptual construction upon conceptual construction, moreover, the word in the subtitle of this paper too should be replaced with a *"koan"* or *"teisho"*—without the pretension of being a Zen master—on Barthes's *Empire of Signs*. It also should not escape our attention that "phenomenological reduction" *(epoche)* may be called *conceptual emptying*—the technique of "suspending" all prejudgments so that the observer may construct his thought based directly on actual experience rather than piling concept upon concept (i.e., conceptual sedimentation). Zen thinking *(nen)* is compared with phenomenological reduction in Katsuki Sekida, *Zen Training*, ed. A. V. Grimstone (New York: Weatherhill, 1975), pp. 188–92. It is of course beyond the scope of this paper to compare and elaborate on Zen and phenomenology including what, as contrasted with phenomenological reduction, Alfred Schutz calls the *"epoche* of the natural attitude" which suspends "doubt" rather than "belief" in the reality of the outer world. (See *Collected Papers*, vol. 1, *The Problem of Social Reality*, ed. Maurice Natanson [The Hague: Nijhoff, 1962], p. 229.) Zen can be a free variation on both types of *epoche* and more.

37. For an emphasis on the system of intersubjective meanings relevant to our discussion here, see Charles Taylor, "Interpretation and the Sciences of Man," *The Review of Metaphysics* 25 (September 1971): 3–51; Paul Ricoeur, *Hermeneutics and the Human Sciences*, trans. John B. Thompson (New York: Cambridge University Press, 1981); and Clifford Geertz, *The Interpretation of Cultures* (New York: Basic Books, 1973), especially chap. 1, "Thick Description: Toward an Interpretive Theory of Culture," pp. 3–30 and *Local Knowledge* (New York: Basic Books, 1983), especially chap. 3, " 'From the Native's Point of View': On the Nature of Anthropological Understanding," pp. 55–70. In *The Conflict of Interpretations*, ed. Don Ihde (Evanston: Northwestern University Press, 1974), Paul Ricoeur develops most fully the idea of hermeneutical phenomenology as compared with structural semiology. Cf. David Carroll, *The Subject in Question* (Chicago: University of Chicago Press, 1982), p. 15: "The structuralist critic in his effort to be *for* language, *for* the 'text,' will be for the most part militantly anti-subject. In fact the problem of the subject soon passes into obscurity, into a space radically outside that is no longer analyzed, no longer pertinent. The insistence on the subject and the whole problem of consciousness associated with it is considered by structuralists to have obscured, if not negated, the problem of language (the work of the signifier); and so now, through a reversal of the problematic, language negates, displaces, and replaces the subject as origin. The subject remains only as a skeleton of its former self, as a function of language." In *The Subject of Semiotics* (New York: Oxford University Press, 1983), Kaja Silverman explores the *human subject* as the *subject* of semiotics.

38. Cf. Dalby who writes that "it is often said with justification that Japanese food is more a feast for the eyes than for the palate, so even if I didn't get to taste the banquets

I witnessed, I at least got to view the beautifully orchestrated composition of dishes" (*Geisha*, p. 113).

39. The expression *hors jeu* is used by Richard Macksey during the questioning of Jacques Derrida's talk entitled "Structure, Sign, and Play in the Discourse of the Human Sciences." (See Macksey and Donato, eds., *The Structuralist Controversy*, p. 268.) The limits of the "theatrical" understanding of the world is explored by Bruce Wilshire in *Role Playing and Identity* (Bloomington, Ind.: Indiana University Press, 1982).

40. Zenkei Shibayama, *Zen Comments on the Mumonkan*, trans. Sumiko Kudo (New York: Harper and Row, 1974), p. 10.

# Ponge on Braque: The Visible Object

## Serge Gavronsky
*Barnard College*

LET us begin with a simple question: why would Francis Ponge find such pleasure in expressing his pleasure over Georges Braque's work? The answer is already in the question. There is no communication without the pleasure of the text finding its expression, the text as being onto itself. Since all Ponge's works can be considered as material objects, the duality is ever present between perception and translation, between the viewer's sensitivity and the encodation through language, both initially set into motion by the pleasure principle, suggesting not only the truth of Freud's observation but equally that of classical treatises on rhetoric which confirmed the exemplary position of the laudatory function of speech. Thus the connection between the eye of the viewer and the "I" of the text converges in the specificity of language. Far from allowing some sort of automatism to operate, or even allowing the automatic compulsion (as Lacan suggests) to define the structure of the text, the ever-watchful Ponge assumes full responsibility in his "veneration"[1] of the visible object, his own as well as Braque's. In fact, Ponge declares rather straightforwardly that Braque is great, an adjective one rarely encounters in Ponge's vocabulary, but then Ponge qualifies this greatness since he considers Braque's inspiration greater than any thinker, poet, or philosopher, greater than either a statesman, a scientist, or a man of religion.[2] In his most recent text on Braque, dated May 1982, Ponge called Braque "the greatest pictorial genius of the century."[3] Praise is thus inspired, as Plato would have said about the poet's practice.

In this hyperbolic exercise the poet defines not only his own aesthetic sensitivity but also, and in time, works out his own poetics, making his language go through its paces to perfect it as well as its capacity to translate the material, objective world.

As a consequence, one should equally appreciate the form of praise *and* the object that the poet praises, refusing to acknowledge any distinction between signifier and signified. In his first text on Braque, written in 1946, a year after having first met him, Ponge wrote that he had to think of his text as a kind of poem,[4] and years later, in 1971, he considered his work as "an Ode to Georges Braque,"[5] that is, anchored both in his familiarity with the painter and the consecration of a mode of representation in the text.[6]

Whether in an introduction to an exhibit or in a catalog, the double discourse is ever present since Ponge refuses to separate the theoretical from the poetic. The unity of language traverses writing itself as the poet seeks to revalorize language by attending to its whims and its sources, its reasons and its resonances. In so doing, the shape of the text emerges in its adequate configuration. The most classical is that one which most directly defines the thought of the text, thereby assuring the congruence between the boundaries of both.

But, as I observed in another context, the poet's reflections on the text must also be construed as forms of autoportraiture, and this singular affection for Braque, then, should be envisaged as a sign of narcissism in its largest sense since the poet's intentions reflect simultaneously his own poetics and the image of the Other.[7] This conjugation of needs is exemplified throughout Ponge's texts on Braque. Side by side the theoretical adheres to the poetic, the praise of the painter with self-reflective praise. Each text is a metadiscourse as well as an aesthetic one. The visibility of both never escapes the reader's attention.

To emphasize this nearly tactile quality, Ponge, in his first attempt to describe Braque, played on an underlying homophonic motif as he situated Braque halfway between Bach (pronounced in French with a *k* sound) and Baroque, both words initially sharing the letter *b* and reminding the poet of a bark with the vowel *a* suggesting the sound of an oar and the *q* recalling both the shape of a spoon and a hand mirror.[8] The first level of language is thus its fundamental components, but then Ponge equally acknowledges the function of those turns, those tropes within the text that call attention to the text itself. Describing Braque's lithographs, Ponge suggested a running metaphor that began with the initial transformation of the catalog into a "sort of very precious vulgate or let us say a plenary missal, to be used by those for whom modern art today replaces religion."[9] This metaphor is then expanded, since for Ponge this particular religion has no dogma; it is pure practice and, as a consequence, considered as highly dangerous by both Hitler and Stalin, both of whom violently reacted to modern art.[10] Ponge once again alluded to the same metaphor when, a few pages further on, he referred to Braque's work as "holy images."[11] He concluded with an appreciation of these same images as colored flags.[12] A derivative metaphor is also elaborated as Ponge defined these lithos as "apostolic acts."[13]

This rhetorical surdetermination has a triple justification. The first justification depends on a powerful emotion generating the text. Rhetoric encompasses the pretextual need to find and to found an expression. Without this emotion the text cannot be born. When it reaches the page, its essence as well as its existence, its materiality, are reflected and present. For Ponge, this initially occurred in 1923 when he saw Braque's cubist painting, *Violin,* dated 1912–13, hanging on Jean Paulhan's wall. His reaction was instantaneous and would never flag. This particular type of reaction was to reoccur on two other occasions.

During the war, as Ponge, his wife, and daughter moved from place to place, only two cheap reproductions decorated their walls. One was Picasso's *A Woman's Head* and the other was Braque's *Banjo.* So strong were the impressions made on the poet by these two paintings that he believed they justified his wartime efforts. Such artists had to be saved.

The third and crucial reaction occurred in the early days of 1945, shortly after the war's end when men's reactions may have been exacerbated by hunger or so it seemed to Ponge when he wrote about that exceedingly rare "aesthetic sob"[14] welling inside him when he first saw Braque's *Fish on a Plate.* Paulhan had taken him to see Braque, who had expressed his pleasure upon reading Ponge's *Le Parti pris des choses,* a collection of poems published by Gallimard in 1942. On leaving, after an hour spent in the artist's studio, listening and looking at Braque, Ponge caught sight of the painting in question, and at that time, though Ponge might not appreciate the analogy, he experienced one of those nearly ineffable experiences. These three visual events constitute the first justification for Ponge's hyperbolic praise of Braque.

I have already alluded to the second justification, one which the art critic Patrick Granville also underlined when he commented upon the similarities between *Le Parti pris des choses* and Braque's own still lifes.[15] These resemblances are first and foremost of a materialist kind. Both poet and painter have (though not exclusively) shunned the grandiose, the classic subjects of representation. Both have found pleasure in fruits and things rarely found in either painting or poem. As they decry the reign of ideas, they raise to high consideration a common appreciation of the exterior world, breaking with excessive anthropomorphism, a fact of civilization ever since the Renaissance. Only when man puts himself aside, according to Ponge, and finds his proper place in the universe, will he express the better part of himself.[16] Braque says the same thing when he insists that we must first set ideas aside and then disgorge an aesthetic object.[17] That moment, which Ponge refers to as the new order,[18] reminds us both of Nietzsche and, more recently, of a rather unfortunate use of that term in the thirties. And yet that need was generally felt, in art as well as in politics. As the new language of poetry had to reveal the surface dear to itself, so the painter had to go beyond and reveal the innermost secrets of Nature.[19] Whatever depths poet and painter were able to reveal, both shared a common sensitivity to reality, or perhaps, using Flaubert's understanding of the term, to realism. Was it first and foremost the acknowledgment of concept and of matter?[20] Ink, paper, and phonolexemes for the poet, and for the painter, the paint he utilized.[21]

The last justification for Ponge's hyperbolic homage to Braque centers on the similarity between Ponge's autoportrait as a superior being and his reference to Braque as a French genius. In what might appear to be traces of Maurras's vitriolic denunciation of romanticism, Ponge not only claimed Malherbe as his distant ancestor, but has, over the fourteen years I have known him, frequently alluded to the concept of a French race, despite the tragic overtones of that concept during and before World War II. Nevertheless, Ponge uses that idea of race as a way of defining the distinctiveness of the French. In this perspective, he remarks about Braque that "nothing is as French as he is, that he is an essential organ of our country."[22] Were one to speak of grandeur, adds Ponge, one should use that term cautiously, for in France, *grandeur*, the type that Braque represents, is found neither in expansive gestures, loud voices, violence, nor in theatrical attitudes.[23] For the most part, observes Ponge,

Braque's works are framed by the painter himself and are frequently found inside square yards (carrousels) where, like old-fashioned armies, they confront each other in orderly lines.[24]

Similarities exist on still another level, the level of signature. In fact, this act represents a microtext, the vestigial presence of self transferred to the text and yet existing outside of it, adding to it a dimension of provenance, authenticity: its difference.[25] Braque's signature is a sign of "noble intimacy."[26] It is another sign of his race, of his reality incorporated through this simulacrum into the order of things.

In the case of the poet the play of signature is best illustrated by the conclusion of the *Pré* (The Meadow) where Ponge summons the typographers to place, at the end of the poem, in lower case, quite naturally, except for the initial letters of Fennel and Parsley, his name which tomorrow will grow above Francis Ponge. Through this poetic conceit, words and things are interchangeable and the poet's signature coexists both below the ground of the meadow and throughout the meadow itself. To quote Ponge's laconic formula, "A PARTY FOR THINGS equals AN ACKNOWLEDGMENT OF WORDS."[27] Both the painter's signature as well as the poet's are therefore equidistant from the text and the world and yet both signatures are part of the text-world in their "weightiness, their thickness, their awkwardness, the weakness and the precariousness of creatures."[28]

A case in point is Braque's signature on his 1961 *Bird in the Leaves*. On an unlimited newspaper background that blocks out the space of the composition, encircled in a dishlike secondary frame, heavily accentuated in black, a black bird flies through a scattering of symbolic leaves—black brush passage, uniformly applied.[29] Within this other frame, as if the text also belonged to an acknowledged secondary mimetic transfer, there is a painted dish, a symbolic representation, that is, a painting. Within this confine, Braque boldly affixed his initials in black in the lower right-hand corner. His initials appear to have an importance almost equal, in disposition, in elegance, to the subject of the secondary topic: the bird itself. Thus the painter recognizes his work and, in the signatory act, completes it. But there is another signature, this time in full, and slightly to the right of the first one, delicately drawn this time, and emphasized by two short unequal lines below it. One line scores the initial three letters of his name: *Bra*. This is followed by a strong vertical slash marked by the isolated *q* and then completed by another shorter line under the last two vowels: *ue*.

The double field within which the signatures appear and play a significant visual role matches quite neatly Ponge's own description of the duality of his own practice both in the *Meadow* and in other texts signed in the Latin manner, that is, with the Latin transcription of his name.[30] There are no distinctions here to be drawn, and as a result, the two systems of signatures compose a fully ornamented and abbreviated text. In both the *Meadow* and the *Bird in the Leaves*, the incorporation of the signature, the sign, the design, testify to the absolute need of confirming the evidence. As a result, the image and the text's authenticity not only depend on a *resmimesis*, a concordance with that world we cannot render simultaneously, given our lack of ubiquity, but also on the signature, on that symbolic abbreviation of self, it too a *mimeme*, the inescapable materialization of Nature, the image, and the text.

So far I have spoken of pleasure, measure, and signature, but in so doing, the idea of authenticity has entered the arena. In fact, nothing exists in isolation, as Ponge comments on his reactions to Braque's oeuvre, clearly, part of the weight of the reaction is determined by the poet's appreciation of a text whose rumors belong to the exterior world, a text finally liberated from an excessive and immodest anthropomorphism. Ponge, commenting on these birds, observes that they "are much heavier than air, as birds are, in reality. They fly better than other painted birds, because like 'real birds' they take off from the ground, swoop down again for food and take off once more."[31] These birds are thus true to themselves as they allow us to apprehend new things *(res)*, to quote the Lucretian term in the *Nature of Things*. These things are made up of atoms of the so-called exterior world; they contain both the obscurity and the luminosity of things that cast light on one another.[32] *Ita res accendent limina rebus*, writes Lucretius, quoted by Ponge, both in the beginning of his essay on Braque and in the body of the text as well.

Without ever falling into that other dualistic representation of the world, I mean the Christian one, Ponge ascribes meaning to both his own text and Braque's *because* they confer validity to their own means, the text qua text, and on the text as emancipated from sentimental overlays that have rendered anterior efforts nearly incapable of truth in representation, in presentation as well.

The object, liberated from its ideational scaffolding, a key concept for Braque,[33] can, as we have seen, be "true" both to itself and to what it seeks to duplicate. Neither imposition annuls the others. In this fashion, objects depicted by Braque as well as things defined linguistically by the poet are not solely to be judged by the accuracy of the mirroring procedure but by the manner in which both adhere to classical rhetoric, essentially, to a metaphorical transcription, in order to seduce the eye into accepting the totality of the visible object.

There are no other phantoms here but those of etymology and literature as a referential corpus. The text itself is aware of it. Braque keeps a number of his unfinished canvases aligned in his studio as the poet himself rereads his anterior texts on Braque in the process of composing a new one.[34] Such is the practice that Ponge, much like the painter, uses black as a differential color to mark off his corrections and his additions.[35] In a pithy statement that Ponge quotes in his latest catalog, a modest exhibit marking the painter's birth in his hometown of Argenteuil, Braque writes: "that each state is always complimentary to the preceding one."[36] To appreciate the "truth" of the text, would then imply a weighing of the text's concern for its own being as well as its ability to convey, in a secondary degree of presentation, the aspects of the exterior world therein depicted.

Both poem and painting, when they achieve their object, can thus validate their affinity to the world and their preoccupation with the matter used to assure this resemblance. In the same way that the viewer is never fooled by a painting, and perhaps especially by a *trompe l'oeil* that paradoxically reaffirms the autotelic nature of the text, so a reader, less aware of the obgame, as Ponge calls it, needs to be trained in the levels of pleasure involved in decoding the play of perceptions, the metaphorical grid and the object—it too thereby established (placed on the table) at the crucial intersection. Only then can the fully visible constructive circumstances assure the reality of the object, its references perceived both within and outside of itself.

The truth of representation thus depends on a series of homologies, on the principle of recognition as well as on the means avowedly used to constitute the identity of the object.

The truth of it is—and unavoidably—its propriety, in effect, an acknowledgment of its properties, those that will define its lasting values, and, in measured terms, its monumentality whether on a bookshelf or on a museum wall. A monument, which is to say, something which denies periodicity, which attains to the stature of an intemporal work of art. The denaturalization of the object is thus part of its property.

In this matter still lifes have had an ambiguous status. They have abused their objects, metamorphosized them into aesthetic forms, or have chosen to express symbolic meaning through them. They have also evolved before poetry itself those qualities that both Ponge and Braque consider of primary significance.Whether a 1950 *Vase* with its stark flowers and leaves, or the 1954 *Apples on a Black Background,* or, going back to 1921, the lithography *Still Life, III,* Braque's efforts to claim part of the physical world, to sign it, is founded on a principle he himself postulated in his *Cahier:*

> Writing is not describing
> Painting is
>         not depicting
> +++
> Verisimilitude
>     is but a
>         trompe l'oeil.[37]

Would this definition be in opposition to Ponge's poetics? I think not. As I have tried to show, Ponge has significantly maintained both an insistence on referentiality and on the need to reveal, through the visibility of the metatext, the functioning of the meaning in linguistic-rhetorical terms, much as Lautréamont had before him in his *Songs of Maldoror.* The dual face of the sign is at all times present: this is what makes Ponge's *La Chèvre* (The Goat) such a precious object and animal, and, in similar terms, what makes Braque's work priceless for the poet who is charged with writing introductions for his exhibits and his catalogs. Like Van Gogh's shoes, it is no longer a question of knowing to whom they belong[38] but rather how they relate to things around them.

We are now able to appreciate the very markers of a new classicism wherein the painter and the poet, no longer restricted by formal rules of composition of a traditional rhetoric, can now become faithful to their own innermost drives, their understanding of the need to short-circuit the artificial exigencies of the academy. Dismissing the scaffolding, the boat now slides into the ocean, as efficiently as possible. When the painter succeeds in turning his weakness into a virtue, when he manages to realize that he cannot emulate the Old Masters, then he finds his true hand, and the poet, his true voice, when he systematically refuses to cover up the eruption of both object and language in the new order of poetry.

## Notes

1. Francis Ponge, "Georges Braque, un méditatif à l'oeuvre," in *Atelier contemporain* (Paris: Gallimard, 1977), p. 294. All translations are my own. Hereafter, this work will be cited as *AC*.
2. "Braque-Japon," *AC*, pp. 122–23.
3. *Georges Braque, Eaux-fortes, Lithographies* (Municipalité d'Argenteuil: Galerie du Centre Culturel, May–June, 1982), n. p.
4. "Braque le réconciliateur," *AC*, p. 58.
5. Francis Ponge, *Manuscrits-Livres-Peintures* (Paris: Centre Georges Pompidou, 1977), p. 62.
6. All these introductions and presentations are included in *AC* except for the Argeneuil catalog (see n. 3).
7. Serge Gavronsky, "Art Criticism as Autoportraiture," *Esprit Créateur* 22 (1982): passim.
8. "Braque le réconciliateur," *AC*, p. 59.
9. "Deux textes sur Braque," *AC*, p. 237.
10. Ibid.
11. Ibid., p. 238.
12. Ibid., p. 244.
13. Ibid., p. 239.
14. "Georges Braque, un méditatif à l'oeuvre," *AC*, p. 300.
15. Patrick Granville, "Braque au Mai de Bordeaux," *Le Monde*, 27 May 1982, p. 17, col. 3, and mentioned again in the following column.
16. "Braque le réconciliateur," *AC*, p. 63.
17. Ibid.
18. "Braque ou l'art moderne," *AC*, p. 76.
19. "Braque-Japon," *AC*, p. 126.
20. Ibid., p. 127.
21. "Braque, un méditatif à l'oeuvre," *AC*, pp. 306–7.
22. "Braque-Japon," *AC*, p. 128.
23. "Deux textes sur Braque," *AC*, pp. 242–43.
24. Ibid., p. 243.
25. "Braque le réconciliateur," *AC*, p. 66.
26. Ibid.
27. Francis Ponge, "My Creative Method," *Le Grand Recueil* (Paris: Gallimard, 1961), 2:19.
28. "Deux texts sur Braque," *AC*, p. 245.

29. Ponge has also commented on Braque's framing of a picture within a picture. See "Braque, un méditatif à l'oeuvre," *AC*, p. 294.

30. Jacques Derrida, "Signéponge," *Digraphe* 8 (1976): 34–35, and "Signéponge," *Francis Ponge: Colloque de Cerisy* (Paris: Edition générale, 1977), p. 138.

31. "Deux textes sur Braque," *AC*, p. 245.

32. "Braque, un méditatif à l'oeuvre," *AC*, pp. 312–13.

33. "Braque ou l'art moderne," *AC*, p. 74.

34. Francis Ponge, *Manuscrits-Livres-Peintures*, p. 62.

35. Georges Braque, *Eaux-fortes, Lithographies*, n.p.

36. Ibid.

37. *Cahier de Georges Braque, 1917–1947* (New York: Curt Valentin, 1948), p. 31.

38. Jacques Derrida, *La Vérité en peinture* (Paris: Flammarion, 1978), p. 296.